Creating Classroom Communities
of Learning

NEW PERSPECTIVES ON LANGUAGE AND EDUCATION
Series Editor: Professor Viv Edwards, *University of Reading, Reading, Great Britain* and
Series Advisor: Professor Allan Luke, *Queensland University of Technology,
Brisbane, Australia*

Two decades of research and development in language and literacy education have
yielded a broad, multidisciplinary focus. Yet education systems face constant
economic and technological change, with attendant issues of identity and power,
community and culture. This series will feature critical and interpretive, disciplinary
and multidisciplinary perspectives on teaching and learning, language and literacy
in new times.

Full details of all the books in this series and of all our other publications can be found
on http://www.multilingual-matters.com, or by writing to Multilingual Matters,
St Nicholas House, 31–34 High Street, Bristol BS1 2AW, UK.

NEW PERSPECTIVES ON LANGUAGE AND EDUCATION
Series Editor: Professor Viv Edwards

Creating Classroom Communities of Learning
International Case Studies and Perspectives

Edited by
Roger Barnard and
María E. Torres-Guzmán

MULTILINGUAL MATTERS
Bristol • Buffalo • Toronto

Library of Congress Cataloging in Publication Data
A catalog record for this book is available from the Library of Congress.
Creating Classroom Communities of Learning: International Case Studies
and Perspectives
Edited by Roger Barnard and María E. Torres-Guzmán.
New Perspectives on Language and Education
Includes bibliographical references and index.
1. Interaction analysis in education--Cross-cultural studies.
2. Classroom environment--Cross-cultural studies. 3. Communication and
education--Cross-cultural studies. 4. Language and education--Cross-cultural
studies. 5. English language--Study and teaching--Foreign speakers--Cross-
cultural studies.
I. Barnard, Roger, 1946- II. Torres-Guzmán, María E.
LB1034.C74 2008
372.1102'2--dc22 2008026648

British Library Cataloguing in Publication Data
A catalogue entry for this book is available from the British Library.

ISBN-13: 978-1-84769-113-2 (hbk)
ISBN-13: 978-1-84769-112-5 (pbk)

Multilingual Matters
UK: St Nicholas House, 31–34 High Street, Bristol BS1 2AW, UK.
USA: UTP, 2250 Military Road, Tonawanda, NY 14150, USA.
Canada: UTP, 5201 Dufferin Street, North York, Ontario M3H 5T8, Canada.

The policy of Multilingual Matters/Channel View Publications is to use papers that
are natural, renewable and recyclable products, made from wood grown in sustainable
forests. In the manufacturing process of our books, and to further support our policy,
preference is given to printers that have FSC and PEFC Chain of Custody certification.
The FSC and/or PEFC logos will appear on those books where full certification has
been granted to the printer concerned.

Typeset by Techset Composition Ltd., Salisbury, UK
Printed and bound in Great Britain by the Cromwell Press Ltd

Contents

Contributors

Fred E. Anderson is a Professor (*kyooju*) of English Linguistics at Kansai University, Osaka, Japan. He frequently teaches courses in Sociolinguistics and Teaching English to Speakers of Other Languages (TESOL) at Temple University Japan, and has also taught at universities in the United States and Sweden. His published work includes a chapter on Japanese classroom interaction in *A Handbook for Teaching English at Japanese Colleges and Universities* and a co-authored paper on Ainu language revitalization in *Studies in Japanese Bilingualism.* His major work on Japanese language socialization, represented by his 1995 doctoral dissertation in linguistics (University of Hawaii), is the topic of the present book chapter as well.

Roger Barnard, a Senior Lecturer at the University of Waikato, has been teaching on a range of graduate and undergraduate programmes in applied linguistics since 1995. Before taking up his present post, he worked in Britain, Europe and the Middle East as a teacher, teacher developer and English Language Adviser to Ministries of Education. Recently, he has accepted Visiting Professorships/Fellowships in Japan, New York and Hanoi. He is currently researching aspects of language teacher cognition and beliefs. Among his recent publications are R. Barnard and T. Glynn (eds) (2003) *Bilingual Children's Language and Literacy Development.* Clevedon: Multilingual Matters.

Ching-Yi Tien is currently an Assistant Professor at I-Shou University. Her research interests include codeswitching, language and culture, classroom observation, ESP (English for specific purposes) and teaching methodology. She has presented several papers at various international conferences on the topic of codeswitching in classroom practice and the use of English in Taiwan. She is enthusiastic about second and foreign language teaching and is an applied linguist, educator, and the author of the *General English Placement Test* book for English language learners. She has also been developing online language teaching and learning material with her colleagues and a computer software company.

Pearl Chua-Wong Swee Hui is currently Senior Education Officer in the Curriculum Development Department of the Ministry of Education, Negara Brunei Darussalam (Brunei), having previously served in senior positions in secondary schools. Her major research interests are in the field of interaction in the language classroom, and she has presented papers on this topic at a number of regional and international conferences. In 2007 she completed a 'Leaders in Education' programme in Singapore, during which she was able to replicate her earlier Brunei research, which highlighted the distinction between procedural and content talk in language lessons.

Patricia A. Duff is Professor of Language and Literacy Education at the University of British Columbia. Her research mostly involves ethnographies of classroom communication with second language learners in English-medium and other (e.g. Chinese) language environments, language socialization and task-based research. She has published widely on these topics in the major journals in the field and in over 20 edited volumes, has co-edited two books and written another, and has also given invited lectures internationally. Patsy has taught English as a second/foreign language and applied linguistics in several countries in Asia as well as in North America.

John F. Fanselow's interest has been analysis of interactions. His publications reflect this interest. 'Beyond *Rashomon*' and 'Let's see', two of his seminal papers in the *TESOL Quarterly*, have been reprinted in many anthologies. 'Beyond *Rashomon*' was the basis of *Breaking Rules* (Longman, 1987) and 'Let's see' was the basis of *Contrasting Conversations* (Longman, 1992). He has been president of New York State TESOL and TESOL and Program Chair of the 1976 TESOL Convention. After he became Professor Emeritus at Columbia University, Teachers College, he became president of a private college in New Zealand focusing on staff development through observation.

James McLellan has worked in the Department of General and Applied Linguistics at the University of Waikato, Aotearoa/New Zealand since 2004. After working as a secondary-level teacher of French and German in the UK and of English in Malaysia and Brunei, he taught in the Department of English Language and Applied Linguistics at the University of Brunei Darussalam from 1989 to 2002. He obtained his PhD from Curtin University of Technology in 2005. His current research interests include Malay–English language alternation, Borneo indigenous languages in education, classroom discourse and language policy in education in Southeast Asia.

Vijay Kumar is a senior lecturer with the Department of English at Universiti Putra, Malaysia. He obtained his PhD in Linguistics from the University of Otago, New Zealand. He has 27 years of teaching experience. Vijay's research interests are in postgraduate development and academic writing. Among his published and on-going research include: providing feedback to doctoral candidates, hedging in PhD dissertations and publishing during candidature. Vijay is an invited member of the

International Doctoral Education Research Network. His recent publication 'An analysis of written feedback on a PhD thesis' appears in a UK-based journal, *Teaching in Higher Education.*

Rhonda Oliver currently holds the chair in education at the South-West Campus of Edith Cowan University, Western Australia. She has worked in the field of Education, Applied Linguistics and TESOL for a number of years. As an ESL teacher she taught in reception and transition classrooms, and supported mainstream teachers. Her research interests include second language acquisition, specifically conversational and interactional studies, particularly those pertaining to children, oral language development (for both first and second language learners), as well as studies of mainstream teaching practices. She has published numerous papers in a number of international scholarly journals.

María E. Torres-Guzmán, Professor of Bilingual/Bicultural Education in the Department of International and Transcultural Studies at Teachers College, Columbia University, has taught and conducted research throughout the United States and in various parts of the world, including Puerto Rico, Spain, Japan and New Zealand. Her research has primarily focused on the Spanish-speaking populations within the United States but it has extended beyond to centre her research on how teachers think about the spaces of freedom within the context of strong forms of bilingual education and how they create and recreate linguocultural spaces in multicultural classrooms.

Sylvia Wolfe studied for her PhD in the Faculty of Education, Cambridge, UK where she continues to work as a tutor on the Primary Post Graduate Certificate of Education (PGCE) and Master of Education (MEd) courses. She also works as a lecturer in Educational Enquiry and associate researcher for The Open University. Sylvia is currently involved in a study using multimodal methodologies to explore preschoolers' literacy practices around new technologies. Before entering Higher Education, Sylvia worked as a class and language support teacher. In her doctoral thesis she explored the conditions that appeared to support a dialogic pedagogy. She has experimented with a variety of approaches to analysing discourse.

Wong Bee Eng is Associate Professor in the Department of English at the Faculty of Modern Languages and Communication, Universiti Putra Malaysia. She obtained her PhD in Linguistics from the University of Essex. She teaches courses in linguistics and applied linguistics. Her main research interests are in the areas of syntactic and vocabulary development in Second Language Acquisition (SLA) and second language assessment. She has published papers (including journal articles) in these areas. She has also edited three books, one individually (*Second Language Acquisition: Selected Readings* 2005, Sasbadi) and the other two as a co-editor.

Transcript Conventions

#1, #2	number of extract
#1b, #1c	interaction which follows immediately after previous extract
01, 02	speaker turn
T	teacher
Ro, Ma	initial letters of student's name
S1, S2	unknown students
Ss	more than one student speaking
]	overlapping speech
/, //, ///	pause (length of seconds)
bold	emphasis given by speaker
(xxx)	unintelligible speech
(hello)	guessed speech
{ }	activity associated with the speech
< >	interpretive comment
italics	translation of original speech in vernacular

NB: All names of teachers and students are pseudonyms (except where specifically stated to the contrary).

Foreword

When I first received the proposal for this book, I experienced mixed emotions in my role as series editor. On the one hand, I felt confident that the topic – the creation of classroom communities of learning – would be of interest to a broad readership. It was also clear that the geographical coverage by respected researchers was excellent – Japan, Australia, Brunei Darussalem, USA, Taiwan, UK, Malaysia, New Zealand and Canada. This proposal, then, had potential.

But, on the other hand, I was less confident about the Take 1, Take 2, Take 3 approach espoused by the prospective editors who were unhappy with unidimensional interpretations of transcript data. They were proposing that each paper would begin with Take 1 – a discussion of the sociocultural context of the learning community under study, followed by an illustrative transcript of classroom interaction and an explanation of their interpretive framework. Another contributor to the volume would then be responsible for Take 2, where the same data would be explored from a second perspective. To complete the chapter, in Take 3, the reader would be invited to comment on another transcript from the same community of learning from their own perspective and experience. The aim, then, was to create a conversation not only among the contributors but also with the readers of the volume. The emphasis would be on understanding that there is no single 'truth' and on exploring alternative insights.

While this seemed fine in theory, I was hampered by my own lack of experience of this highly innovative approach. How would it pan out in practice? I was also painfully aware that overworked contributors to edited volumes have difficulty meeting deadlines for their own contributions and was therefore sceptical as to whether it was realistic to also ask them to offer perspectives on the transcripts of other authors. The fact, however, that all the authors shared such an obvious commitment to understanding the co-construction of learning finally won the day. I took a leap of faith.

My trust in the editors has been amply rewarded. The introduction – innovative and accessible – takes the form of a conversation between Roger Barnard, María Torres-Guzmán and John Fanselow. It thus demonstrates the same dialogic approach adopted throughout the volume. The chapters not only identify a very wide range of communities of learning but, as promised, provide refreshingly different takes on the illustrative transcripts. The additional transcripts provided by the first authors have the potential not only to draw in individual readers but also make exciting teaching material, extending the conversation still further. John Fanselow's Afterword brings the collection to a satisfying conclusion. He reminds us of the key reasons for analysing transcripts – to move beyond our initial interpretation and judgment and to expand the range of our teaching practices – and reviews a range of issues that can usefully inform future discussion.

This, then, is a book which speaks to teachers, teacher educators and researchers, inviting us to move beyond the more usual unidimensional approach to learning, to co-construct our understandings of the nature of knowledge, and to grow both personally and professionally in the process.

Viv Edwards
University of Reading, UK

Introduction

ROGER BARNARD, MARÍA E. TORRES-GUZMÁN AND
JOHN F. FANSELOW

JOHN: Let's start this conversation by discussing the meaning of the title
of this book – *Creating Classroom Communities of Learning.*

ROGER: The title reflects its main purpose, which is to illustrate how
schoolteachers in specific communities of learning induct young learners
into appropriate attitudes and behaviours. We try to achieve this purpose
by presenting and interpreting transcripts of teaching and learning in a
variety of international contexts.

JOHN: Usually we talk about *classrooms* rather than *communities of learning*.
What is a community of learning and who creates one?

MARÍA: Perhaps we can put it this way: a classroom is a place; a community of learning is a relationship (Lave, 1996). According to Wenger (1999),
a community of learning is when people come together in shared histories
of activity and discourse associated with the learning enterprise. Central to
Wenger's thinking is the notion of the expert who teaches the apprentice
not only the specific tasks associated with the primary activity of the learning community, but also the pragmatic, interpersonal conventions appropriate to carrying out those tasks. As the relationship between experts and
apprentices develops within a spatial and temporal context, a cultural
boundary concomitantly forms to identify this group as a particular sub-
culture. The community of learning is characterised by attitudes and
behaviours that are deemed appropriate to that specific setting.

ROGER: In Wenger's model, the more expert partner seeks to transform
apprentices on the periphery of a community of *practice* – whether this is
craft, professional or academic – into full participants. However, the
apprentices, by co-constructing meaning in dialogue with the expert, also
assist the creation of the rules and conventions that underlie, and identify,
a particular community of *learning*. In this dialogue, a close relationship
between expert and learners, and among learners, is created and sustained.

MARÍA: It is in the relationships established between student and teacher
that the teacher plays a role in creating interest in academic learning as
part of the life projects of the students (Lave, 1996). The students enter the

classroom with their own individual and socially-based histories that interact in the dynamic that develops in classrooms. Engaging students in the
local learning project is a process of negotiation within the context of the
larger social transformational life project. The teacher is constantly negotiating his/her social and individual conception of academic learning within
the students' social and individual identities. It is within this negotiation
that culturally specific notions of *good learners* and *appropriate attitudes and
behaviours* emerge. Every classroom, thus, negotiates anew the developmental and situational aspect of the learner's identity.

ROGER: In other words, these small learning communities are not isolated;
they are influenced by the wider social environment in which they are
located. In order to interpret what is happening at the micro-level – for
example the learning community in schools – we need to understand the
political, linguistic and educational factors operating at the macro-level
which position that setting.

MARÍA: And that is why we are looking for understandings of the relationship between what occurs in classrooms as a specific community within a
wider context and have used 'international perspectives' as our subtitle.

JOHN: I'd like to come back to the issue of the particular contexts related
to international perspectives explored in this book a little later, but first let
me ask – who is going to use this book?

ROGER: I think that it will be useful for many educators in different countries – whether teachers, prospective teachers or teacher educators. In particular, it will appeal to researchers and practitioners who are interested in
developing their thinking about 'exploratory practice', which Allwright
(2003: 131) regards as 'a mutually beneficial enterprise of working together
towards understanding something of common interest' – the key word
there being *understanding*. Also, because of its international scope, the book
will be of interest to teachers and researchers in fields such as comparative
education and the ethnography of schooling – those who are interested in
looking at classrooms from a variety of perspectives, and sharing with
international colleagues insights derived from diverse cultural and theoretical backgrounds. We hope this book will stimulate conversations among –
and indeed beyond – its readers.

JOHN: You invited authors working in Japan, Australia, Brunei, the United
States, Taiwan, the UK, Malaysia, New Zealand and Canada to contribute
to this book. Why these?

ROGER: Essentially, because we are a group of teachers and classroom
researchers – 'practical explorers', to coin a phrase. As can be seen from the
brief biographical notes, we come from various backgrounds in language
education, and have extensive experience of living and working in many
different international/cultural contexts. We have met at various times and
places and found that we have a profound interest in common – the attempt
to understand the co-construction of learning and the creation of learning

communities. More particularly, we believe that the foundations of cognitive, linguistic, and conceptual development are firmly laid in the primary schools and these foundations pre-dispose, or shape, the students' incorporation of subsequent learning processes as part of their changing social and personal identities.

MARÍA: When Roger first approached me to co-edit this book, what most intrigued me was the interactive format, which is intended to be a sort of conversation not only among the contributors of the chapters but also involving the readers. It is an innovative way of breaking with the usual ways that books of case studies are put together. I asked him where he got the idea from.

ROGER: In 2005, John and I wrote a chapter for a book on classroom observation called *Take 1, Take 2, Take 3: A Suggested Three Stage Approach to Exploratory Practice* (Fanselow & Barnard, 2005), and this was the basis for my thinking about this book. The three-take approach was a kind of reaction against what John and I saw as a consistent convention of unidimensional interpretation of transcript data in many, many papers and books. Typically, in books about teaching and learning, a set of transcript data is selected, presented and interpreted to make a single point, or to substantiate a single line of thought.

JOHN: In our chapter, we said that teachers/researchers must be exposed to approaches that presented multidimensional viewpoints. Thus, we laid out a process by which teachers and researchers could move to richer understandings of classrooms.

MARÍA: And what was that process?

JOHN: We selected a number of lesson transcripts that had been commented upon in published books or papers, and our first 'take' was to reproduce the original interpretation. We assumed that the author had an inside knowledge of the context and was thus able to provide a well-informed interpretation. Without wishing to invalidate this perspective, we then showed each transcript (but not the interpretation) to two other teachers and asked them to comment on it from an 'outsider' point of view – in other words to provide other 'takes' on the data. They invariably came up with entirely different interpretations.

MARÍA: I'm not surprised. But, if the second commentators did not know the context, would you say that they were likely to come up with misleading or invalid interpretations?

ROGER: More than likely, but are such 'off the wall' interpretations really misleading? Perhaps they throw up valuable insights on the negotiations between the teacher and the student precisely because the data were seen through fresh eyes. Paradoxically, prior knowledge of the specific setting or the emphasis on the larger context may blind us to achieving understanding of the complexity of what is occurring because too much may be taken for granted.

JOHN: Implicit in the approach is the understanding that our roles as teachers, teacher educators, researchers, and learners overlap as we are all involved in co-constructing understanding about the nature of knowledge – a point emphasised by Allwright (2003, 2006) and also myself (Fanselow, 1987, 1992). As we were developing the chapter, as well as since its publication, I have presented the transcripts in many workshops. So far, in those workshops, I have not had a person write an interpretation of the transcripts in our paper in the way the authors had. No, on reflection, I think I had one out of approximately 300 people attending these sessions who came up with the same interpretation as the original. One of the transcripts in our 2005 paper was from a study I did so I am not trying to cast aspersions on people who wrote papers about interaction with single interpretations.

ROGER: Just as John has tried the three-take approach in many workshops, I have used it with students in my graduate courses, with teachers and with other researchers. It has proved to be fruitful because it makes people realise that there is no 'objective' truth to be discovered amid the complexities of classroom interaction – only a multiplicity of interpretations, each depending on the perspective of the observer. So I approached María and we thought it would be enriching to explore the method, in a book format, with contributors who are researching teachers and young learners in different parts of the world.

MARÍA: The method permits us to illustrate the process of assembling and taking apart meaning and to gain a richer understanding about the complexity of what is occurring in classrooms. This is sometimes difficult to get my graduate students to understand. But I hope by having a range of authors in different countries share their perspectives it will make my students more aware of the diversity of perspectives.

ROGER: In 2007, five of the book's contributors also shared the idea of the book, and a run-through of the three-take approach, during a colloquium at an international conference on social and cognitive aspects of second language learning (Batstone, in press).

MARÍA: For me, the colloquium was important as I was seeing the approach in action. We took data from a Canadian context (Chapter 9 in this book) and suggested two very different interpretations – one by Patsy Duff who had an insider's knowledge of the context, and the other 'take' by Rhonda Oliver (whose data from an Australian classroom are interpreted in Chapter 2), an 'outsider' who had read only the transcript data and some brief introductory material. We also sought the interpretations of the colloquium participants – a lot of 'third takes'. I could see that the differences in interpretations came from both experiential as well as theoretical backgrounds and that no matter what the interpretations were, there was always room for one more interpretation, for a deeper, broader and different understanding.

JOHN: I still think we have some unpacking to do – which brings me back to the word in your first comment, Roger, that immediately caught my attention and which you have not yet defined, 'induct'. What does it mean?

ROGER: Well, perhaps the most important role that primary teachers have is to introduce new beliefs, knowledge and ideas to their students and then scaffold (Wood *et al.*, 1976) their understanding. Of course, many of these new concepts relate directly to the subjects in school curriculum – maths, language arts, social studies, and so on. But there is invariably another underlying agenda – a 'hidden' curriculum – which concerns the ways by which students (Wenger's apprentices) are inducted into the relevant pragmatic norms associated with effective learning. It is now quite common to refer to this process by using Vygotsky's (1978) term, the zone of proximal development (ZPD), in which the teacher inducts – or scaffolds – the development of the learner from his or her present conceptual, cultural or pragmatic knowledge and skills to an expanded appropriation of its use in the real world. Central to the notion of a ZPD is the process of assembling and taking apart meaning by intersubjective dialogue wherein the teacher inducts the learners in and through the language of classroom discourse.

JOHN: In and through language?

ROGER: The distinction is frequently made in the literature on language socialisation theory (e.g. Ochs & Schiefflin, 2008). Socialisation *in* the language occurs, for example, when a teacher tells her students how to bid for a turn, how to formulate an appropriate response or how to address her or each other. In Chapter 1, for example, Fred Anderson explores socialisation in language in the context of a class of six- and seven-year-old Japanese learners. Patsy Duff also draws on language socialisation theory when she interprets the interaction in a class of older learners in Canada (Chapter 9). The Australian teacher (Chapter 2) also explicitly draws her students' attention to the appropriate use of language, but Rhonda Oliver interprets this from a perspective derived from the Initiation-Response-Follow-up (IRF) discourse framework (Coulthard, 1986); originally described by Bellack *et al.* (1966); the IRF structure is also used to interpret the very different interactions in a Taiwanese learning community (Chapter 5). Socialisation *through* language, on the other hand, 'concerns the use of language to encode and create cultural meaning' (Poole, 1992: 595) and is usually more pervasive precisely because cultural values underlying effective learning are often only implicitly communicated, and thus left to be inferred by the students.

JOHN: The wide range of interpretations you just mentioned in the chapters seems to be different from your use of the word scaffolding. Aren't these kinds of terms in fact one way to limit our perspective to one dimension?

ROGER: That's right. Using a specific term, or a framework, to analyse data does restrict our vision, but it also allows the data to be closely and coherently explored.

MARÍA: I agree that sometimes our terms limit our perspective. But a term like infer, which Roger just used, can broaden rather than limit our interpretation if – while we are looking at the transcripts – we consistently apply an associated theoretical framework. So, if we think that the learner makes an 'inference', we can look at the transcripts to compare and contrast it with what we mean by that term; thus the data allow us to interrogate our framework.

ROGER: So, while the framework provides a perspective with which to view the data, the data in turn allow us to reflect on, and perhaps alter, the perspective.

MARÍA: Right. Going back to the point that terms can lead to one-dimensional thinking, let me remind you that there are different meanings to the same terms. For example, in my opinion, even though one could interpret Roger's use of *infer* above as passive, it can also be interpreted as interactive. The socialisation through language that you refer to is essentially an interactive process in which learners and teacher jointly co-construct meanings through the discourse of learning. Wong Bee Eng and Vijay Kumar (Chapter 7), in their interpretation of interaction in a Malaysian setting, bring in Sonnenmeier's (1993) definition of co-construction: an active skill which contributes to the understanding of a conversation, and which depends on the nature of the relationship. If we are to accept this more interactive definition of inferencing, to a greater or lesser extent students actually shape the shared meanings by their active participation in what Tharp and Gallimore (1990) referred to as 'instructional conversations' – as you discuss, Roger, with regard to the New Zealand setting (Chapter 8).

ROGER: I think the implicit socialisation through language, and active inferencing, is very clearly illustrated in the primary school in England (Chapter 6): Sylvia Wolfe interprets the teacher's encouragement of the collaborative construction of knowledge in terms of Alexander's (2001) 'dialogic teaching'. And, of course, a similar process of socialisation applies in your own setting, María, which is a bilingual classroom in New York (Chapter 4); here, you apply the concepts of *respeto y cariño* (respect and caring) derived from Valdes (1996). On the other hand, opportunities for active co-construction of understanding among learners and teachers may be limited by educational policies that restrict interactive dialogue, as may be seen in the data from Brunei (Chapter 3), which James McLellan and Pearl Chua-Wong Swee Hui interpret using Chick's (1996) construct of 'safe-talk'. Here, the teacher and students keep the discourse within superficial, and unchallenging, bounds because of their implicit understanding of the rules of engagement that apply within their educational environment.

MARÍA: The learner comes to the classroom with some sociocultural understanding of communication rules – who they are, what and who a teacher is, what they are supposed to do at schools, and so forth. For example, by age three my trilingual grandchild, like many other children, can identify which language system is spoken by what grandparents. She knows how to tell stories, how to request things she wants, and is pretty sophisticated in getting attention from the adults. Most children are capable of this and more by the age they go to school. In the Japanese classroom (Chapter 1), the teacher builds on such emerging understandings to induct the six- and seven-year-old children to distinguish and use the polite, the formal and the colloquial registers of Japanese in the classroom – and, by participating, the children co-construct the social value of these registers with the teacher.

JOHN: While it is true, as you say María, that in some cases the children co-construct understanding through interaction it is also true that some do not. And to me this is a key value of this book. We see that our often stated claims that when we do X, the result is Y is true in some instances but not in all. A key purpose of the three-take approach is to remind ourselves that scaffolding, inducting, co-constructing or whatever, happens in some cases and does not happen in other cases. As we look at transcripts over and over we can see ways we could, on another occasion, alter the interaction to include more in the induction! We have to remember how many school dropouts there are. So we have to always ask how is what we are doing failing to induct as well as facilitating induction.

ROGER: That's very true. And although those prior 'dispositions' (Bourdieu, 1990) are derived from the primary socialisation provided by parents and other early caregivers, such as older siblings, or by their previous experience at school, they have different consequences for different learners. There are many different social life projects, so to speak, entering the classroom. What they learn in the classroom may or may not be integrated into their life projects. Maybe what is integrated is a confirmation that the classroom project is not for them. In any society, there will be a wide variety of such assumptions resulting from social, cultural and individual differences among students and teachers, and this is clearly shown in all of the settings discussed in this book, even in the linguistically homogenous settings in this book – Japan, Taiwan and England (Chapters 1, 5 and 6), and perhaps more in bilingual classrooms such as those in Brunei, the United States and Malaysia (Chapters 3, 4 and 7).

MARÍA: In today's partially globalised world, the extent of such differences is considerably expanded by the fact that classrooms in many countries now comprise learners of diverse linguistic and ethnic backgrounds, as a result of immigration, temporary employment of parents, the desire for international education, the seeking of asylum and so on. The classroom populations of Australia, the United States, New Zealand and Canada (Chapters 2, 4, 8 and 9) are extremely diverse, and the interactions between the teacher and the students with respect to co-constructing what it means to create a community of learning can be even more complex.

ROGER: When learners move from one educational context to another, or when there is a profound internal change within a system, adjustments have to be made – either by the learner or their teachers or (less likely) the system – to accommodate to the new situation.

MARÍA: And, of course, in addition to the differences between different individual teachers and their classes, the educational systems vary quite considerably as well.

ROGER: Yes. To explain some of these variables, our authors begin each chapter with an introduction in which they set out the broad sociocultural context in which the particular classroom is located. In some cases, our authors discuss educational policies regarding the use of languages in schools; in others, the authors' attention is focused on the breadth and limits of national curricula. The extracts of classroom interaction which are subsequently presented and interpreted in each chapter are intended to illustrate the discourse between teachers and learners in that particular setting.

JOHN: Are these contexts typical in any way?

ROGER: No, not at all. Given that every learning community is a unique culture, these case studies cannot be regarded in any way as typical, either of education in any particular country, or even of the learning culture of primary schools within the particular system.

JOHN: OK, it is true that each community of learning is unique. However, aren't there some common features of classrooms across the board?

ROGER: Well, yes – but this is why our distinction between a community of learning and a classroom is important. Anyone entering a classroom in most parts of the world would instantly recognise what it is. First of all, school classrooms across the world look very similar: there is usually one teacher and a large number of learners – 15 to 50, or even more. The teacher is usually positioned at the front of the room with a chalkboard or whiteboard behind him or her. The teacher has freedom to move around the room at will, the learners less; in many cases very little liberty of movement at all. The classroom is dominated by the teacher's voice – usually two-thirds or more of the talking time is taken by the teacher, who almost invariably initiates and concludes any discussion, with learners' contributions (often thinly) sandwiched between. Typically, though not invariably, students sit at desks, and often in rows, facing the teacher, as is the case in the Taiwanese, Bruneian and Malaysian settings (Chapters 3, 5 and 7): the situation described in England, the United States and New Zealand (Chapters 4, 6 and 8) show that this arrangement is not universal. Almost always, the content and activities of a lesson are pre-determined by the teacher to meet aims set by her or by an imposed curriculum.

MARÍA: That's true, but the transcripts in this book do show, to a greater or lesser extent, that the learners share in the shaping of both content and activity. For example, the learners in Brunei (Chapter 3) and Malaysia (Chapter 7) appear to conspire with the teacher to keep the structure and discourse of the lesson 'safe' for both parties. By contrast, in the New Zealand setting (Chapter 8), we see the learners being encouraged to actively shape not only the learning activities, but also the conceptual content of the lesson.

ROGER: Exactly. Within the physical similarity of classrooms, the teaching and learning is culturally specific, and it is only by a close analysis of the classroom discourse that a real sense can be gained of how communities of learning are created. If the observer attends closely to what is being said and done, some understanding can be achieved. However, to get a deeper and richer interpretation it is necessary to record and transcribe key elements of the interaction. This book is based upon examples of such transcripts.

JOHN: Of course, there are some limitations of this type of analysis.

ROGER: Yes. First, longitudinal studies are really necessary to obtain a deep understanding of any classroom culture. However, in the chapters of this book, the interactions are extracted from only a few lessons, and sometimes only one.

JOHN: So, it is not possible to gauge the way that relationships between teachers and learners, and among learners themselves, change over time and across settings. This is very important for our readers to understand.

ROGER: Yes, but despite this obvious limitation, we believe that plausible interpretations can be made from thoughtful analysis of transcript data of even a single lesson. Another limitation is that even carefully written transcripts can only provide the *verbal* aspects of classroom discourse. So much meaning in any communicative event is conveyed by nonverbal means – by intonation, gesture, eye-contact and even in how and where people are positioned in relation to each other.

MARÍA: Of course, much of this nonverbal activity could be captured if lessons were video-recorded.

ROGER: Yes, this was done in almost all of the settings in this book (elsewhere, the lessons were audio-recorded) and the authors' interpretations are enriched by their having observed the classes, and by reference to these recordings as well as field notes taken during the observations, and reflective notes made afterwards.

JOHN: Wouldn't it have been illuminating to have included these recordings with this book – on a CD-ROM, perhaps?

ROGER: Well, we considered this possibility, but there were two major difficulties. The first was that the technical quality of many of the recordings was, understandably, not of a high standard. More important however, is that the publication of video data raises complex ethical issues relating to confidentiality and anonymity. So, although only a fraction of the actual interaction can be covered in written form, we believe that the transcribed lesson extracts in these chapters do allow a range of interpretations of how learning and teaching may be co-constructed in specific contexts, and how these patterns can differ from one setting to another.

MARÍA: So, from a methodological viewpoint, we have established a unit of analysis as a starting point for all the contributing authors – the interactions of the teacher and students in specific lessons, but there are some significant variations in how the authors approach an analysis/their interpretation.

ROGER: Right. In each chapter, after the introduction to the sociocultural context, the authors explain the framework they have employed to assist their own interpretation of the transcript data.

JOHN: But even if the authors have a sound understanding both of the background circumstances and the specific context, this doesn't mean that the interpretations of what is going on are very complete – both in the sense of being an incomplete human being which makes it possible to take up the same issue from another mind frame and in the sense of being, in some way, always biased as what you see is from your own subjectivities.

ROGER: Very true. All of us involved in exploring classroom learning are all too aware of the partiality, tentativeness and – as you say – subjectivity of our own explanations of what is really happening in any learning context. Ideally, in order to obtain fuller explanations of what is happening in any lesson, the investigation should involve, and include the interpretations of, those directly involved – in other words to apply ethnographic principles and procedures.

MARÍA: There are many ways to get at how the actors in a situation think about what they are doing. Some are through interviewing, doing stimulated recall discussions before and after classroom observation, joint video viewing and reflection, interactive journal writing, and in participant observations and collaborative research, informal conversations play a significant role in getting to what participants mean when they speak and act.

ROGER: Yes – to elicit the underlying intentions and meanings of the teachers and learners involved. In practice, however, it is not always possible to do this, and for various reasons we were unable to adopt ethnographic procedures for the data in this book and so we chose alternative means of interpreting the data.

MARÍA: So, let's talk about what we have come to understand as 'take two' – an alternative interpretation.

ROGER: In each chapter, there is a second commentary by other contributors to the book. So, for example, Sylvia Wolfe, the author of the chapter with a British setting, reinterprets Fred Anderson's transcripts from the Japanese context; Fred comments on the Taiwanese data, and María reviews (re-views) the Brunei transcript, originally interpreted by James McLellan and Pearl Chua-Wong Swee Hui. And so on.

MARÍA: So the data are explored though another lens, so to speak.

JOHN: I would like to suggest we substitute *the lens* metaphor, María, to *camera*. For one thing, our idea for both the title of our paper and the concept – Take 1, Take 2 and Take 3 – comes from the film industry. As we know, an important difference between 'legitimate' theatre and the film industry is that while filming, directors take many shots of the same scene. They change the focus of the lens from close up to long range, from clear to not clear, the lighting, perhaps the filters on the lens etc. So to highlight our different perspective, we might start to use the camera metaphor rather than the more common lens metaphor.

ROGER: In order not to prejudice the second commentators, they were not shown the first take, nor did they know the camera or the angle used by the original author: they were provided with the sociocultural introduction and only the transcript data – no other interpretation. They were then asked to comment on any aspects of the transcript data that struck them as being interesting.

MARÍA: So, each set of data is given more than one interpretation – to provide alternative perspectives on the same events through another camera, as John suggested, with a range of lenses, speeds and types of filters. The second commentary may or may not focus on aspects of the situation that were overlooked or highlighted in the first interpretation, or it may actually coincide at some level with the first.

JOHN: Focusing on events with one particular framework will highlight key features associated with that angle of vision. However, this may lead to overlooking other important aspects. Thus the second commentator, by using another camera, can focus on and discuss different issues that may come into view. Sometimes, the researcher who is an insider to the situation they study cannot see what someone else examining the data can see – precisely because they are too close. The second commentator may bring in a more distant or outsider's perspective.

MARÍA: And thus add to the richness by viewing the data through a different camera.

ROGER: Exactly. And there is one more level in each chapter. To provide two perspectives on the same data can lead to a sense of contrasting, or conflicting viewpoints, and thus set up an unhelpful dichotomy. But in reality, there is no single 'truth' to be found in any communicative event. So, at the end of each chapter, we provide another set of transcript data taken from the original context. We invite the readers to read and interpret this new dataset in the light of the previous interpretations and – more importantly – from their own perspective and experience. And so we seek a third 'take' on the data, from which an even richer palimpsest of interpretations can be built.

JOHN: So this is a form of triangulation.

MARÍA: Yes. The notion of triangulation derives from the method used by surveyors to map out an area by tracing a network of triangles from a baseline; in this way, they can determine the accuracy of their measurements. The metaphor has been taken up in educational and other research to strengthen the validity of the data which has been collected. In this book, we are triangulating the data from different points of view.

JOHN: Yes, but I think our method is different from triangulation. In the three-take approach, it is not *accuracy* we are looking for, but alternative insights.

MARÍA: I think so too. In some ways we had a baseline for the book, like the surveyors. We had some ideas about how learning communities might be created in classrooms. Two reasons gave us impulse to find out more about what we already know. One is the understanding of the importance of context, as we have already stated. The other reason is embedded in who we are as academics and the need to know a phenomenon more deeply. So, we wanted to know how the phenomenon is the same and different in the diverse international contexts as they compare to what we already know.

Our own conference call conversations,[1] however, are somewhat different. They are reflective dialogues that bring together what we would like to see, what we have learned in the process of putting together the book, our perspective on what our contributors bring to it, and the individual subjectivities each one brings to it. The baseline is different. Yes, we have the book, we have our past relationships and we have a disposition to be open to multiple ways of seeing and interpreting the world. But, in our conference call conversations we are 'in the moment' creating our own community of learning and creating our individual learning at the same time. We are three individuals in search of a collective understanding of learning communities and so on. We are not one individual looking for different ways of measuring. We are three individuals trying to create joint understandings.

ROGER: As we converse, we are co-constructing an understanding of some of the central ideas and features of this book. Each of us brings our own ideas to the surface of the dialogue, and we share our understandings in a dialectic process. Thus, one conversation occurs on the surface between three people, but as Ushakova (1994) says, there are three other unspoken conversations going on: each of us is having a private internal conversation within our self – between 'I' and 'me' – in which we refine and make personal sense of the understandings reached on the surface. The external dialogue continues when each of us brings these newly appropriated (Bakhtin, 1981) constructs back into the conversation.

MARÍA: And as Barthes (1977) would say, we also come into the conversation with our reading of many prior authors in conversation within and between us. I see spaces of freedom in how each of the contributors has taken up the call for contributing to a discussion about how the teachers and students have taken up the task of creating a community of learners. It is in the very acts of defining, negotiating, and sustaining what 'appropriate learning behaviours' means. Teachers must step into their personal spaces of freedom (Greene, 1988) to negotiate the individual's unique and personal code as well as personal choice in language learning (Brumfit, 2001) within his/her social life project. Teachers need to have the freedom to move in different ways that will engage the diversity (at a variety of levels) of learners in their classrooms.

ROGER: But in schools in many places, teachers do not have such freedom to act; they may be constrained by pressure from examinations, classroom layout, school authorities, parents and even their own learners.

JOHN: There is still another level that is very important for this book. It is the freedom that teachers can come to when they realise that what they have to say about their own classrooms is just one more turn in a conversation. It does not have to be right or wrong. It is not an argument. It is an assertion. This can be very freeing for the teacher to understand that she is a knowledge maker as well as a learner in a conversation she/he has with other teachers, teacher trainers, researchers about what happens in her/his or anybody else's classroom.

ROGER: And that is how we would like the readers of this book – especially teachers – to respond. There is a third part of each chapter, containing additional transcript data from the original context. Having read the first and second interpretations by contributors to this book, they can consider the new transcript data and take their turn in the conversation. Or, perhaps, start a new one of their own with colleagues and friends, knowing that there are no 'right' or 'wrong' interpretations, but rather different viewpoints each of which may contribute to a growing understanding of classroom activity, and of the multifarious ways in which teachers in different contexts can be seen to induct their students.

Note

1. We used SKYPE, which is a freeware through which the international computer to computer calls are at no cost and this kind of technology enabled us to do the type of collaboration that could not be carried out until recently.

References

Alexander, R. (2001) *Culture and Pedagogy: International Comparisons in Primary Schools.* Oxford: Blackwell Publishers.

Allwright, R. (2003) Exploratory practice: Rethinking practitioner research in language teaching. *Language Teaching Research* 7 (2), 113–141.

Allwright, R. (2006) Six promising directions in applied linguistics. In S. Gieve and I. Miller (eds) *Understanding the Language Classroom* (pp. 11–18). Basingstoke: Palgrave MacMillan.

Bakhtin, M. (1981) *The Dialogic Imagination.* Austin, TX: University of Texas Press.

Barthes, R. (1977) *Image, Music, Text.* Glasgow, Scotland: Collins Fontana.

Batstone, R. (ed.) (in press) *Sociocognitive Aspects of Language Use and Language Learning.* Oxford: Oxford University Press.

Bellack, A.A., Kliebard, H.M., Hyman, R.T. and Smith, F.L. (1966) *The Language of the Classroom.* New York: Teachers College, Columbia University.

Bourdieu, P. (1990) *In Other words: Essays Towards a Reflexive Sociology* (Matthew Adamson, trans.). Stanford, CA: Stanford University Press.

Brumfit, C. (2001) *Individual Freedom in Language Teaching: Helping Learners to Develop a Dialect of their Own.* Oxford: Oxford University Press.

Chick, K. (1996) Safe talk: Collusion in apartheid education. In H. Coleman (ed.) *Society and the Language Classroom* (pp. 21–39). Cambridge: Cambridge University Press.

Coulthard, M. (1986) *An Introduction to Discourse Analysis*. London: Longman.

Fanselow, J.F. (1987) *Breaking Rules*. White Plains, NY: Longman.

Fanselow, J.F. (1992) *Contrasting Conversations*. White Plains, NY: Longman.

Fanselow, J.F. and Barnard, R. (2005) Take 1, Take 2, Take 3 – A suggested three-stage approach to exploratory practice. In S. Gieve and I. Miller (eds) *Understanding the Language Classroom* (pp. 175–199). Basingstoke: Palgrave MacMillan.

Greene, M. (1988) *The Dialectic of Freedom*. New York, NY: Teachers College Press.

Lave, J. (1996) Teaching, as learning, in practice. *Mind, Culture, and Activity* 3 (3), 149–164.

Ochs, E. and Schiefflin, B. (2008) Language socialization: An historical overview. In P. Duff and N.H. Hornberger (eds) *Encyclopedia of Language and Education: Vol. 8 : Language Socialization* (pp. 2–15). Boston: Springer.

Poole, D. (1992) Language socialisation in the second language classroom. *Language Learning* 42 (4), 593–616.

Sonnenmeier, R. (1993) Co-construction of messages during facilitated communication. *Facilitated Communication Digest* 1 (2), 7–9.

Tharp, R. and Gallimore, R. (1990) A theory of teaching as assisted performance. In P. Light, S. Sheldon and M. Woodhead (eds) *Learning to Think: Child Development in Social Context 2* (pp. 42–61). London: Routledge.

Ushakova, T.N. (1994) Inner speech and second language acquisition: An experimental-theoretical approach. In J.P. Lantolf and G. Appel (eds) *Vygotskian Approaches to Second Language Research* (pp. 135–136). Norwood, NJ: Ablex Publishing Co.

Valdes, G. (1996) *Con Respeto: Bridging the Distances Between Culturally Diverse Families and Schools: An Ethnographic Portrait*. New York, NY: Teachers College Press.

Vygotsky, L.S. (1978) *Mind in Society: The Development of Higher Psychological Processes*. Cambridge, MA: Harvard University Press.

Wenger, E. (1999) *Communities of Practice: Learning, Meaning, and Identity*. Cambridge: Cambridge University Press.

Wood, D., Bruner, J.S. and Ross, G. (1976) The role of tutoring in problem solving. *Journal of Child Psychology and Psychiatry* 17, 89–100.

Chapter 1

Under the Interactional Umbrella: Presentation and Collaboration in Japanese Classroom Discourse

TAKE 1: FRED E. ANDERSON
TAKE 2: SYLVIA WOLFE

TAKE 1

Introduction

While formal education plays an important role in the socialization of children in any culture, the role of Japanese schooling in socialization cannot be overemphasized. There are a number of reasons why it may be even more important than school socialization in other societies, particularly Western societies. Japanese children spend a great deal of time at school, with the number of designated school days ranging between 220 and 225, compared with 175–180 days for American children (Wray, 1999). In addition, there are school attendance days, where pupils are expected simply to show up for formal ceremonies, even during vacation periods. Moreover, as has been pointed out by a number of authors (e.g. Peak, 1991; Tobin *et al.*, 1989), modern Japanese children tend to be indulged at home. Hence, much of the socialization necessary for teaching them to be productive members of a community takes place only after they enter preschool. To borrow Peak's words, 'learning to go to school' appears to be a more significant result of preschools than content learning. This emphasis on socialization continues well into the primary school years. As noted by White (1987: 123): 'For the Japanese child, social lessons are everywhere to be found, meaning all activities during the school day are valued, not just those with explicit academic content.'

Children's communities of learning as found in school classrooms both reflect the adult society and serve as systematic preparation for it. Values necessary to succeed in the adult world are developed in the classroom explicitly, through formal instruction, and implicitly, through participation in culturally significant verbal and nonverbal activities. The present chapter examines language socialization in a Japanese lower primary school classroom as reflected in the classroom discourse. The focus is on three recurring routines that are seen to be representative of Japanese socialization more generally. The first is an *aisatsu* or 'greeting' routine used to open and close lessons; the second a *happyoo* or 'presentation' routine, through which students present ideas in response to a teacher's questions; and the third a *hannoo* or 'reaction' routine through which classmates formally respond to each others' presentations.

Setting

The principal data for the study were collected ethnographically in a first-/second-grade classroom in Fukuoka Prefecture, southern Japan. As is customary in Japanese primary schools, the students and teacher remained together as a unit for two academic years. The examples used in this chapter were extracted from 65 hours of participant observation: 23 of these hours were audio or videotaped, and 16 were fully transcribed with the help of native Japanese-speaking research assistants. After an initial period of general observation, social studies lessons were singled out as the main focus of the study for two reasons. First, they were rich with the routines that were seen as integral to Japanese language socialization. Second, the explicit emphasis in the social studies curriculum was on learning about society, especially the local community, and not on language per se; hence the lessons could provide a window on the process of language development as related to more general sociocultural learning.

Theoretical Framework

The study was conducted within the general framework of language socialization, defined as 'socialization to use language' and 'socialization through the use of language' (Schieffelin & Ochs, 1986: 2). The language socialization perspective sees the development of language and world view as occurring in tandem and being mutually influential. The analysis that follows is a condensation of themes discussed in more detail in Anderson (1995). Although this research was, to my knowledge, the first extensive study of Japanese classroom discourse presented in English, related analyses have since been carried out in Japanese first-language environments (Cook, 1999; Dotera, 1998; Walsh, 1998); in the context of teaching and learning Japanese as a second language (Kanagy, 1999; Ohta, 1999); and in relation to the teaching of English as a foreign language in Japanese schools (LoCastro, 1996). The body of research developing in this area allows me to theorize with a greater degree of confidence than was previously possible.

The basic unit of analysis used in the present study is the 'interactional routine' (Gleason, 1976; Kanagy, 1999; Ohta, 1999; Peters & Boggs, 1986), defined as 'a sequence of exchanges in which one speaker's utterance, accompanied by appropriate nonverbal behavior, calls forth one of a limited set of responses by one or more other participants' (Peters & Boggs, 1986: 81). In classroom discourse, it is normally the teacher who initiates the sequence, and students who provide responses, individually or as a group. Although Peters and Boggs's definition specifies that the possible responses are limited, the form of a response may vary in a continuum from formulaic to flexible depending on the initiation. Formulaic responses – such as *aisatsu*, and to some extent *hannoo*, in the present study – require presentation of language in memorized chunks. Flexible responses – such as *happyoo* in this study – do not require specific phrases, but are still culturally constrained by what Peters and Boggs refer to as 'modes of speaking', such as the use of a particular style or register. Nevertheless, whether the response is formulaic or flexible, it is possible to predict at least some aspect of it. Furthermore, 'its predictable structure affords an arena for practice and reinforcement' (Peters & Boggs, 1986: 84), and in this way interactional routines 'can provide "building blocks" for social and linguistic interactions at a time when a child has few linguistic resources at her disposal' (Peters & Boggs, 1986: 86).

Classroom Interaction: Three Classroom Routines and their Cultural Foundations

The *aisatsu* 'greeting': Transitions and teamwork

The routine commonly referred to as *aisatsu* by Japanese teachers and students is a highly formulaic one. It is used to demarcate the beginnings and endings of lessons and other classroom events. The most common English dictionary translation of *aisatsu* is the word 'greeting', but the Japanese concept of *aisatsu* is more inclusive. In the present data *aisatsu* is a short, collectively constructed proclamation that a new lesson is about to begin (or about to end); it can be thought of as a performative speech act (Austin, 1962) where the proclamation itself serves as the beginning (or ending) of the lesson. Similar types of *aisatsu* occur outside of the classroom as well, including – very commonly – in adult interaction. In one study of Japanese business practices, for example, an *aisatsu* is described as the 'formal greeting *ceremony*' preceding negotiations (Hall & Hall, 1987: 118; emphasis added).

In its purest form the classroom *aisatsu* proceeds as in Extract 1 below. Students had been practicing the routine throughout the year and were well versed in its enactment by the time this example was recorded. The data, both here and in ensuing extracts, are presented in the original Japanese

followed by English translations. The first extract below is the opening of a
social studies lesson:

Extract #1:

01   T   Hai / Hajimemasu! *Okay, let's begin!*
02   Ss   <two class monitors> Shisei! / / Ima kara shakai no obenkyoo o
          hajimemasu / rei! *Sit up straight! We now begin the social studies
          lesson. Bow.*
03   Ss   {All students bow}
04   T   Hai / / minna no kooen to iu obenkyoo de ... *Okay. The lesson is
          called Everybody's Park ...*

In the above example, the teacher's first utterance calls for two designated
monitors (Ss) to recite the speech formula that will open the lesson (02). This
formulaic utterance, which can be thought of as the core of the routine, is
called out in a loud, clear voice, using a formal register of Japanese. The
Japanese word *shisei* ('posture' in a direct translation, but translated here as
'sit up straight') carries the dual function of calling the lesson to order while
simultaneously emphasizing the importance of proper non-verbal behavior.
Finally (03), the monitors' classmates acknowledge non-verbally, through
bowing, that the lesson has been opened, which in turn serves as a cue for
the teacher to begin the instructional phase of the lesson (from 04).

A parallel performance of *aisatsu* was later used to close the same lesson:

Extract #2:

01   T   Nooto o atsumegakarisan te o agete kudasai / / ja kyoo wa mae
          no hoo no / migigawa no joshi atsumegakarisan / / aisatsu ga
          sundara motte kite kudasai / / owarimasu. *Workbook-collection
          monitors, raise your hands. Let's see, today's collection monitors are the
          girls at the front right. After we've finished the aisatsu, bring them up
          here. Let's finish now.*
02   Su   Hai. *Okay.* <aside>
03   Ss   <two class monitors> Shisei! / / kore de shakai no obenkyoo o
          owarimasu. / / Rei! *Sit up straight! We now end the social studies
          lesson. Bow.*
04   Sa   Nijikanme taiiku desu. *The second period is P.E.*
05   T   Saa / moo kigaete kyooshitsu de / hora. *Okay, hurry up and get
          changed, in the classroom.*
06   Ss   {Chat informally}

Other than the brief aside (02), the closing *aisatsu* mirrors the *aisatsu* used
to open the lesson. The teacher completes the instructional phase of the

lesson (01), and provides the cue – 'Let's finish now' – which elicits a performance of the *aisatsu* formula (03). This serves as the formal ending of the lesson, after which pupils have a short break during which they are free to chat using a more informal register of Japanese (as in 04 and 06). The teacher herself (05) uses informal Japanese to address the students, as they are now operating outside of the formal lesson mode.

Extracts 1 and 2 together show that *aisatsu* tend to occur in opening and closing sets, and for this reason the routine is not simply a 'greeting' in the Western sense, but rather a device for *framing* classroom events. Similar framing devices have been discussed in studies of Japanese school interaction at other levels as well. Walsh (1998) has revealed how 'ceremonial boundaries' similar to the *aisatsu* of my study are used to frame junior-high-school class meetings. Tobin *et al.* (1989) have related the verbal framing of preschool activities to the Japanese concept of *kejime*, a uniquely Japanese term that implies the clarifying of boundaries between social situations requiring different behaviors. In the classroom, the opening and closing *aisatsu* function as explicit *kejime* to distinguish situations in which formal verbal and nonverbal behavior are required – such as the lessons themselves – from those in which less formal behavior is acceptable – such as recesses and the lunch break. Moreover, the switching between formal and informal registers according to situation is a pattern found not only in school classrooms but in society more generally. Lebra (1976), for example, has described 'situational interaction' as a primary characteristic of Japanese behavior.

So far the *aisatsu* routine has been discussed as a fixed conversational entity. In the remainder of this section, we will consider it from a developmental perspective. The extracts that follow illustrate how, through teacher feedback, students are socialized into proper use of the routine in cases where they do not carry it out according to protocol. In Extracts 3 and 4 – again, both openings of social studies lessons – the teacher emphasizes the importance of nonverbal parameters of the routine.

Extract #3:

01　T　Hajimemasu. *Let's begin.*
02　Ss　<two class monitors> Shisei! // ima kara shakai no obenkyoo o hajimemasu./ Rei! Sit up straight! *We now begin the social studies lesson. / Bow.*
03　T　Shisei ga warui kara / moo ichido shimasu. *Your posture is bad, so let's do it once more.* <It is not clear whether she is addressing the monitors or the other class members.>
04　Ss　Shisei! // Ima kara shakai no obenkyoo o hajimemasu. / Rei! *Sit up straight! We now begin the social studies lesson. Bow!* <This time the performance is accepted>

Extract #4:

01 T   Hajimemasu *Let's begin*
02 Ss <monitors> Shisei! // Ima kara shakai no obenkyoo o hajimemasu /
        Rei. *Sit up straight! We now begin the social studies lesson. Bow.*
03 T   Hai. *Okay.* <Corrects students who have not bowed properly>
04 T   Ii ne // moo ichido onegai shimasu. *That's better. Once more please.*
05 Sa <monitor> Shisei! // Ima kara shakai no obenkyoo o hajimemasu.
        / Rei. *Sit up straight! We now begin the social studies lesson. Bow.*
06 T   Minna ni iroiro kaite moraimashite / kyoo wa kore no happyookai
        o shitai to omoimasu. *I've had everyone write something, and today I'd
        like you to present what you've written.*

In Extract 3, the teacher (03) requests a reenactment of the routine due to deficiencies in the pupils' posture. In Extract 4, it is the way of bowing that does not meet the standards, so this is corrected nonverbally in 03. This is followed up (04) by a call for a reenactment, which takes place in 05. With the lesson now officially opened, the actual instruction begins in 06.

One final example, Extract 5, illustrates a more complex version of the routine. In this example, which is the opening of a Japanese language arts lesson, the teacher explicitly socializes the students through the use of language on several levels.

Extract #5:

01 T   <Gives cue for students to perform routine>
02 Su <monitor> Hai // Shisei // Ima kara kokugo no... *Okay. Sit up
        straight! From now language arts...* {uttered in a quiet voice}.
03 T   Dame! *Stop!* <emphatically> Shisei / Ichi ni! *Sit up straight!, one,
        two!* <loudly and clearly>
04 Su Shisei / Ichi ni. *Sit up straight! One, two.* <playfully>
05 Ss Wa ha ha ha ha. *Ha ha ha ha ha.*
06 Sa Ichi made iu n ja nee. *You don't have to go so far as to say one.*
07 T   Imura-kun *(Mr.) Imura.*
08 Im Hattori-kun wa ... *(Mr.) Hattori is ...*
09 Su Shisei // Ima kara ... *Sit up straight! From now ...*
10 St Piisu. *Peace* <aside>
11 Su kokugo no obenkyoo o hajimemasu. / Rei. *We begin the language
        arts lesson. Bow.*
12 Ss {Bow}
13 T   Shisei to iu no wa / Sensei no hoo o muite / Ima kara benkyoo
        desu // Onegai shimasu // Sensei mo obenkyoo sasete moraoo
        onegai shimasu. *Sit up straight! Means that you face toward the*

> *teacher, and think, 'It's time to study now.' You also ask the teacher to*
> *help you study.*

14 T <Addresses student who has entered late> Daisuke-kun / ohayoo. *Daisuke, good morning.* <Gentle voice>

15 T Hai / Onegai shimasu. *Okay, please go ahead.*

16 Su Shisei // Ima kara kokugo no obenkyoo o hajimemasu / rei. *Sit up straight. We now begin the language arts lesson. Bow.*

17 T Onegai shimasu to iitai keredomo / saito-kun … *I'd like to move on, but (Mr.) Saito is …*

18 Si <Warns classmate> Saito-kun. *(Mr.) Saito.*

19 T Hai / rasto wan // Hai / moo ichido // onegai shimasu. *Okay, last one. Okay, once more. Let's go.*

20 Su Shisei // Ima kara kokugo no obenkyoo o hajimemasu. / Rei. *Sit up straight. We now begin the language arts lesson. Bow.*

21 T Hai / Mazu hinichi to namae o kaite kudasai // sakki to onaji desu. *Okay, first write the date and your names please. The same as before.*

In Extract 5 above, a student monitor begins to produce the *aisatsu* formula in 02, but – apparently because of poor voice quality – the teacher aborts the *aisatsu* and calls for a reenactment (03). She may also be responding to an overall lax attitude by other class members. In the fourth and ensuing turns, one can see that by the end of the second grade, when this extract was recorded, students had become comfortable enough with the routine that they could take liberties in manipulating it. The monitor (04) playfully mocks the teacher by repeating her request verbatim rather than producing the expected response, which gives rise to extraneous laughter and discussion (05–08). Following this light-hearted interlude, the monitor is able (09) to recommence delivery of the formula, and the routine is completed with the classmates' bows (12). However, it is apparent (13) that this enactment is still insufficient. Here the teacher lapses into a metalinguistic explanation of what the routine means and why they are practicing it. This is a type of discourse that is relatively rare in the data, but significant in that it addresses students on a more intellectual level than when they are simply repeating pat phrases. After two more renditions (16 and 20) interspersed with additional distractions and requests, the teacher begins the content phase of the lesson (21), which also serves as implicit acknowledgment that the *aisatsu* has been accepted. In considering this extract as a whole, one thing that stands out is that there is a formal metastructure that defines the routine, but within this structure a degree of informality and extraneous chatter is permitted.

Aisatsu were performed many times throughout the day; not only to open and close individual lessons, but also to announce the beginning and end of the school day, or to frame special events such as class meetings.

While the routine is linguistically simple and at first blush may be dismissed as unimportant, the attention granted it by the teacher points to a cultural significance that surpasses its surface simplicity. This comes through especially clearly in Extract 5, where the teacher refuses to accept the students' lax performance, despite the fact that they are obviously well versed in the mechanics of the routine.

Through these multiple enactments, young pupils are continually reminded of the importance of collaborative activity, and of maintaining situational boundaries. As mentioned earlier, similar routines are ubiquitous in Japanese adult society as well, being used to frame all varieties of meetings, ceremonies and even parties. In this way, socialization to use language, and through the use of language, develops early but continues throughout the lifespan.

The *happyoo*: Presenting the public self

The Japanese classroom activity referred to as *happyoo* in many ways parallels the question-and-answer sequence that is ubiquitous in Western classroom discourse (Gallimore & Tharp, 1990; Mehan, 1979). The term, however, suggests differences from the Western sequence. The most common dictionary translations of *happyoo* are 'announcement' and 'presentation', though the latter is probably a more appropriate English depiction of the event as it occurs in the classroom. In either case, the *happyoo* is constrained by Japanese modes of speaking, though it is not formulaic like *aisatsu*. In my observations, students making *happyoo* would stand and present their ideas formally using a polite, standard register of Japanese (known as *hyoojungo*, literally 'standard language'), while often attempting to construct sentences that were more complex than what they would utter in everyday conversation. The overall effect was that of a simulated public mini-speech. The first of four turns of Extract 6, a social studies lesson, illustrate the *happyoo* in its simplest form.

Extract #6:

01	T	Ne ... de wa ... kore wa ... Nan no tame ni reitooko ni ireru deshoo ka? *Okay ... well ... let's see ... why do we put (fish) in the freezer?*
02	Ss	{Raise hands} Hai! *Yes!*
03	T	<Calls on student> Yonekawa-san. *(Ms.) Yonekawa.*
04	Yo	<Stands> Kusaranai yoo ni suru tame desu. *It is so that it does not rot.*
05	Sa	Ii desu! *Good!*
06	Su	Onaji desu! *I have the same!*
07	T	Kusaranai yoo ni suru. *So that it doesn't rot.*

The teacher initiates the sequence (01) by asking students for the answer to a simple question based on a lesson in the textbook. Students then bid to answer (02), raising their hands high while shouting *hai!*, literally 'Yes!' but probably closer conceptually to the English 'Me!' or 'Here!' One student is then called upon to answer (03), in this case a girl student, Yonekawa. She immediately stands up straight and presents her answer in Japanese *hyoo-jungo* (04). In this case the student's presentation is acceptable, and the sequence hence progresses into the *hannoo* phase (05 and 06), which will be discussed in greater detail in the next section of this chapter.

As was the case with *aisatsu*, *happyoo* do not always proceed according to expectation. An extended sequence may emerge, where the teacher provides feedback to steer a student toward a more desirable answer or form. The following short example in another social studies lesson shows how a boy student, Hattori, modified his *happyoo* as a result of the teacher's feedback.

Extract #7:

01 Ha Boku mo harada-san to onaji desu // atsui tebukuro o shite imasu. *I have the same as (Ms.) Harada. They are wearing thick gloves.* <Student is looking at workbook, responding to question about how workers in a bread factory keep from getting burned.>
02 T <Models more appropriate linguistic form> Shite iru to **omoimasu**. *I **think** they are wearing thick gloves.*
03 Ha <Self-corrects> Shite iru to omoimasu. *I think they are wearing thick gloves.*

Above, Hattori presents an answer (01) which is grammatically and lexically correct. Nevertheless, the teacher seems to feel that he should soften it by adding 'I think', which she models (02), and which Hattori adopts (03).

Through the activity of *happyoo*, school children appear to develop their ability to express ideas using the polite register of Japanese, and, simultaneously, to construct a public, outward looking face to complement the colloquial language and private face of more intimate interactions. In the following section, this process should become clearer, as further examples of *happyoo* and their treatment by the teacher will be shown together with the *hannoo* routine.

The *hannoo* reaction: Acknowledgment and consensus

The third routine, *hannoo* ('reaction'), falls between the fixed and flexible ends of the spectrum proposed by Peters and Boggs (1986). In Extract 6 above, immediately following the first student's *happyoo* (04), classmates react to the content of the presentation by calling out speech formulas chosen from among several pre-instructed possibilities. The two most common formulas in my focus classroom, and the first two that the students had learned, appear in 05 and 06 of this extract. *Ii desu!* ('Good') is simply an acknowledgment that one is listening to one's classmate. *Onaji desu!* ('I have the same') takes the acknowledgment a step further by indicating that one actually agrees with the classmate's presentation, and therefore does not wish to modify or challenge it. The teacher immediately (07) confirms the student's answer, 'So that it does not rot'. This simultaneously serves as a positive evaluation of the *happyoo-hannoo* sequence as a whole, and as a closing out of the sequence.

As with *aisatsu* and *happyoo*, my data include numerous examples of pupils being explicitly socialized into the prescribed use of *hannoo*. Extract 8 shows teacher treatment of inappropriate style during *happyoo/hannoo* interaction, again in a social studies lesson:

Extract #8:

01	T	Hai / ja / mine-kun. *Okay, let's see, (Mr.) Mine.*
02	Mi	Shinbunshi ya fukuro o burasagete imasu. *They hang down newspaper or bags.*
03	Sa	{Raises hand} Hai! // Hai! // Chotto. *Yes! Yes! Let me …*
04	T	Ima / mine-kun ga happyoo shite minna ii desu to ka itte nai kara / mada te o agenai. *Don't raise your hands yet, until you respond ii desu (Good) or something like it, to (Mr.) Mine's happyoo (presentation).*
05	Ss	Ii desu! *Good!*
06	T	Hai. *Okay.*
07	Im	Sawada-kun to mine-kun ni / nan te iu ka ne / iitai koto ga arucha. *I don't know quite how to say it, but I have something to say to (Mr.) Sawada and (Mr.) Mine.*
08	T	Hai / Iitai koto ga arimasu. *Okay, I have something to say.* <Correcting inappropriate speech style from line 07>
09	Im	Hai / Iitai koto ga arimasu. *Yes, I have something to say.* <Self-correction, following teacher; uses formal 'arimasu' rather than colloquial 'arucha'>
10	T	Hai / imura-kun. *Okay, (Mr.) Imura.* <Allows him to continue speaking after correction>
11	Im	<Continues in formal style>

In the above, a boy student, Mine, makes a *happyoo* presentation in (02). Immediately following this, a classmate attempts to gain access to the floor (03) without first reacting to Mine's *happyoo*. The teacher hence intervenes (04) by cautioning the students that they must react to the presenter's *happyoo* before they themselves can speak. This in turn brings about a round of *ii desu!* reactions (05), which the teacher acknowledges (06). The next turn

(07) introduces a new element into the discourse. Imura, a boy student, informally tries to gain access to the floor so that he can respond to his classmates, Sawada and Mine. However, his speaking style is judged as too informal, even including an element of the local dialect (the expression *arucha*), which the teacher corrects through modeling (08). Imura then repeats the correct phrase (09) and is granted the floor (10). This short interchange shows the importance of maintaining appropriate style and register within formal classroom routines. Moreover, explicit correction of this type in my data is generally limited to the formal interactional routines, which further points to the significance of the routines as a vehicle for language socialization.

Two additional reaction turns, *tsukekuwaemasu!* ('I have something to add') and *chigaimasu!* ('I have something different'), were taught later in the year. As evident in the following extracts from a later social studies lesson, these moves also serve as gambits through which reacting students can gain access to the floor and then formulate their own *happyoo*.

Extract #9:

01	T	Nan to iu sakana o sodatete imasu ka? *What kind of fish are they raising?* <Referring to picture in the textbook>
02	Ss	{Raise hands} Hai! *Yes!*
03	T	Hai / ja / mori-kun. *Okay, let's see, (Mr.) Mori.*
04	Mo	{Stands} Hamachi desu. *It is yellowtail.*
05	Ss	Ii desu! *Good!*
06	Ha	Tsukekuwaemasu. *I have something to add.*
07	T	Hai / ja / hattori-kun. *Okay, let's see, (Mr.) Hattori.*
08	Ha	{Stands} Hamachi no kodomo ya / hamachi no naka kurai ya / hamachi no ookii no desu. *There are baby yellowtail and medium-sized yellowtail and large yellowtail.*
09	T	Hai / soo desu ne // hai / demo / sakana wa **hamachi** to kaite imasu / ne? *Yes, that's right. Okay, but, the fish is called **yellowtail**, isn't it?*
10	T	Hai. *Yes.* <Calling on Ozawa.>
11	Oz	{Stands} Hattori-kun to nan ka chotto chigaimasu // nan ka / ippai hamachi o sodatete imasu. *I have something, like, a little different from (Mr.) Hattori. Like, they are raising a lot of yellowtail.*
12	T	Ippai ne // demo / donna sakana tte iu no wa hamachi desu ka? *There are a lot, aren't there. But as for the kind of fish, can we say it is yellowtail?*
13	Oz	Eetto ne // namae wa ii kedo / nanka / nanka / Ippai iru to omoimasu. *Uh, the name is okay but, like, like, I think there are a lot of them.*
14	T	Hai / soo ne. *Yes, I see.*

In Extract 9, following the *happyoo* sequence (01–04), and the first reaction move (05), Hattori uses the *tsukekuwaemasu* formula (06) to gain access to the floor (07) and present his own *happyoo* (08). This leads into a short evaluation by the teacher, in which she questions Hattori's answer (09); and a *happyoo* from Ozawa (11), for which he uses a variant of the *chigaimasu* gambit. In turns 11–14, the teacher engages in a short discussion with Ozawa regarding the appropriateness of his proclamation, and in the end appears to accept it grudgingly.

Extract 10 provides further examples of interaction and socialization through the *happyoo* and *hannoo* routines, and through teacher feedback.

Extract #10: Social Studies

01　T　De wa / misuzu-san no shitsumon. // Jikokuhyoo ga tsuite iru n desu ka? // naze? *Okay, Misuzu's question. Is there a schedule (on the mailbox)? Why?* <Referring to a question by a character in the textbook>

02　Ss　{Raise hands} Hai! *Yes!*

03　T　Kore wa ne / chotto kaite iru hito sukunakatta kedo. // Hai / ja / matsuzaki-kun. *It doesn't look like many of you wrote down the answer. Okay, let's see, (Mr.) Matsuzaki*

04　Ma　{stands} Okurenai yoo ni da to omoimasu. *I think it is so that they will not be late.*

05　Ss　Onaji desu! *I have the same!*

06　Sa　Hoka ni arimasu. *I have something else.*

07　T　Minna / okurenai yoo ni de imi ga wakaru no? // Ja / Sensei shitsumon shimasu // matsuzaki-kun ni shitsumon ga arimasu // hai / nani ga okurenai yoo ni desu ka? *Everyone, do you understand the meaning of okurenai yoo ni (so that they will not be late). Now, I'll ask a question. I have a question for you, (Mr.) Matsuzaki. Okay, what are you referring to when you say so that they will not be late?*

08　Ma　Yuubin o haitatsu suru hito ga / tegami o motte iku no ga okurenai yoo ni. *The people delivering the mail, so that they don't come late with the letters.*

09　Ss　<Matsuzaki's classmates comment informally on the side about his response>

10　Ma　Tegami o haitatsu suru hitotachi ga / tegami o yuubinkyoku e motte iku no o okurenai tame desu. *It is so that the people delivering the mail will not be late in bringing, in bringing the letters to the post office.*

In the above, *happyoo* and *hannoo* are enacted in 01–06; and although the specific reaction move presented in 06 is not common as a speech formula in my data, it corresponds semantically to *chigaimasu* ('I have something different'). The final four turns introduce a new element of language social-ization, namely the teacher developing the students' language skills through metalinguistic awareness. As was the case with explicit correction and modeling, this type of activity seems to occur only within the confines of formal classroom routines.

The notion of classmates reacting and building on one another's presen-tations is pervasive in my data, yet not limited to it. Cook (1999), in her research on third-/fourth-grade Japanese classroom discourse, has identified similar 'reaction turns'. She has discussed these in relation to the develop-ment of 'attentive listening', which was a theme in my earlier work as well (Anderson, 1995), albeit to a lesser extent than in Cook's. Dotera (1998), while not referring to reaction turns specifically, has discovered a similar interac-tional pattern in first-/second-grade classrooms, namely 'idea piling', which emphasizes active participation above strict display of academic knowledge. One can thus see how formal interaction in Japanese classrooms may serve as implicit preparation for culturally valued adult communication practices. Particularly, there would seem to be a relation to the development of 'listener talk' (Yamada, 1997), where the primary responsibility for making sense of a conversation is with the listener rather than the speaker. One can also specu-late on how the collaborative verbal construction of ideas seen in the class-room discourse leads to the process of consensus building that is viewed as central to Japanese adult decision making (Hall & Hall, 1987).

Discussion

The *happyoo* and *hannoo* routines together form an instructional sequence that can be analyzed as consisting of four moves, abbreviated in my own work (Anderson, 1995), and in that of Cook (1999), as Initiation (I), Presentation (P), Reaction (Rx) and Evaluation (E). The validity of this sequence in the wider context of Japanese school culture is further sup-ported by the work of LoCastro (1996), who discovered, in Japanese secondary-school English lessons, a parallel 'four-part teacher soliloquy' (Solicit–Response–Assessment–Acknowledgment) where the teacher played all the 'roles.' In my research, the IPRx-E sequence is defined as follows:

(I)   The teacher elicits a response from students, through questioning or other strategies.

(P)   Students bid to answer through handraising. Selected student stands and presents answer or opinion using standard, polite Japanese (*hyoojungo*).

(Rx)   Classmates react to presentation using formulaic phrases to acknowledge (*ii desu!*), agree (*onaji desu!*), add to (*tsukekuwaemasu!*), or disagree (*chigaimasu!*). The latter two formulas may also lead to new presentations (P), which are in turn subject to classmates' reactions (Rx). In this way, Rx often loops back into P.

(E)   The teacher provides feedback on presentation, especially where revision is required; or on P and Rx moves together.

While the four-part sequence was not the only vehicle of instruction that I observed, it did account for a substantial proportion of the teaching, especially in social studies lessons. A closer look shows that the ceremonial *aisatsu* also follow this model:

(I)   The teacher initiates *aisatsu* sequence with a short phrase such as 'Let's begin now' or 'Let's end now'.

(P)   Designated student monitors recite *aisatsu* formula.

(Rx)   Classmates acknowledge *aisatsu* nonverbally by bowing.

(E)   The teacher evaluates sequence (negatively) by calling for a reenactment; or (positively) by carrying the lesson into the next phase.

Although the IPRx-E sequence is to a large extent an idealized depiction of the discourse, it does have explanatory power when contrasted with the three-part IRE (Initiation–Response–Evaluation) sequence widely described as a cornerstone of Western classroom instruction (Cazden, 1988; Mehan, 1979). It begins in a similar way as the IRE sequence, with students bidding to respond to a teacher's elicitation, together with hand raising. However, the Japanese bid is also accompanied by a distinctive verbalization, *Hai!* ('Yes!' or 'Me!'), which would be seen as inappropriate in western classrooms. In the Japanese classroom, however, it is an expected part of the bid, related, it would seem, to acknowledging one's role as listener. One student (in both Japanese and Western classrooms) is then called upon to respond, but in the Japanese case the response is formal, and hence is labeled 'presentation' (*happyoo*) rather than simply 'response'. But as an outsider conducting ethnographic research within the Japanese system, what initially struck me as the strangest aspect of the discourse was the reaction turns. For these I could identify no clear counterpart in the American school system where I had been raised. The practice of 'calling out' formulaic reaction phrases without first being granted access to the floor was a practice that would likely be highly discouraged, if not forbidden, in classrooms in my culture. Yet it was positively sanctioned, and even subject to explicit instruction and correction, in the Japanese classroom.

Despite differences, however, Japanese and Western instructional sequences do seem to be products of a common metastructure, through which the responsibility for regulating lesson interaction is ultimately assigned to a teacher. This meta-structure may be present in some form – albeit with variations reflecting local cultural norms – in classroom settings in all modern, industrial societies. Viewed within such a universalist framework, the P and Rx turns of the Japanese sequence can be seen together as forming a collaborative response equivalent to the R of the Western IRE sequence. In my previous work (Anderson, 1995) and in that of Cook (1999) this participation structure has been referred to as an 'interactional umbrella'. It suggests that the role of the Japanese teacher is primarily to *structure interactions among students*, rather than to engage in dyadic interaction with students individually, as is more common in the West. While I arrived at this hypothesis strictly from examination of the discourse data, it is interesting that non-linguistic accounts of Japanese early education (Tobin *et al.*, 1989; White, 1987) point to a similar role for the teacher.

The interactional umbrella, like the dyadic interaction of Western classrooms, is above all a means of regulating talk and other activities. However, under the interactional umbrella one may find more collaboration, attention to one's peers, and situational sensitivity than one finds in Western classrooms. And while the structured and often formulaic nature of the routines may create the impression of highly controlled interaction, there is also room for informal talk, laughter, play and sometimes even chaos. In other words, top-down control at this level is not excessive, as some stereotypes of Japanese education might lead one to believe.

TAKE 2

Educational goals are social constructs, translated into action by policy makers, administrators and teachers and reflecting cultural values and notions of identity existing in the wider communities at any particular time in history. These values and priorities are indexed or 'voiced', to use a Bakhtinian term (e.g. Bakhtin, 1986), in the discourses accompanying all social activities and are therefore theoretically accessible for investigation, provided of course that the flow of talk is captured for posterity. The data in this chapter are offered as instantiations of routine exchanges typical of Japanese society today and taught explicitly to children in Early Years and primary settings. They support the view of linguistic anthropologists, Duranti and Ochs, that the classroom is just one example of an 'environment in which socialization through language and socialization to use language take place' (Duranti & Ochs, 1988: 189).

Rules, routines and rituals mediating pedagogic activity can be inferred from the accompanying discourse and offer insights into the issues of concern and values warranted by a particular group of students and their teacher (Alexander, 2001; Christie, 2002). Nevertheless, the meanings transacted are often unclear, even to the participants themselves, supported or negated by features of the physical environment and routine ways of thinking, acting and interacting that operate at a subconscious level of human action – the semiotic conditions mediating interaction. The more contextual information available to the analyst, the richer the interpretation of pedagogic activity becomes, hence my interest not only in linguistic discourse, filled out by observations of non-verbal behaviours, but also in the material and semiotic conditions prevailing in particular activity settings and their wider contexts of interaction. With these assumptions in mind, I begin my commentary on the data submitted.

In the contextual notes accompanying this chapter, Anderson identifies the dominant goal of formal schooling in Japan: to socialise children into the values and norms of behaviour of society at large. He draws attention to the formality of Japanese society, the importance of ritual and deference to authority (children are expected to attend ceremonial occasions, even when on holiday) and their function in equipping children to become 'productive members' of the wider community.

From this background information, we might infer that education in Japan is regarded in a strongly utilitarian light: childhood serves as a preparation for adult life rather than a unique phase of development through which children are nurtured and afforded opportunities to develop their full potentials as human beings. This 'child-centred' view is typically associated with the 'progressive' tradition in education, an ideology inspired by figures such as Friedrich Froebel (1782–1852) and John Dewey (1859–1952) that has resurfaced in various different forms in primary schools in England since the 1960s (Alexander *et al.*, 1995). In contrast, close analysis of the transcripts of classroom discourse presented by Anderson and expanded by the dimensions alluded to above, reveal a preoccupation with ritual and authority in some Japanese educational practices.

The first set of extracts (#1–5) focus on a highly patterned, almost formulaic greeting (*aisatsu*) in which teacher and students engage at the beginning and end of lessons. Without further contextual detail it is, of course, difficult to test the author's claim that the data are 'representative of Japanese socialization more generally' since the extracts might simply capture one teacher's unique way of interacting with his/her children, a quirky mannerism perhaps. It is interesting to observe the nature and quality of relationships mediating these pedagogic interactions and especially the roles assumed by participants in, what I assume to be whole class settings. The teacher is clearly in control, using student 'monitors' to assist his/her organisation of the lesson. Selecting children to collect books at the end of a lesson (#2) is not at all uncommon in English primary schools but the role of '*class* monitors' seems more unusual, at least from my anglicised perspective. Has the teacher delegated authority to the individuals involved or are they representative of the collective body of students? Whichever is the case, the climate of authority appears to be tempered by an ethos of respect that extends to children. Teachers *and* students address each other formally by their titles (Mr/Ms) and in Extract #5 (14) the teacher adopts a kindly tone to welcome a latecomer. In Extract #4 children chat 'informally' whilst getting ready for PE. Perhaps we might interpret these exchanges as indication that although Japanese society is organised hierarchically, it is not ipso facto authoritarian. Let us now take a closer look at what we can learn about the concerns and values prized by participants in these exchanges, by focusing on regulatory aspects of classroom discourse.

Once the teacher signals his/her intention to start (e.g. #1, 3, 4 and 5) the class monitors formally call their peers to attention and announce, with an accompanying bow, the subject of the lesson to follow. The teacher's directions are precise and focus unequivocally on correct performance; how to speak (loudly and clearly, #5: 03) and when/how to bow (#3 and 4). The clearly articulated definition of 'attention' (#5: 13) lends an interesting insight into what it means to be 'doing school' for young children in Japan. Students are required to, 'face the teacher', orientate themselves to study, and 'ask the teacher' for help. These procedural instructions position teachers as the source of all information and children as novices, dependent on the teacher's expertise. Indeed students appear to understand their role in this particular social practice and collude with each other to ensure compliance with instructions (#5: 10, 18).

The linguistic and non-verbal behaviours noted above are typical of traditional models of instruction and an epistemological view of knowledge as objective truths, in a world that is ordered and 'knowable'. The teacher's role is to impart information and 'test' children's understandings (i.e. recall) with simple question/answer routines. The sequence of exchanges in Extract #9 seems to support this interpretation of the enactment of teaching and learning in Japanese classrooms. The teacher is concerned to elicit a 'correct', factual response from students by asking a closed question (What kind of fish are they raising?) and refusing to be drawn into discussion of the size or quantity of 'yellowtail' in the picture. Nevertheless, it would be premature to view this as confirmation of strict, didactic instruction, without understanding either the teacher's purpose or the point in the lesson when these exchanges occur. What is of interest, however, is the way in which students are inducted into the formal processes of presenting opinions and reaching agreement in a public forum.

Although Anderson distinguishes between the routines for 'presenting the public self' (*happyoo*) and 'acknowledgement and consensus' (*hannoo*) the subtle shifts in discourse only become clear to less well-informed readers through the teacher's reminder in Extract #8 (04). It seems that once a student's bid to respond to an opening question has been accepted by the teacher, s/he 'stands' to present an idea (*happyoo*) using a particular form of words. In Extract #7 the antecedent, 'I **think** ...' is required and the teacher models the construction, emphasising the omitted verb. At this stage in the routine other students are expected to concur or otherwise with the proposition using a phrase such as 'ii desu' (good) and without raising their hands. It is only when this phase is exhausted that they might contribute an alternative idea by raising a hand and being selected to speak.

Again, there are clear expectations about the form of words required for injecting fresh ideas into an exchange ('I have something to say' #8: 07–09). Although the author's notes indicate that this formal style differs from colloquial speech the nuances of tone that appear to be at stake (the words are the same) are lost in the processes of translation and transcription. The entire process appears to play out in Extracts #9 and 10 and it is interesting again to observe that although the exchange sequences conform to a predetermined pattern, or script, there is an expectation that students will think for themselves and respect each other's points of view.

What sense, then, can be made of these episodes and what questions do they generate for an observer unfamiliar with Japanese language or culture? First, no information is given about the age of children in these extracts although the subject labels, 'Social Studies' and 'Japanese Language Arts' suggest to an English practitioner accustomed to the less esoteric terms Personal, Social and Health Education (PSHE) and Literacy/English, that students are possibly in the middle years of their primary education, about seven- to eight-years old. Some are clearly able to write (#4: 06) and work independently from work/textbooks, nevertheless it is difficult to know whether students have prepared written answers as a rehearsal for talk (e.g. #7, #10) or are making-meaning from pictures only, as appears to be the case in Extract #9. It would be interesting to discover the age at which children in Japan are expected to participate in formal presentation of their ideas through talk? What is the relationship between print and oral literacies? Is talk valued as a medium for learning in its own right or is it subordinate to writing, so typical of literacy practices in the West? These are of course, questions generated by my own interests. The intention of the author, let us remind ourselves, is to demonstrate 'recurring routines' that are 'representative of Japanese socialization more generally' and it is in this light that I offer my final comments.

The extracts presented suggest that Japanese schoolchildren are introduced to and required to participate in genres of communication that will prepare them for aspects of life in a hierarchically organised society where there is great deference to authority and interactions are respectful and highly coordinated social events. It would have been an interesting addition to the data to have seen examples of similar communicative sequences drawn from business or professional life in Japan. Comparisons between these sources might demonstrate how interaction behaviours learned in school manifest themselves in adulthood and any transformations that occur or are required in new contexts and situations, for example when Japanese men and women operate in global marketplaces where different social practices are juxtaposed.

Of course, it is difficult to gauge the extent to which a preoccupation with authority actually dominates the discourse in Japanese classrooms. In England today, many primary school teachers introduce lessons with clear statements of learning objectives and explicit expectations of pupil behaviour. Nevertheless, although these introductory exchanges might be classified as 'routine', the tenor of a whole lesson will often vary according to the topics of study and shifting goals at different points in a lesson. Sadly, the extracts in this chapter are stripped of lesson context that would allow readers to discover themselves how typical such exchanges are of the whole and whether Japanese children are exposed to alternative communicative possibilities.

TAKE 3

This extract is from a social studies lesson in the middle of the year.

01	T	Hai / de wa / kono mae / tochuu datta ne / kore. // Hai, kono ue no migi no shashin / nan no shashin deshoo ka? *Yes, well, last time, we were in the middle of something, here. Okay, this photo at the top right, what is it a photo of?* <Referring to a photo in the textbook.>
02	Su	Hai! / Hai! *Yes! Yes!*
03	T	(xxx) Hai / ikkai itta kara ne. // Hai. / Takahashi-kun(xxx) *Okay, you only need to say it once. Let's see, (Mr.) Takahashi.*
04	Ta	{Stands} Jitensha okiba desu. *It is a bicycle parking lot.*
05	Ss	Ii desu! *Good!*
06	Ss	Takahashi-kun to onaji desu. *I have the same answer as Takahashi.*
07	T	Hai / 'onaji desu!' dake de yokatta ne. *Yes, but 'onaji desu' is enough, okay?*
08	T	Sono shita / nan deshoo ka? *Below that, what is it?*
09	Ss	{Raise hands} Hai! *Yes!*
10	S1	Sensei / kore / nan te ieba / ieba ii tcharoo ka. *Teacher, this, what do you, what do you call it?*
11	T	Hai / u / muzukashii // yasui-kun. *Yeah, hmm, that's a hard one. (Mr.) Yasui.*
12	Ya	{Stands} Okujoo desu. *It is the rooftop.*
13	Ss	Ii desu! *Good!*
14	S1	Yasui-kun ni tsukekuwaemasu! *I have something to add to (Mr.) Yasui.*
15	S2	Yasui-kun ni tsukekuwaemasu! *I have something to add to (Mr.) Yasui.*
16	T	Hai/ jaa / Ushida-kun. *Okay, let's see, (Mr.) Ushida.*
17	Us	{Stands} Okujoo no asobu tokoro desu. *It is the rooftop play area.*
18	S3	Chigaimasu! *I have something different!*
19	S4	Chotto chigaimasu! // Sensei … *I have something a little different! Teacher …*
20	S5	Chotto chigaimasu. *I have something a little different.*

21   S6   Asobiba yaroo? *Is it really a play area?* {aside; mumbling to self}
22   T   Hattori-kun. *(Mr.) Hattori.*
23   Ha   {Stands} Okujoo no geemu sentaa desu. *It is the rooftop game center.*
24   T   Geemu sentaa? *Game center?*

Guiding questions for Take 3

(1)   What are the rules for turn taking? How does the teacher establish the rules for the students' response?
(2)   From the text reading, when is it appropriate for a student to speak? What does it signal with respect to the teacher's expectation? What does standing up mean in this setting?
(3)   How does the teacher deal with the student's side comment in line 21?

Acknowledgements (by Fred E. Anderson)

The data collection, transcription and early analysis for the author's research were made possible by grants from the Wenner-Gren Foundation for Anthropological Research and from the Japan Association for Language Teaching. Later analysis and writing were supported by a doctoral fellowship from the East-West Center, Honolulu, Hawaii; and by a grant from the Joint Committee on Japanese Studies of the Social Science Research Council and the American Council of Learned Societies with funds provided by the Andrew W. Mellon Foundation. The author would also like to express his deep gratitude to the teacher and pupils in the class; as well as to student assistants and colleagues at Fukuoka University of Education (where he was employed at the time) who helped to make the research possible.

References

Alexander, R. (2001) *Culture and Pedagogy: International Comparisons in Primary Education.* Oxford: Blackwell Publishers.
Alexander, R.J. with Willcocks, J., Kinder, K. and Nelson, N. (1995) *Versions of Primary Education.* London: Routledge.
Anderson, F.E. (1995) Classroom discourse and language socialization in a Japanese elementary-school setting: An ethnographic-linguistic study. Doctoral dissertation, University of Hawai'i at Manoa. Ann Arbor, MIUMI Dissertation Services Document No. 9604132.
Austin, J.L. (1962) *How to Do Things with Words.* Cambridge, MA: Harvard University Press.
Bakhtin, M.M. (1986) *Speech Genres and Other Late Essays.* Austin, TX: University of Texas Press.
Cazden, C.B. (1988) *Classroom Discourse: The Language of Teaching and Learning.* Portsmouth, NH: Heinemann.
Christie, F. (2002) *Classroom Discourse Analysis: A Functional Perspective.* London: Continuum.
Cook, H.M. (1999) Language socialization in Japanese elementary schools: Attentive listening and reaction turns. *Journal of Pragmatics* 31, 1443–1465.
Dotera, I. (1998) Idea piling: Verbal interaction in elementary Japanese language arts. *Language, Culture and Curriculum* 11, 28–46.

Duranti, A. and Ochs, E. (1988) Literacy instruction in a Samoan village. In E. Ochs (ed.) *Culture and Language Development: Language Acquisition and Language Socialization in a Samoan Village* (pp. 189–209). Cambridge: Cambridge University Press.

Gallimore, R. and Tharp, R. (1990) Teaching mind in society: Teaching, schooling, and literate discourse. In L.C. Moll (ed.) *Vygotsky and Education: Instructional Implications and Applications of Sociohistorical Psychology* (pp. 175–205). Cambridge: Cambridge University Press.

Gleason, J.B. (1976) The acquisition of routines in child language. *Language in Society* 5, 129–136.

Hall, E.T. and Hall, M.R. (1987) *Hidden Differences: Doing Business with the Japanese*. Garden City, NY: Anchor Press/Doubleday.

Kanagy, R. (1999) Interactional routines as a mechanism for L2 acquisition and socialization in an immersion context. *Journal of Pragmatics* 31, 1467–1492.

Lebra, T.S. (1976) *Japanese Patterns of Behavior*. Honolulu: University of Hawai'i Press.

LoCastro, V. (1996) English language teaching in Japan. In H. Coleman (ed.) *Society and the Language Classroom* (pp. 40–58). Cambridge: Cambridge University Press.

Mehan, H. (1979) *Learning Lessons: Social Organization in the Classroom*. Cambridge, MA: Harvard University Press.

Ohta, A.S. (1999) Interactional routines and the socialization of interactional style in adult learners of Japanese. *Journal of Pragmatics* 31, 1493–1512.

Peak, L. (1991) *Learning to go to School in Japan: The Transition from Home to Preschool Life*. Berkeley, CA: University of California Press.

Peters, A.M. and Boggs, S.T. (1986) Interactional routines as cultural influences upon language acquisition. In B. Schieffelin and E. Ochs (eds) *Language Socialization Across Cultures* (pp. 80–96). Cambridge: Cambridge University Press.

Schieffelin, B.B. and Ochs, E. (1986) Language socialization. *Annual Review of Anthropology* 15, 163–191.

Tobin, J.J., Wu, D.Y.H. and Davidson, D. (1989) *Preschool in Three Cultures: Japan, China and the United States*. New Haven, NJ: Yale University Press.

Walsh, J.M. (1998) Building ideology: Linguistic ritual in a Japanese junior high school. Unpublished Masters dissertation in Applied Linguistics, Macquarie University.

White, M. (1987) *The Japanese Educational Challenge: A Commitment to Children*. New York: The Free Press.

Wray, H. (1999) *Japanese and American Education: Attitudes and Practices*. Westport, CT: Bergin & Garvey.

Yamada, H. (1997) *Different Games, Different Rules: Why Americans and Japanese Misunderstand Each Other*. New York: Oxford University Press.

Chapter 2

Teaching Content, Learning Language: Socialising ESL Students into Classroom Practices in Australia

TAKE 1: RHONDA OLIVER
TAKE 2: JAMES McLELLAN

TAKE 1

Introduction

This chapter is an exploration of the interactions that occur in a classroom that consists predominantly of students from linguistically and culturally diverse backgrounds. Some students have low levels of English proficiency and struggle with the English language requirements of the mainstream curriculum. In the class the teacher works to develop their English, teach content, but at the same time socialise the students into the culture of mainstream learning.

Observations were made in the middle primary class once a week for an entire 10 week school term. Recordings, both audio and visual, were then made of a 'typical' school day. Transcripts of the resulting discourse show that within the classroom there are a range of interactional exchanges that occur. Further, it appears that the pattern of these classroom interactions is determined by the focus of the task in which the teacher and students are engaged. Specifically the task context influences both the flow of information and the nature of the teacher's feedback to her students. At the same time, the tasks reflect the range of pedagogic intentions of the teacher. Thus, this chapter demonstrates the fine balance that occurs in the exchanges as the teacher attempts to give content instruction, whilst at the same time helping her students learn English (the medium of instruction) and socialising them into the classroom practices of Australian schools.

The curriculum of this class follows that used by mainstream primary school teachers throughout Western Australia. As such there is a strong focus on developing literacy and this includes working to improve students' speaking and listening skills, as well as those skills related to reading, writing and viewing (i.e. media and visual text analysis). For the students in this study these literacy aims are particularly important because of their need to further develop their English language proficiency. Mathematics is also covered by this and other Western Australian teachers, as is science, 'society and environmental' studies and the arts. In order to cover all these areas, wherever possible the curriculum is integrated. The teacher in this study does this by selecting reading texts that can be used as a basis for discussion and activities in other curriculum areas. As shown in the transcripts below some of the talk that emerges about the reading text is then recycled when the class begins a science activity. At the same time the science activity is structured in such a way that the students have the opportunity to work on their speaking and writing skills.

Setting

The data for this study was collected in a school located in an inner city suburb of Western Australia. The population of the school is multicultural with a variety of languages spoken in many of the students' homes. Because of the nature of the local community, the school is an English as a Second Language (ESL) reception school where newly arrived migrant children are supported through intensive English instruction. After a period ranging from approximately six to 12 months, these 'reception' students are then moved into classes that are designed to facilitate their transition into mainstream schooling. It is a class such as this that is the focus of the current study.

Using participant observation, the class of nine and 10-year-olds was observed for a full day, weekly for one school term. As such the researcher became part of the class during this time – she responded to questions from students if they asked, and provided individual assistance on request, however, generally during teacher fronted lessons, individual activities and even group work tasks, she observed and when possible took field notes based on her observations. Towards the end of this school term video and audio recordings were made of the class for one full 'typical' school day. These recordings formed the basis of the transcripts from which samples were selected and analysed.

Classroom Interaction

This current study builds on previous research undertaken with a similar cohort of learners which indicated that particular patterns of interactions occur in classrooms (Oliver & Mackey, 2003). In particular, Oliver and Mackey explored whether or not negative feedback, that is the information provided to learners that indicates the acceptability and/or appropriateness of the language they produce (a construct that has been the focus of numerous second language acquisition studies), occurs and is used more often in some classrooms contexts than it is in others. The findings did, in fact, indicate that this was the case: Teachers were most likely to provide feedback in exchanges that were focused on explicitly teaching language or curriculum content, whereas learners were most likely to use feedback provided in explicit language focused exchanges. Feedback was rarely used by the learners in content exchanges and never when the focus was of a management kind.

In a similar way to this previous study an examination of the current transcript data shows that the teacher interacts with her students in a variety ways, but that there seems to be a systematic pattern in the way she does so. Specifically it appears that the nature of the interaction seems to be very context dependent: further, this context impacts upon the type of language that is used in the classroom, and in particular, on the way that the teacher communicatively engages in the classroom. The context also appears to shape the flow of information – at times this is unidirectional (from teacher to student) and at other times it is a more egalitarian, two way flow. It also shapes whether or not the teacher provides feedback, and if she does so – the form that it takes. Thus it would seem that the tasks and the related interactions that are the centre of the various classroom contexts reflect the various intentions of the teacher. These include her apparent aims to informally interact in communicative ways with her students; to manage behaviour; to teach mainstream content; and, to further develop the English language proficiency of her charges. Examples of these patterns are illustrated below.

Communicative exchanges

In all classrooms there are times when teachers interact in communicative ways. During such times informational exchange is genuine (as distinct, for example, from situations where teachers ask display questions – questions to which they already know the answer) and the flow of information is two way between the teacher and her students. Therefore, in these contexts the teacher and her students work together to share information and jointly construct meaning. As such, the teacher appears to be working in ways to socialise the students into appropriate ways of communicating with other English speakers. The following exchange occurs during a 'news sharing' activity at the beginning of the day and demonstrates one such communicative exchange.

Extract #1a

01   Ma   On Saturday, I went to watch the movie 'Liar Liar'
02   T   Liar, Liar, did you like it?

03   Fr   Funny /
04   T   Did you want to ask a question to Pia?
05   Fr   {shakes head}
06   T   Any questions?
07   Fr   Is it fun?
08   Ma   Yes
09   T   Was it a funny movie?

Mark shares information about an activity he did on the weekend. The teacher follows this with a genuine question asking whether the student liked the movie. At this point Frederique joins the conversation. Unfortunately, the question she asks is incomplete and thus unclear, but when prompted she initially declines the opportunity to clarify the question. However, when the teacher opens up the floor, inviting all the students in the class if they have questions, Frederique attempts her question again. Although the form the question takes is non-target-like (in that it is not said in the same way a native speaker would say it), it is clear that Mark understands and responds accordingly. Next the teacher provides form-focused, but meaning oriented feedback repeating the same question asked by Frederique, but in a target-like way, that is the teacher provides a recast (Long, 1996: 234, defines recasts as 'utterances that rephrases a child's utterance by changing one or more sentence components (subject, verb or object) while still referring to its central meanings').

By reformulating the question in this way she is able to maintain Frederique's intended meaning, but also provides a model for both this student and the entire class. However, as can be seen in Extract 1b, Mark ignores this repetition and continues with his recount.

Extract #1b

10   Ma   I don't know why it was-um-it was only for-um-eighteen-to
          eighteen-to eighteen-um, it wasn't for little-
11   T   It wasn't for girls and boys?
12   Ma   Yeah, it wasn't meant-
13   T   But was it OK?
14   Ma   Yeah, and there were lots of little people-
15   T   There]were
16   Ma   Yeah, and]
17   T   [And
18   Ma   [More small than me
19   T   Smaller than you?
20   Ma   {Nods}
21   T   All right then, thank you very much

Once again Mark's production is non-target-like, but this time the teacher responds with a confirmation check (11) – thus engaging in what has been described in much of the second language literature (initially described by Long, 1980) as negotiation for meaning. However, the teacher not only checks the meaning of Mark's previous utterance, but actually reformulates it into a more meaningful form. The conversation proceeds with the teacher asking another genuine question 'But was it OK?' (13) and then prompting the students in order to progress the conversation further, including another recast in the form of a confirmation check (19). Thus, in this exchange the focus is very much on genuine two-way information exchange, and even when there is a focus on form (specifically feedback relating to the structure of a student's turn), the sharing of meaning remains central to such a communicative exchange. This pattern of interaction continues when the teacher turns to another student and again engages in meaning oriented communication:

Extract #1c

22	T	Where did you go?
23	St	I go to New Coles.
24	T	Coles. What did you buy at Coles? Food?
25	St	Yep – and vegetables.
26	T	And which-. Do you know the name of the Coles?
27	St	Perth. Perth
28	T	The Perth Coles.
29	St	Yep
30	T	What did you buy there? Food?

Once again the teacher prompts a sharing of information by asking the genuine question 'Where did you go?' Steven responds with the name of a particular store. The teacher recasts Steven's contribution from 'New Coles' – the name written on the store to that in common usage 'Coles' (24). Without providing an opportunity for uptake (i.e. for the student to incorporate this lexical change) the teacher proceeds with the conversation asking further questions 'What did you buy there? Food?' Therefore, it can be seen that even in this small exchange there is a two way flow of information, and although the teacher provides reformulation (as a recast) the focus appears to be very much on meaning rather than form, once more highlighting the way the teacher appears to socialise her students into appropriate ways of conversing.

Management interactions

At other times it was apparent that the teacher was more concerned with directing the students' actions and socialising them into appropriate ways of behaving within the classroom than she was about working to develop her students' language and understanding. As a consequence the information generally flowed in a one way direction: specifically it was provided by the teacher for her students. When the students did contribute to the interaction, the teacher appeared to pay little attention to its form. Further, she did not appear to react with any strength to the communicative intent of the students – so that in this context she did not ask questions to clarify student meaning. Thus, the illocutionary intent of these exchanges appeared to be very much about getting the student to do as they were asked.

In the following extract, the students are seated and are working in groups around the room. The teacher gets their attention and instructs them on how to undertake a new task. She does this by providing a series of directives and then by exemplifying these.

Extract #2

1	T	Alright, now you're going to stay in your groups.// This time, I want you to think of your favourite reptile
2	Ro	(xxx)
3	St	Oh cool
4	T	Right, now I want you to say]
5	Ch	[Alligator
6	T	[Don't-just think it up here {Point's to head} / What you have to say to your group is 'I like the alligator **because**'/// Now you think why you like it
7	St	(xxx)
8	T	Right, now back in your groups//the same first, second, third/ right. // Back you go quickly.

The teacher begins with the discourse marker 'Alright', she then provides two instructions – 'stay in your groups' and 'think of your favourite reptile'. Even when Robin and Steven make comments about the task, the teacher simply ignores them, even though the form of their comments (2 and 3) is both unclear and possibly non-target-like. When Charles proffers an example of a reptile that he likes, the teacher does expand on this, but only in terms of using the lexical item as a way to further explain what the students must do in their groups. It is clear that she intends to get them working both efficiently on the set task – listing in an ordinal way things that must occur (i.e. first, second, third) and with speed (i.e. go quickly). As such she is clearly setting the parameters around what is expected in school and in doing so, socialising students in appropriate ways of behaving in the classroom.

In Extract #3 the teacher is again focused on having the student act in appropriate school ways, that is, her interactions are primarily concerned with socialising the students into acceptable school behaviours. This time she does interact briefly with students Jacob and Warren when they indicate that they have finished the assigned task 'Are you finished? Good ...' (03), however, it is simply to reward them for completion and then to again reinforce the appropriate classroom behaviour 'Right, it's not playing games, we're reading.' The exchange once again ends with her listing, in order, the tasks that must be done 'You pack up yours please, and put it away.'

Extract #3

1	T	Right, did you put your name up the top and put the date?
2	Ja	Yes, I'm finished
3	T	Are you finished? // Good, I just have to hear these people read.
4	Wa	I'm finished
5	T	And you've finished yours? I just have to collect it. // Right, it's not playing games, we're reading. / Right, you pack up yours please, and put it away

In Extract #4 a similar pattern emerges with the teacher providing all the information in a one way direction to her students as she transitions from one part of the lesson to another. Thus she provides instructions and explanations without involving the students in any part of the discourse. Even when a student attempts to question her, the teacher's response is actually formulated in such a way that enables her to continue providing her directions.

Extract #4

1	T	Right, let's have a look here. Jack, don't worry about what's over there, just sit down- sit down and look this way. Now we need to think very carefully.
2	Ja	Why?
3	T	You're going to try and help me do a little bit of writing.

Content interactions

An examination of the transcripts shows that when the teacher focuses on the content of the curriculum this results in didactic interactions. Many of the exchanges in this context include the stereotypical Initiation-Response-Feedback (IRF) and drill/display pattern of teacher directed talk. In this way the students are invited to participate, but the communication is directed by the teacher and as such the information generally flows in a one way direction. The IRF pattern of interaction has been well documented (e.g. Cazden, 1988; Coulthard, 1986). In fact, as Hall and Walsh (2002: 189) indicate 'the ubiquity of the Initiation–Response–Evaluation (IRE) pattern of interaction in the second and foreign language classrooms' has been confirmed time and time again. This was clearly the case in the data taken from this classroom as illustrated in Extract 5 below:

Extract #5

1	T	OK, K it's your turn
2	Ka	I like turtles/
3	T	Because/
4	Ka	Because it's not dangerous, and/ That's it
5	T	All right, because it's not dangerous, and/ {turns towards Ben}
6	Be	I like sea turtle (?) because it can swim and is no dangerous
7	T	What was that?
8	Be	Is no dangerous
9	T	Not dangerous, right-come here-yes-come here // Is everybody finished?

The teacher uses this pattern as part of the language 'drill' of the classroom – using the pattern to refine the students' production, but also as a way to scaffold further development. Despite this, if a problem with the form of a student's contribution occurs the teacher provides feedback, and does so in a meaning oriented way, such as through the use of confirmation checks or clarification requests. The teacher initiates the exchange by nominating a student to participate (01). In response, Kath provides her answer (02) but then falters in her attempt to explain why she likes turtles. The teacher in her feedback to this provides a prompt in the next turn using the word 'Because' with rising intonation to indicate that Kath needs to complete this turn. Kath does so, but finishes her initial attempt with the conjunction 'and'. When she is unable to expand further, she changes direction and claims 'That's it' (04). The teacher then initiates an interaction with another student by using the form provided by Kath and using the same incomplete utterance ending with 'and' to invite a response, thus using one student's contribution to scaffold the form for the entire class. Ben responds providing an additional piece of information 'it can swim' (06), but also appending it to the meaning provided by Kath. However, the form he uses is incorrect and so in response the teacher provides corrective feedback, and in this case in the form of a clarification request 'What was that?' (07). Note, however, it is not explicit feedback – the teacher does not state 'No that's wrong' or 'You don't say it in English like that', rather it is done in a conversational and implicit way. In response Ben repeats his non-target-like production saying 'Is no dangerous', but this time the teacher provides a partial recast stating 'Not dangerous' (09). Without providing an opportunity for Ben to incorporate this correction, the teacher moves to a more management-focused exchange as she concludes this part of the lesson. Thus it can be seen that within the context of these exchanges the teacher focuses on the form of the students' language and where it does not conform to that which is expected (i.e. target-like production) the teacher provides corrective linguistic feedback, and does so in an implicit and conversational, rather than in an explicit way. Despite the conversational nature of this feedback the direction of the exchange is controlled by the teacher – she is always the one to initiate the exchange and to provide the feedback. The students' role in these types of exchanges is simply to respond in an appropriate way to the teacher.

As noted in the introduction this class is situated in a large multicultural school. The purpose of this and similar classes is to facilitate the transition of the students into mainstream learning. There is a great deal of English that the students in the class still have to learn. In the following extract it can be seen how the teacher works during a reading lesson to provide opportunities for language learning and in particular to develop her students' vocabulary and understanding of words. Thus there is a focus on the form of the English language (in this case mostly lexical) and this includes talk by the teacher about components of the English language (i.e. metatalk), or what Swain and Lapkin (1998) refer to as Language Related Episodes.

Extract #6

1	T	Now this morning we're going to look at a new big book./ Now our new big book comes from New Zealand and it's a Mäori story.
2	Fr	Mary?
3	T	No Mäori. Mäori are special people that come from New Zealand, and this is the story.
4	St	Oh, I know this one
5	T	Well, you keep quiet then / This is 'Hachu Pachu and the Bird Woman' and this is Hachu Pachu. Okay, this is the bird woman
6	St	Yukky
7	T	Yes, very yukky / <reading> 'Let me tell you about Hachu Pachu, of the Arawa people. One day in the forest, Hachu Pachu met the bird woman. She was a bony old woman, she had bony legs, and bony fingers and feathers on her bony arms.'/ What do I mean by bony? Pia?
8	St	Bones
9	T	Right, where are your bones? Feel your bones
10	St	Here
11	T	Good, you can feel inside you've got bones. 'Young Hachu Pachu tried to run, but the bird woman pounced on him and took him to her house in the forest.' She pounced on him.

Unlike in the IRFs described in Extract #5, the students in this extract have the opportunity to initiate these exchanges. For example, Frederique uses a confirmation check 'Mary?' (02) to negotiate meaning with the teacher. The teacher then uses this opportunity to explain the meaning of the word Mäori. Also in these exchanges, unlike that which occurs in the management exchanges the teacher responds to, rather than ignoring, the comment when Steve calls out 'I know this one' (04). Further, in this context, the teacher will also change direction (07), in this case interrupting the reading of the story to engage the class in a discussion about the meaning of the word 'bony'. Thus she takes the opportunity to enhance her students' vocabulary and to maintain a meaningful interaction with them. However, when she has concluded reading the story, as shown in Extract #7 below, the teacher moves back into a didactic pattern of interaction, questioning the students about their knowledge and understanding of the story:

Extract #7

1	T	Now let's go back to the bird woman. Who can tell me something about the bird woman? Look at what she has. What her hair is like/ What her arms are like? C?
2	Ch	She has a long leg, and a skinny leg, and a sharp claws
3	T	Right, long skinny legs with sharp claws. Very good. O?
4	Og	She has green eyes
5	T	Good. She has green eyes. Good. One more?
6	St	And feathers
7	T	Right, and feathers on her arms
8	Di	She has got beak
9	T	Right, and she has a beak like a bird. I think that is why she's called Bird Woman, and because she's got feathers. P?
10	Pe	She's got black colour
11	T	Right, she is a black colour. Something else A?
12	An	She's got long hair
13	T	And she's got long hair like that. Y?
14	Yo	She's got no clothes
15	T	Right, she's not wearing clothes because she's called bird woman, she's part bird, part woman. Yes, C?
16	Ch	She body is very skinny
17	T	Right, her body is very skinny, very thin. E?
18	Er	I've forgotten.
19	T	You've forgotten. / Okay, let's have a look. {Puts up a picture of the bird woman and puts the book away} Right, now here is the bird woman. The only thing I haven't got there- what colour were her eyes?
20	Ss	Green
21	T	Green

In this extract it can be seen how the teacher quite clearly indicates to the class that the topic of the discussion will be about the text they have just read: 'Now let's go back to the bird woman.' She asks for descriptions about the bird woman and scaffolds her questions so that the students can respond appropriately: 'Look at what she has. What her hair is like. What her arms are like' and then she nominates a student to respond (01). When Charlie does and provides his answer in a non-target-like way, she commends him on the content of his answer 'Right' and 'Very good', but recasts it into a more target-like form – 'long legs with sharp claws'. She then embarks on a cycle of IRF exchanges eliciting responses from a number of students. In her feedback she provides a recast for Charlie's reply (03), repeats Ogga's response (05) and elaborates Steve's (06) brief contribution. She then provides a summary and provides the class with a rationale for why the character is called the bird woman (09). She then continues further IRF cycles (09–19) with her students – getting their responses and providing feedback that both affirms their answers and also reformulates their responses towards more target-like forms (e.g. 10, 15 and 17). She even invites a choral response from the class about the colour of the woman's eyes (19). And so this pattern of exchange continues until the completion of this discussion about the story of the bird woman.

Discussion

The examples of interactions provided above serve to illustrate the various ways that the teacher interacted with her students. They also show that when there is a communicative focus the interactions are less formal and the meaning is shared in a two way direction between teacher and student(s). During such exchanges, when a problem occurred with the way a student formed his or her responses, although the feedback from the teacher was form-focused it was primarily meaning oriented (and included the use of recasts and negotiation strategies). In contrast, when the teacher was focused on managing student behaviour, particularly in relation to socialising the students into acting appropriately in class, the information flowed in a one way direction, and in addition, the teacher rarely provided feedback related to the form of a student's utterance. Similarly, a curriculum and/or content focus resulted in didactic interactions with information generally flowing in a one way direction – from teacher to students. Many of these exchanges also included the asking of display questions and the use of the stereotypical IRF pattern, sometimes in the form of drilling. However, unlike in the management exchanges if there was a problem with the form of a student's contribution, feedback was provided and it was usually meaning oriented. Also evident in these content exchanges was comment by the teacher about aspects of the English language (i.e. metatalk), labelled by some as Language Related Episodes (Swain & Lapkin, 1998).

Thus, the examples of interactions provided in this chapter demonstrate the fine balance that the teacher works towards as she undertakes to teach content, whilst at the same time helping her students learn English (the medium of instruction) and socialising them into the classroom practices of Australian schools.

TAKE 2

It is assumed that these extracts occur consecutively, apart from Extract #5, which seems to follow from Extract #2. It is evident that the teacher has both a pedagogical and a socialising agenda. These are operationalised simultaneously throughout the seven extracts. Hence in this 'Take 2' commentary, the interactive features and the pedagogical aspects of the instructional task are considered together, rather than under separate headings.

The pedagogical agenda is the development of the students' capacity to participate in classroom interaction using English, so as to 'facilitate their transition into mainstream schooling', as mentioned in the introduction. This includes contributing meaningfully and accurately to the interaction, and involves initiating as well as responding, as in Extract #1a, in the target language.

The socialising agenda can at times be in conflict with the pedagogical. Classroom socialisation, defined in Chapter 3 (this volume) on Brunei as 'the ways in which students become attuned to the interactional expectations of teachers and other stakeholders', involves students learning about the constraints on participation. An example is found in Extract #6, where the student's grammatically accurate comment, 'Oh I know this one' (04), is not evaluated positively by the teacher, who asks the student to keep quiet and not spoil the novelty of the story for the others.

Socialisation in these extracts also involves ensuring that students follow the structural frame provided by the teacher during their group-work, as demonstrated in Extracts #2 and #5, where they are expected to follow the prescribed model 'I like (name of reptile) because ...'. The teacher seems insistent that this should be the pattern used in Extract #5, supplying the prompt 'Because' (03) when the student hesitates.

Likewise, as part of their socialisation they are required to understand the 'activity frame' (van Lier, 1984) in which the teacher is operating at any particular time, especially as this can change. This is noticeable at the end of Extract #1b, when the end of the 'news sharing activity' is explicitly signalled by her closing move 'All right then, thank you very much' (21). Likewise, in Extract #3 the teacher feels the need to make the activity frame explicit by saying 'Right, it's not playing games, we're reading' (05).

There is a risk that students, as recently-arrived migrants to Australia and coming from a variety of linguistic and cultural backgrounds, may experience some measure of confusion as to what is expected of them in terms of their participation in oral interaction. They receive mixed messages. In Extract #2, responding to the teacher's prompt (01), the student produces the word 'Alligator' (05). The teacher's evaluation in the following turn is not positive, partly because this single-word response is deemed to be structurally insufficient, but also because the transcript shows this as an interruption of the teacher's instruction (04).

On the pedagogical side the teacher's evaluative follow-up moves are worthy of close analysis. In the news-sharing Extracts #1a, 1b and 1c, there is next to no actual student–student interaction, although this is what she is trying to encourage at this point. Her comment (04) represents a negative evaluation of the student's single word comment 'funny'. Eventually, after initial reluctance (05), a question is offered and responded to appropriately (07 and 08). However, the teacher then reverts to a form-focused activity frame which runs contrary to the fluency-oriented news sharing agenda, by offering an expanded reformulation of the question, shifting the tense to the simple past, 'Was it a funny movie?', (09). A similar form-focused reformulation occurs in Extract #1b, where 'More small than me' (19) is corrected to the correct comparative form 'smaller'.

Elsewhere student contributions are not recognised, and there are instances where the teacher interrupts a potentially meaningful and grammatically accurate student comment, such as in Extract #1b, 'Yeah it wasn't meant ...' (12). The teacher's interruption (13) actually shifts the topic initiated by the student, who has produced a lengthy contribution commenting on the unnecessarily high (18+) rating given to the movie 'Liar Liar'. Her reformulation, 'But was it OK?', is asking the student to comment on the suitability of the movie for a younger audience. The student answers this with a cursory 'Yeah' (14) and reverts to the topic (s)he wants to share with the class, that in spite of the 18+ category there were plenty of younger people in the audience.

In Extract #5, where the students are working in groups practising the formulaic pattern 'I like (name of reptile) because ...', the teacher closely monitors the group's output for accuracy, and to ensure that they remain on task. Having accepted the student's contribution (04–05), she prompts another student to make a longer contribution. Ben adds some new information 'because it can swim' and also repeats the phrase used two turns previously by the other student, 'is no(t) dangerous'. The function of the teacher's question (07) is uncertain: either a signal that she has not clearly heard what B said, or else it is an evaluative move inviting the student to pay closer attention to accuracy and to notice that the negative 'no' is an error. The student interprets the question as the former, and repeats 'Is no dangerous'. The teacher corrects this to 'Is not dangerous' (09), then immediately signals the end of this group-work activity. Whilst group-work tasks are more usually fluency-focused, in this case the teacher attempts to monitor closely for grammatical accuracy of the students' output.

Throughout Extracts #6 and #7 student contributions are dealt with somewhat curtly, as the activity frame here is the teacher recounting a story from a big book, with the students expected to be passive listeners until prompted to contribute. In Extract #6, the student mishears 'Mäori' as 'Mary' (02) uttered with a rising intonation, requiring further explanation from the teacher about who the Mäori people are. The student's reaction to the picture 'Yukky' (06) is accepted, but she immediately reverts to reading. She then feels the needs to negotiate the meaning of the key word 'bony', which occurs four times in succession in the book text. The student's response 'Bones' (08) suggests that this is understood, but the teacher decides that further negotiation is required and, leaving the book text, elicits a physical response by instructing students to feel their bones. 'Bony' and 'pounced' (11) are identified by the teacher as items in the book text which may be problematic for the students to comprehend, and therefore require a form of meaning negotiation beyond a mere comprehension check. This can be seen as a one-sided form of negotiation for meaning, since – apart from the example of Mäori – it is the teacher who determines which words represent items of possible misunderstanding.

The shifting activity frames throughout these extracts can be presented in Table 2.1. The extracts show that there are issues relating to control and management of the interaction by the teacher. She presumably sees it as her responsibility to demonstrate by example, and thus transmit to the students a sense of what is and what is not legitimate language and the ground rules of legitimate participation in the Australian classroom. At the same time, one is left wondering just what mixed messages the students are taking from this lesson, about what kind of contributions they are expected to make, about whether they should focus more on accuracy of expression, on taking longer turns, or on communicating meaning fluently. Although, as shown in Table 2.1, the teacher attempts to make her expectations explicit, there must be a risk that students will not immediately interpret the signals which indicate the activity frame, as this changes according the different transactions determined by the teacher in her lesson plan.

TAKE 3

This interaction follows immediately from Extract #7 above.

1 T Her eyes were green. So maybe I'll put green here for her eyes.
     Now we're going to call her/ She's called 'Bird Woman'. Now C,
     I like some of the things that you told me. You tell me something
     about the lady/ You said something about she had long/
2 C Long, skinny legs
3 T She has long skinny legs/ and the last one?
4 Ss Sharp claws

Table 2.1   Analysis of activity frames and expectations

Extract	Activity frame	Teacher's signal of activity frame	Expected student behaviour	Focus
1 (a, b, c)	News sharing	Beginning (not given in the extract) End: 21, 'All right then, thank you very much'	Initiate and develop conversation topics	Fluency
2	Group-work	06 'what you have to say to your group is …'	Form sentences following a pattern	Controlled structural practice
3	Transition to reading activity	05 'Right, it's not playing games, we're reading'	Finish and submit scripts, then listen in silence	Aural comprehension
4	Transition to writing activity	03 'You're going to try and help me do a little bit of writing'	01 "…think very carefully"	Pre-writing planning
5	Group-work	(as in Extract 2)	Accurate output: forming sentences following a pattern	Controlled structural practice
6	Reading	01 'we're going to look at a new big book'	Listen in silence	Aural comprehension
7	Answer questions on the reading and picture	01 'Who can tell me something …'	Describe a picture from memory; respond to teacher elicitations	Display understanding and recall

5	T	Right, I didn't hear that. Sorry, C you say it again
6	C	With the sharp claws
7	T	Right, 'has long, skinny legs and sharp claws- '
8	O	On his feet
9	T	Do you want to say where they were?
10	T	No, let C say.
11	O	On his feet
12	T	Do you want to say where they were? No, let C say.
13	C	On her feet
14	T	'- on her feet'. Right, O you tell me something about/ like you told me about her eyes.
15	O	And sharp claws on her-
16	T	On her fingers
17	A	And the feathers
18	T	She has feathers. All right. On her ends of her fingers she has sharp claws. Now what were you saying about the feathers? She has feathers/
19	Ss	On her arms
20	T	She has feathers on her arms/
21	F	But she can't fly.
22	T	I think she can a little bit, but it didn't exactly tell us how she moved around. So, she has feathers on her arms. Now what you have to do is what I've just done. Say some things about the Bird Woman. No, you can use the words to help you/ Now remember long skinny legs and sharp claws on her feet. Now, if you need a word from the book like bony, maybe I'll write bony on the board. I'll put bony over here- 'bony arms'. Right, there's the word bony. Now, here's your paper. It's already called it Bird Woman for you. You can colour the eyes in green, and you say all the things about how the Bird Woman looks.

Guiding questions for Take 3

(1) What are the elements of the interaction that establish the teacher's expectation about the academic learning goals for the students?

(2) How does the teacher communicate appropriateness of turn-taking in this passage?

(3) How does the teacher support the students' thinking before the activity of colouring and writing about the Bird Woman begins?

References

Cazden, C. (1988) *Classroom Discourse: The Language of Teaching and Learning.* Portsmouth, NH: Heinemann.

Coulthard, M. (1986) *An Introduction to Discourse Analysis.* London: Longman.

Hall, J.K. and Walsh, M. (2002) Teacher-student interaction and language learning. *Annual Review Applied Linguistics* 22, 186–203.

Long, M.H. (1980) Input, interaction, and second language acquisition. Unpublished doctoral dissertation, University of California, Los Angeles.

Long, M.H. (1996) The role of the linguistic environment in second language acquisition. In W.C. Ritchie and T.K. Bhatia (eds) *Handbook of Research on Language Acquisition: Vol. 2. Second Language Acquisition.* New York: Academic Press.

Oliver, R. and Mackey, A. (2003) Interactional context and feedback in child ESL classrooms. *Modern Language Journal* 87 (4), 519–533.

Swain, M. and Lapkin, S. (1998) Interaction and second language learning: Two adolescent French immersion students working together. *Modern Language Journal* 82 (3), 320–336.

van Lier, L. (1984) Analysing interaction in second language classrooms. *English Language Teaching Journal* 38 (3), 160–169.

Chapter 3

Socialisation and 'Safetalk' in an Upper Primary English Language Classroom in Brunei Darussalam

TAKE 1: JAMES McLELLAN AND PEARL CHUA-WONG SWEE HUI
TAKE 2: MARÍA E. TORRES-GUZMÁN

TAKE 1

Introduction and Conceptual Framework

This chapter investigates aspects of socialisation in an upper primary English language classroom in Negara Brunei Darussalam, as exemplified in an extract from a lesson taught by a Bruneian teacher. Socialisation is defined as the ways in which students become attuned to the interactional expectations of teachers and other stakeholders, including school principals, inspectors and Ministry of Education officials. Teachers are constrained by these stakeholders, as well as by the wider Bruneian community, to socialise their students in ways that are exemplified in the data extract discussed in this chapter.

The main conceptual framework is the notion of 'safetalk' and 'safe' language practices (Arthur & Martin, 2006; Chick, 1996, 1998; Hornberger & Chick, 2001), addressed in the discussion section in relation to the lesson extract. The notion of 'safetalk' derives from the work of Chick (1996), who analyses interaction in a Mathematics lesson in Kwazulu-Natal, South Africa, during the apartheid era:

> safetalk is a style of interaction that subordinate groups socialise one another into as a means of coping with the overwhelming odds they face in social and policy contexts ... where children are taught through the medium of a language not their own. Chick (1998: ¶2.0)

Summarising the features of interaction in English-language and English-medium subject classrooms in Brunei, Cath and McLellan suggest that

[t]he talk between teachers and pupils becomes something of a cooperative venture or a game played according to local rules: pupils do not expect to be given long turns at speaking or to be asked many open questions, and teachers are content to meet these expectations. (Cath & McLellan, 1993: 14)

This observation can be linked with Chick's 'safetalk' notion and can be considered as an example of 'safe' language practices.

In addition, van Lier's (1984: 161) concept of 'activity frames' in the discourse of language classrooms is used in the discussion of the language-related tasks. Activity frames correspond to the teacher's agenda or expectations for what she expects the class to do at any point in the lesson: whether to repeat what she says or reads out, or whether to respond to her elicitations, prompts and questions. The turn-taking rules, and other conventions of language classrooms, 'do not follow the rules of general conversation' (van Lier, 1984: 162).

Sociocultural Context

An outline of the roles, status and functions of language use in the classroom and in the wider society is a prerequisite to the more focussed investigation of the lesson extract. We draw on Chua-Wong (1998) and McLellan and Chua-Wong (2002) as major sources for the following sections outlining the Brunei classroom context.

Language policy in education in Brunei Darussalam

Negara Brunei Darussalam is a small independent Muslim monarchy situated on the north-west coast of the island of Borneo, with a population of some 380,000 (Wikipedia, 2006, Demographics of Brunei). Of these, 28.1% are between the ages of 0 and 14 years, a relatively high figure compared to other nations. About two-thirds of the total population are classified as Brunei Malays: this figure also includes the other indigenous groups known as *'puak jati'* (native races). Chinese, Iban, Penan and foreigners employed in Brunei account for the remainder. There is a high level of individual and societal multilingualism (Martin & Poedjosoedarmo, 1996; Noor Azam, 2005), with very few monolinguals aside from monolingual English-speaking expatriates. Nothofer (1991), describing the languages of Brunei, distinguishes between Standard Malay (*Bahasa Melayu*) which is almost identical to the Standard Malay of the Malay Peninsula but with identifiable Bruneian features, and the local vernacular and *lingua franca* Brunei Malay. The two varieties are closely related and are thus mutually intelligible (Nothofer, 1991: 153). For the majority of Bruneian citizens, Brunei Malay is the first language, the language of the home and other informal domains, whilst the Malay that is prescribed as an official language and a medium of education under the *Dwibahasa* policy is the standard *Bahasa Melayu*, which is alike in most respects to the national languages of Brunei's neighbours in Southeast Asia, Malaysia and Indonesia (Martin, 1996, 2005b: 227). For a significant minority of students from other indigenous ethnic groups such as Dusun and Lun Bawang, English is the third or even fourth language. There is ongoing language and cultural shift from all the minority indigenous groups towards 'the Malay centre' (Martin, 2005a: 74), and towards Brunei Malay (Noor Azam, 2005).

From 1985 onwards a bilingual system of education, known as '*Dwibahasa*' ('two languages'), was gradually implemented (Ahmad bin Haji Jumat, 1991; Ministry of Education, 2004). By 1993, the policy was in place throughout the education system. The languages concerned are *Bahasa Melayu* (henceforth 'Malay') and English. In lower primary years 1 to 3, the medium of education is Malay for all subjects except English Language. Starting from primary year 4, there is a significant change, whereby Science and Geography are taught through the medium of English, whilst History, Physical Education, Malay Language, Civics, Arts and Handicraft and Islamic Religious Knowledge continue to be taught in Malay. This gives a 56 : 44 weighting in favour of the English-medium subject areas, measured by the number of contact hours per week. At secondary level, there is a gradual increase in the weighting in favour of English-medium subjects.

Brunei is an example of the 'separation approach' in bilingual education (Swain, 1983: 40–41), in which different subjects in the curriculum are taught in different languages. An upper primary student's typical school day could begin with 30 minutes of Physical Education (in Malay), followed by 60 minutes of Maths (in English), then 30 minutes of English Language, 60 minutes of Islamic Religious Knowledge in Malay, and so on.

The *Dwibahasa* policy is based on the premise that the use of English as the medium of instruction for certain subjects is not detrimental to the status of Malay. Jones (1992: 103) argues that Brunei has the prerequisites for successful implementation of a bilingual policy: 'the place of Malay is well established and both Malay and English are highly valued in their various domains'. In a survey of the attitudes of students conducted at one Brunei secondary school, Cath (1991) found that they recognised the importance of English for purely instrumental reasons: passing examinations and getting jobs. They did not express any form of integrative motivation towards English.

Hence Malay and English are not perceived as being in competition in Brunei, since they occupy different areas of the linguistic ecosystem: Malay for home and family and many official domains; English for the workplace, especially in the private sector, but also in some of the government ministries (Wood *et al.*, 2001).

Implications of the Dwibahasa Policy

The participants in teaching/learning events in primary English language classrooms in Brunei could be either a Bruneian teacher with

Bruneian students, with almost all having recourse to the same L1, or else Bruneian students and an expatriate teacher who speaks only English. One pre-service student teacher in 2002 expressed the view that as a Bruneian it was unnatural for her to address a class of fellow Bruneians in English. She felt she could not serve as a teacher of English, as this involved contravention of sociocultural norms of politeness and deference towards students coming from families of higher social status, especially those related to the royal family. This perception demonstrates the importance of appropriate language choice according to local norms, and can serve as a partial explanation for Bruneian teachers and students resorting to co-constructed 'safetalk' in primary-level English language lessons. Any meaningful communication would normally take place through the default code, Brunei Malay, so the use of English in the language classroom is akin to a *sandiwara* (a staged, stylised dramatic performance).

Classroom behavioural norms

Classroom practices in Brunei are relatively similar from school to school and, compared to classrooms in western countries like Britain, are highly restricted. In all primary and secondary schools, students stand when the teacher enters the room and, led by the class monitor, chant in chorus 'Good Morning, Teacher' at the start of every lesson and 'Thank-you', at the end, with a marked 'singsong' intonation. If the teacher is a Muslim, then the Arabic greeting 'Assalamualaikum' ('peace be with you') precedes the English greeting, as demonstrated in the lesson extract under discussion here. The teacher is expected to return this greeting with 'Mualaikumsalam' ('with you be peace'), and to instruct the class to sit down before writing the topic of the lesson and the date on the blackboard. School inspectors, Ministry of Education officials and head teachers have been known to comment adversely if these practices are not rigorously observed. Whatever is written on the board is expected to be copied by the class into their exercise books. When nominated by the teacher, students are expected to stand before attempting to respond. If their response is deemed unsatisfactory, they may have to remain standing while other students try to provide a more acceptable answer. Often teachers seek to avoid these time-consuming procedures by accepting a chorused response from the whole class, who stay seated (Arthur & Martin, 2006: 195). The rituals described here are cultural practices which are reproduced in the cycles of daily life in Bruneian classrooms (Cath & McLellan, 1993).

Classroom Interaction

This extract is from the beginning of a designated grammar lesson at Primary year 4 level in Brunei. The teacher is a Bruneian, with 26 years of teaching experience. The class consists of 20 pupils, seven girls and 13 boys.

The lesson was videorecorded by one of the joint authors of this chapter. All names of students have been changed to preserve confidentiality. Turns 1–18 show the formulaic interaction at the start of the lesson.

Extract #1

01	T	Mana lagi? *Where again* Mana lagi? *Where again* Ha? Sit down. Okay
02	Ss	<seated in single rows, stand up>
03	Mo	Assalammualaikum *Peace be with you*, good morning teacher
04	Ss	Assalammualaikum *Peace be with you*, good morning teacher
05	T	Mualaikumsalam *With you be peace*, good morning, sit down
06	T	Now, you have your English revision <writes 'English revision' on the blackboard> Now, what is today?
07	Ss	Today is Thursday
08	T	Again
09	Ss	Today is Thursday
10	T	Yesterday?
11	Ss	Yesterday was Wednesday
12	T	Spell.<writes on the blackboard>
13	Ss	T-H-U-R-S-D-A-Y. Thursday
14	T	Now, what's the date today?
15	Ss	Eighteenth
16	T	Eighteenth of May. Repeat
17	Ss	Eighteenth of May 1995
18	T	Eighteenth of May 1995

The extract was recorded in the month of May. The Brunei school year begins in January, hence it takes place at a time when students should already be familiar with the teacher's expectations in terms of appropriate norms of participation in the language classroom. They are already 'socialised', and there is evidence of this in the extract. Firstly, the students, led by the class monitor, Mohammed, are able to interpret the teacher's 'Okay' (01) as a signal to begin the formal greeting routine. Secondly, in the later exchanges (6–18), they respond in the appropriate manner to the teacher's initiations and cues through chorused replies. Clearly they have been trained to give full-sentence responses, so their responses (7 and 11) are 'Today is Thursday' and 'Yesterday was Wednesday', rather than just the names of the days, which would be sufficient and appropriate replies outside the classroom domain. They also know that 'again' (8) is a cue to repeat in chorus the response they have just provided, and that the teacher's one-word command 'Spell' (12) requires a chorused recital of the letters of the current day, not the previous, which the teacher proceeds to write on the blackboard. Having been prompted to spell out 'Thursday', they then repeat the whole word.

However, the chorused (14–18) response is not accepted by the teacher as sufficient for the date, so the teacher's feedback (16) consists of both repetition and expansion of the inadequate reply, and the prompt 'repeat'. This contrasts with the preceding exchanges where there is zero feedback or evaluation on the part of the teacher (10 and 12). Zero feedback and verbatim repetition in this episode are thus co-constructed by teachers and students as positive. Orientation towards these interactive practices is part of the socialisation process in the classroom context, through which students show whether they are operating in the same activity frame as the teacher.

Extract #2

19	T	Now, we will have your English revision
20	T	/// <writes on the blackboard for 3 mins 11 secs>
21	T	Now, look at the sentences. Rearrange the words to make a good sentence. The first one, 'I eat like to durian *local fruit'*. Don't give the answer first. {reads}Thursday tomorrow be will, we shout mustn't in class. An orange than a grape is bigger, we with cut bread a knife. Now, read this sentence. This one. Read all this. Don't give the correct answer, okay?{reads}I eat like to durian. Thursday tomorrow be will, we shout mustn't in class, an orange than a grape is bigger, we with cut bread a knife. Now, rearrange this sentence to make a good sentence. The first one, I eat like to durian. Maybe you do, go write the sentence.
22	Al	<walks up to the blackboard and pauses>
23	T	I eat like to durian
24	Al	<writes>
25	T	Next one, Number two. Sit down. You, Nurul
26	Nu	<walks to the blackboard, thinks, then writes>
27	T	Three. Diana, try to do number three
28	Di	<thinks, writes, then walks to her seat>
29	T	Number four. Rosdi, try number four
30	Ro	<writes on the blackboard>
31	T	Sit down. And number five. Adi, number five, please
32	Ad	<walks to the blackboard and writes>

The teacher (19) signals the transition from the opening formulaic phase to the main pedagogical task. This involves rearranging the word order of jumbled sentences written on the blackboard. It becomes clear that the blackboard is being used in place of a textbook in this lesson. In this instance the teacher chooses to spend more than three minutes writing up a set of five sentences with incorrect word order on the blackboard, rather than giving out the exercise on a worksheet or dictating the words of each sentence. This may be motivated by a desire to replicate the format of the written monthly test for which the class is being prepared. During this time the class has nothing to do other than look at the board.

The students' task is to come up to the board individually, when nominated, and write out the sentences in the correct word order. In a lengthy turn (21), the teacher twice reminds the class not to anticipate and not to help their peers by calling out the correct answers: 'Don't give the answer first' and 'Don't give the correct answer, okay?'. In imposing these conditions the teacher clarifies the activity frame for this part of the lesson, a strategy which can be viewed as a form of local socialisation. Unlike the chorused responses (6–18 and from 43 onwards), this section of the lesson requires individual students to perform as individuals in public by writing their answer on the blackboard, without assistance from their peers. Individual performance of this type runs counter to the notion of collusive 'safetalk' outlined by Chick (1996), since this task is more face-threatening than nominating an individual student to produce a verbal response, as the students' output is visible to all on the blackboard.

Extract #3

33	T	Okay, see the blackboard. Now, class, look again. Now, the first one. Can you read this sentence?
34	Ss	I eat like to durian
35	T	Now, the answer
36	Ss	I like eat to durian
37	T	Is that correct?
38	Ss	No.
39	T	Who can give the correct answer?
40	Ss	<hands up>
41	T	Mazlan, stand up. You write the answers here {points next to the original answer on the blackboard}.
42	Ma	<walks to the blackboard and writes>
43	T	Now, class read the answer.
44	Ss	I like to eat durian
45	T	Once more
46	Ss	I like to eat durian
47	T	Number two. Read the answer number two.
48	Ss	Thursday tomorrow be will. Tomorrow will be Thursday.
49	T	How to spell Thursday here?
50	Ss	T-H-U-R-S-D-A-Y. Thursday
51	T	Again, Thursday. Again. Once more, spell.
52	Ss	T-H-U-R-S-D-A-Y, Thursday.
53	T	Again.
54	Ss	T-H-U-R-S-D-A-Y.

55	T	What about the word tomorrow?
56	Ss	Tomorrow will be]
57	T	Spell the word tomorrow
58	Ss	T-O-M-O-R-R-O
59	T	Is that correct?
60	Ss	No!
61	T	What is the missing spell? What word is missing?
62	Ss	W
63	T	Next, read once more, tomorrow
64	Ss	Tomorrow will be Thursday
65	T	Number three, read first, we //
66	Ss	We shout mustn't in class
67	T	Now, read the answer
68	Ss	We mustn't shout in class

Interactional features in Extract #3

The student Ali, who wrote an incorrect answer for the first of the five jumbled sentences, has to endure having his answer visible to the whole class on the board, read out by the whole class (36), then judged to be wrong by the class as a whole (38), before finally being publicly corrected on the board by another student, Mazlan (42–44). The same applies to student Nurul, who omits the letter 'w' when writing the word 'tomorrow' on the board, and has this omission publicly corrected (55–62). In turns 55–56 the students misinterpret the teacher's initiation move 'What about the word tomorrow?' Although they have just been prompted to spell 'Thursday', they take the initiation to be a request to read out the answer, in which 'Tomorrow' is the first word. The teacher interrupts the chorused response with a prompt which clarifies her expectation at this point, 'Spell the word tomorrow'. The teacher's aim here is to draw attention to another mistake in the answer which Nurul has written: the omission of the final letter 'w'. The students have been socialised to read out what is on the board in front of them, believing this to be the correct activity frame at this point, so a further two exchanges are needed (59–62) for the teacher to raise the consciousness of the class towards the incorrect spelling.

Aspects of the instructional task in the three extracts

The presentation and exploitation of text in the target language in this extract shows the use of decontextualised text, or citation forms, as distinct from 'real' communicative interaction. The example sentence, written on the blackboard in jumbled order and chorused by the students (64), is 'Tomorrow will be Thursday'. Yet the students earlier focused on the actual date at the start of the lesson, and twice repeated in chorus 'Today is Thursday' (7 and 9). At one point the teacher, in an aside (21), says 'Maybe you do', referring to the nominated student, Ali, who is asked to write out the sentence 'I like to eat durian' with the correct word order. This aside is the only instance where the meaning of the target language text is referred to rather than the orthographic or syntactic form, specifically the word order, which is the main pedagogical objective of this activity.

Throughout the extract it is evident that the teacher's major instructional aim is the production of accurate text in the target language, a prerequisite if the students are to achieve success in the forthcoming monthly test in which a similar exercise will be an item: 'Is that correct?' (37 and 59), 'Who can give the correct answer?' (39), 'What is the missing spell? What word is missing?' (61).

The teacher's instructional agenda for this lesson, 'English revision', does not permit negotiation for meaning between her and the students, as she perceives that the need for the students to be prepared for the forthcoming test is paramount. She does not offer any explanation of the rules of English syntax which determine that 'I like to eat durian' (44 and 46) is the correct target form, whilst the original item 'I eat like to durian' and first answer written on the board, 'I like eat to durian', are both incorrect.

Discussion: 'Safetalk' and Mutual Avoidance of Displays of Incompetence

This lesson extract demonstrates aspects of collusive 'safetalk', described by Chick (1996, 1998), by Hornberger and Chick (2001), and applied to the Brunei classroom context by Martin (1997: 376–378) and by Arthur and Martin (2006).

The preference for chorused repetition in Extracts #1 and #3, the lack of open questions, and the limited level of cognitive load required of the students to perform the task successfully, are characteristic of 'safe practices'. These practices have been observed to occur in a number of postcolonial settings where the former colonial language has been retained as a medium of education (Arthur & Martin, 2006: 177–178). In Brunei classrooms the requirement to use English only may be a cause of stress: both for teachers, whose competence in English may be inadequate for teaching the language at this level, as well as for the students, who are experiencing the sudden increase in the role of English in primary year 4. As noted by McLellan and Noor Azam (2000), English is only used to a limited extent outside the educational domain in Brunei, so students may have limited opportunities to use the English they are learning. Instead of being an arena where learning is promoted through discussion and negotiation and where knowledge is scaffolded by the expert teacher for the novice learners, the classroom is a place of ritual, formulaic public performance, which satisfies local sociocultural norms and elite-group expectations concerning how language lessons should be conducted.

The use of codeswitching between the target language and other languages shared by teacher and students is one feature of 'safetalk', found to occur frequently in the Brunei context, in defiance of imposed policy relating to classroom language use (Arthur & Martin, 2006; Martin, 1997). Malay and Arabic only occur minimally at the beginning of this lesson extract (#1) alongside English, where the teacher is encouraging the students to settle at their desks, using the Malay phrase 'Mana lagi?' literally 'where again', (1) as a class management strategy to direct the students towards appropriate behaviour at the outset of the lesson. In other lessons analysed by Chua-Wong (1998), and in English Language and English-medium classes at the upper primary level discussed by other Brunei-based researchers, codeswitching is a frequent feature, especially when the teacher's focus on class management rather than pedagogic content. Codeswitching is seen by Martin (2005a) as one strategy which can combat the threat posed by the institutional requirement that the lesson be conducted in English only. Safe practices, such as the opening routine using the formulaic Arabic greetings, encourage the maintenance of harmony which is of great importance in the Brunei sociocultural context.

As noted in the analysis of Extract #2, however, the teacher appears to contravene the 'safetalk' concept by asking individual students to write their answers on the board. It is likely that the teacher's aim here is to raise students' awareness of their errors and their failure to attend to orthographic and syntactic accuracy. In this way the revision task is justified as preparation for the forthcoming monthly test: students are made aware of the importance of accuracy and the need to perform well in the test.

Whilst 'safetalk' serves as a useful and highly relevant conceptual framework for the analysis of aspects of socialisation in classrooms in Brunei and elsewhere, the demands made of individually-nominated students in Extract #2 of this lesson appear to be face-threatening, and in contravention to the concept as defined by Chick (1996). Indeed Chick makes specific mention of students being asked to write responses on the board. However, in the lesson extract he discusses, from a year 7 Mathematics class in a Kwazulu school in South Africa, this activity takes place only after 'responses have been well rehearsed' (Chick, 1996: 29). This appears not to be the case in this Brunei lesson extract, since two out of the five nominated students make mistakes when writing on the blackboard.

Aspects of 'safetalk' in this lesson extract thus co-occur with an activity which contravenes the 'safe practices' concept: making the students write answers on the board in full view of their peers. Far from invalidating or challenging Chick's concepts of 'safetalk' and 'safe practices', we feel that the analysis of this lesson extract demonstrates the usefulness of these notions as analytical descriptors for classroom interaction. The patterns of interaction in these extracts show that the students have been socialised to meet the expectations of the teacher and of other stakeholders. Yet misunderstandings are liable to occur within the interaction, at points where the teacher and the students operate within different activity frames.

TAKE 2

Introduction

This chapter investigates aspects of socialisation in an upper primary English language classroom in Negara Brunei Darussalam, as exemplified in an extract from a lesson taught by a Bruneian teacher. Socialisation is defined as the ways in which students become attuned to the interactional expectations of teachers and other stakeholders.

In the first 18 lines of the transcript the interaction is formulaic. Turns 1 through 5 constitute the salutation in Brunei Malay; turns 6 through 18 constitute an instructional activity that serves as the content for teaching English. The content is temporal location and it is also presented in a formulaic sequence such that it assists students in meeting the teacher's instructional expectations and permits the teacher to extend the lesson through questions or commands. The dance of the day is a relatively smooth one, as everyone knows the steps.

The adverbial 'now' (06) in Extract #1 expresses command and makes explicit to the student that the teacher wants their attention as the following statement 'you have your English revision' and the nonverbal writing on the blackboard indicate the teacher's foreshadowing that both subject and language are changing. The students comply. From an outsider's perspective, this immediate compliance indicates familiarity with the form; in other words, there have been previous, repetitive occasions in which the students have encountered the same cue to indicate an entry into the English lesson of the day. It is a routine. The choral response seems to be the default mode of responding in both the salutation and the initial activity in English. The teacher uses various strategies to reinforce the students' knowledge of English, such as, requesting repetition, asking students to name the letters that spell the word while she writes them on the board, and extending their understanding of the meaning by differentiating it from more specific details of the temporal location of their interaction.

In turns 19 to 38, the teacher calls the students' attention to a change in content and the need to remain in the English language; a reinforcement of the language of instruction and the subject of learning. She continues to use the adverbial 'now', yet, in this segment of the lesson the students are not responding chorally. What is different in this segment is that she goes to the board to write before calling attention to the students (the second 'now' in turn 21) and once she has the students' attention, the teacher indicates what her expectation is. Read the sentences written, notice that they are not arranged grammatically, rearrange the word in the order appropriate for the English language, keep what you notice in your head, and do not call it out for all to hear. She repeats this twice in different parts ('Rearrange the words to make a good sentence ... Don't give the answer first ... Now, read the sentence... Read all this. Don't give the correct answer, okay? ... Now, rearrange this sentence to make a good sentence') all within the same turn. The key to the task is that students understand that they need to 'rearrange' what they see on the board in order that it reads as a 'good sentence'. Another difference is that she designates an individual student to respond. Perhaps, what this indicates is that the default is a chorus response unless otherwise instructed. From then to the end of the excerpt, the only thing that is formulaic is the process of the teacher selecting a student, the student complying and going to the board to write the grammatical form they believe to be correct, and walking back to their seat. The students individually are applying a grammatical rule that seems like they have been studying it for some time, that is, that the possibility of this application exercise is due to past teaching. To complete the exercise appropriately the student needs to demonstrate that he/she has a cognitive handle on the grammatical rules of the language being taught – English – and there is no indication of any resistance or deviation to the process or the rules of engagement already established in this classroom.

The third extract (39 to 75) is the immediate feedback the individual students receive with respect to the grammaticality of the English sentences. Here, we get some cues as to how gaps in English grammatical knowledge are identified, negotiated, and corrected in this classroom. In the previous segment, the teacher had requested that individual students' display their knowledge (in some cases, lack of it) by going up to the board to write the answer. She elicits from the students to first read the scrambled sentence she has written and then to read the student's written sentence. As in the previous segments, she uses the adverbial 'now' as a secondary device because she starts with the 'okay'. 'Okay' is an American US colloquialism implying democracy and consent. Yet, as it has come to be commonly used, and used in this setting, it is a weaker version of consent; it is used in a similar way as 'now' – to call attention to the next move: in this case, evaluation. We see the students and teacher go back to the default mode of responding – the choral response – with one exception. While they read the scrambled sentence together, the teacher asks a question ('Who can give a correct answer?') which indicates that she expects, in the next move, an individual response. After turn 54 through the end, however, the class goes back into the choral response mode. The response to the exchange suggests that the teacher was actually wanting to give an example of what she expected the students to do when they responded as a group – a socialization move.

There is one other deviation and it has two parts. When the students come to the word Thursday, she asks them to spell it. This can be interpreted as a reinforcement of the previous turns 12 and 13. The second part comes right after the reinforcement when the students come to the word 'tomorrow' (62–68). The teacher asks, 'what about the word tomorrow?' One can see in these turns the only misunderstanding in the segments provided for analysis, which may give us a clue about how differences in interpretation are resolved in this classroom. When (63) the students seem to be going into the previously encountered formulaic response in the initial excerpt which called for them to say what day would tomorrow be – a content response, the teacher interrupts and gives clearer instructions of her intended expectations – '*spell* the word tomorrow' (my emphasis). One could interpret both of the spelling exercises. The first one focused on Thursday as well as the second which focused on tomorrow, as engaging and preparing students to provide corrective feedback, as a group, about what was written on the board. This deviation appears to be sufficient for the students to understand what was expected of them even if the next command ('What is the missing spell?') is a non-native English construction that could potentially lead to misunderstandings. This is underscored by the next utterance as the teacher asks 'What word is missing' instead of 'what letter is missing' (61) and the students respond by correcting the spelling. The communication dance was complete even if there was some stumbling.

The Dance as a Whole

The pattern of relationship between the teacher and the students is well established in this classroom. One could venture to say that it was either reflective of the broader cultural understandings of what ought to occur in social interactions within schools or that it was a well established relationship reflective of the time which this particular teacher and her class have been together, as the learning dance activity they jointly construct, even when missteps occur, are not major disruptive catastrophes but part of the practice on the way toward refinement.

The latter proposal, that is, that this teacher and his/her students are well into the year when the observation took place, is supported by the commands and responses, by the call to attention, and even by the elegant control the teacher has over the deviations. Even the nature of deviations gives the reader some clues – one can find a purpose for each of them. The two indicators that reflect broader social patterns are the salutation in the native language and the response of the students to the teacher's lack of clarity in turn 68. In the salutation the difference is in both the content and the medium; in the response, it is what is understood and how one treats the person of social status when they make a mistake that can confuse. The salutation is a marker of religious, linguistic, cultural, social identities and beliefs associated with the broader society of Brunei Darussalam; the response is a marker of second language learning and of social and/or role status.

One could find the efficiency and the smoothness of the moves in this classroom and the sequencing of presentation as evidence of the subject matter – English grammar – or of the comfort of the classroom participants with English as a language of instruction, thus, supportive of McLellan's and Chua's (2002) claim that the bilingual policy of instruction is not a threat to Malay.

Yet, they are not distinct in the underlying form – both the salutation and the response take. The form of the salutation, in some respects, becomes itself a framework for working through the learning of English. The teacher signals a transformation of the structure of the salutation into a new language in the first move – where the order of business is locating oneself temporally. Once the students are squarely in the second language, the new learning takes place but within the salutation structure.

As in the salutation, the teacher calls on an individual to lead. The student who is called on must have confidence in having the correct content – 'Who can give a correct answer?' As in the beginning of the salutation, in the beginning of the evaluation of the unscrambled sentences, an individual responds. The group as a collective takes on a prominent role as it is in the group that answers chorally from then on. It is the community of co-learners that together evaluates through reading what was written on the board by both the teacher and by other members of the class. The level of difficulty of the lesson increases and requires the learner to go from listen-and-repeat or listen-and-recall to demonstrating that they know how to apply and evaluate the application of the rules of English grammar, but the cultural form remains throughout.

The dance of this classroom may be reflective of the role and the place of the group and the individual as experienced in the Brunei Darussalam society, but as an outsider, I do not know their dance. At most, I may be able to enjoy its performance.

TAKE 3

01 T Keep away all your books. Do you have your papers? I want you to read your papers silently. Read it slowly and silently. <waits for class to read while a student cleans the duster outside the classroom. Then writes the date, day and topic of the lesson on the blackboard> Hmm. Finished reading? No?

02 S2 Yes

03 T Now. Write your name on the paper. Write your name <walks to the front desks to check on the students> Write your name. Write it clearly. Ya, *yes*, so that I can read your name there. Hmm <picks up the chalk> Now. Look at your passage. Look at the story there. How. Now. Listen. / Before we read the story, I want to ask how

		many of you ever sit in a car? How many of you have been sitting in a car?
04	Ss	<raise hands>
05	T	Now. Yes. Everybody ever sit in a car. Hmm. Now. Which seat do you go and sit? Which seat? Back seat? Front seat?
06	S4	Back seat!
07	S2	Front seat!
08	S5	<hands up>
09	T	How many of you ever sit in front seat?<looks at students>
10	Ss	<hands up>
11	T	Good. Sit down. <points at students> Put down your hands. Now. What is your . . . What do you notice in the front seat?
12	S2	Seat belt
13	T	Yes – safety belt. What must you do with the safety belt?
14	S2	Use it
15	T	Yes. You must use it. Why must you use it?
16	S2	Because it
17	T	Huh? Why must you use it? For your . . .
18	S2	For your safety
19	T	For your safety. Good. Now, if you sit in the back seat of the car, in the back seat of the car, do you have any safety belt?
20	S2	Yes!
21	T	Do you have it?
22	Ss	Yes. Yes
23	T	Yes, if you don't use it, what happens?
24	S2	Accident
25	T	Ah! Ya *yes*. Good If anything happen, or accident or anything happen to the car, so the safety belt will save you from. . .
26	S2	from
27	T	from being thrown out. You will tie yourself there in the car. Now. Let us see passage now. What is the safety belt for? What is the safety belt for? What is it used for? I will tell you what it is use for. Now. Let's see. Read the passage now.

Guiding questions for Take 3

(1) How does the teacher use the student's prior knowledge to connect them to the topic of study?

(2) What cues does the teacher give students with respect to her expectations about their responses? How do students respond to these cues?

(3) In lines 17 and 27, the teacher asks a similar question regarding the use of the safety belt, yet they may signal different interactional meanings to the student. Can you explain the possibly intended differences in meaning?

References

Ahmad bin Haji Jumat, Dato' Dr Haji (1991) *'Dwibahasa'* (Bilingual) System of Education in Negara Brunei Darussalam. Paper presented at *Conference on Bilingualism and National Development (BAND'91)*, Universiti Brunei Darussalam, Bandar Seri Begawan, Brunei, December 1991.

Arthur, J. and Martin, P.W. (2006) Accomplishing lessons in postcolonial classrooms: Comparative perspectives from Botswana and Brunei Darussalam. *Comparative Education* 42 (2), 177–202.

Cath, A. (1991) The social background of Form 3 students in Sekolah Menengah Lambak Kanan and their attitudes to learning English. Unpublished RSA/Cambridge Diploma dissertation.

Cath, A. and McLellan, J. (1993) 'Right. Let's do some ah, mm, speaking': Patterns of classroom interaction in Brunei Darussalam. Paper presented at *BAAL Seminar on Bilingual Classroom Discourse*, Lancaster University, July 1993.

Chick, J.K. (1996) Safe-talk: Collusion in apartheid education. In H. Coleman (ed.) *Society and the Language Classroom* (pp. 21–39). Cambridge: Cambridge University Press.

Chick, J.K. (1998) *Safe-talk, Safetime, and a Culture of Learning*. Linguistics Archive, University of Natal, Durban, South Africa. On WWW at http://www.und.ac.za/und/ling/archive/chic-02.html. Accessed 10.07.08.

Chua-Wong, P.S.H. (1998) A study of teacher talk in upper-primary English language classrooms in Negara Brunei Darussalam. Unpublished MA dissertation, Universiti Brunei Darussalam.

Hornberger, N. and Chick, J.K. (2001) Co-constructing school safetime: Safetalk practices in Peruvian and South African classrooms. In M. Heller and M. Martin-Jones (eds) *Voices of Authority: Education and Linguistic Difference* (pp. 31–56). Westport, CT: Ablex.

Jones, G.M. (1992) Planning language change: Some social and cultural implications for Negara Brunei Darussalam. In Abu Bakar Haji Apong (ed.) *Sumbangsih: Esei-Esei Mengenai Negara Brunei Darussalam* (pp. 94–105). Bandar Seri Begawan, Brunei Darussalam: Akademi Pengajian Brunei.

Martin, P.W. (1996) Brunei Malay and Bahasa Melayu: A sociolinguistic perspective. In P.W. Martin, A.C.K. Ożóg and G.R. Poedjosoedarmo (eds) *Language Use and Language Change in Brunei Darussalam* (pp. 27–36). Athens, OH: Ohio University Center for International Studies.

Martin, P.W. (1997) Accomplishing lessons bilingually in three primary classrooms in Negara Brunei Darussalam: Insights into the 'Dwibahasa' programme. Unpublished PhD thesis, Lancaster University.

Martin, P.W. (2005a) 'Safe' language practices in two rural schools in Malaysia: Tensions between policy and practice. In A.M.Y. Lin and P.W. Martin (eds) *Decolonisation, Globalisation: Language-in-Education Policy and Practice* (pp. 74–97). Clevedon: Multilingual Matters.

Martin, P.W. (2005b) Talking knowledge into being in an upriver primary school in Brunei. In A.S. Canagarajah (ed.) *Reclaiming the Local in Language Policy and Practice* (pp. 225–246). Mahwah, NJ: Lawrence Erlbaum Associates.

Martin, P.W. and Poedjosoedarmo, G. (1996) Introduction: An overview of the language situation in Brunei Darussalam. In P.W. Martin, A.C.K. Ożóg and G.R. Poedjosoedarmo (eds) *Language Use and Language Change in Brunei Darussalam* (pp. 1–23). Athens, OH: Ohio University Center for International Studies.

McLellan, J. and Chua-Wong, P.S.H. (2002) Two languages in the classroom: Clashing codes or coexistence? *The ACELT Journal* 6 (2), 11–19.

McLellan, J. and Noor Azam Haji Othman (2000) The myth of widespread English in Brunei Darussalam: A sociolinguistic investigation. *South East Asia: A Multidisciplinary Journal* 2 (1&2), 37–46.

Ministry of Education, Negara Brunei Darussalam (2004) *The Development of Education in Brunei Darussalam*. On WWW at http://www.moe.gov.bn/development.htm. Accessed 10.07.08.

Noor Azam Haji Othman (2005) Changes in the linguistic diversity of Negara Brunei Darussalam: An ecological perspective. Unpublished PhD thesis, University of Leicester.

Nothofer, B. (1991) The languages of Brunei Darussalam. In H. Steinhauer (ed.) *Papers in Austronesian Linguistics, No. 1. Pacific Linguistics* A-81, 151–176.

Swain, M. (1983) Bilingualism without tears. In M. Clarke and J. Handscombe (eds) *On TESOL '82: Pacific Perspectives on Language Learning and Teaching* (pp. 35–48). Washington DC: TESOL.

van Lier, L. (1984) Analysing interaction in second language classrooms. *English Language Teaching Journal* 38 (3), 160–169.

Wikipedia (2006) *Demographics of Brunei*. On WWW at http://en.wikipedia.org/wiki/Demographics_of_Brunei. Accessed 10.07.08.

Wood, A., Sharifah Nurul Huda Alkaff, Swan, J. and Elgar, A. (2001) Shifting sands: Malay in place of English, English for Malay? – Language in the workplace in Brunei Darussalam. Paper presented at conference on *Plurilingual Hubs in the New Millennium*, Hong Kong Polytechnic University, January 2001.

Chapter 4

Negotiating Appropriateness in the Second Language Within a Dual Language Education Classroom Setting

TAKE 1: MARÍA E. TORRES-GUZMÁN
TAKE 2: VIJAY KUMAR AND WONG BEE ENG

TAKE 1

Introduction

Appropriateness, in this chapter, is interpreted at a variety of levels. There is the appropriateness of student responses to the teacher questions; appropriateness of student interpretations of the text; and appropriateness of the ways of talking, listening and communicating within a classroom. Most importantly, appropriateness refers, within, to the type of relationships between teacher and the students.

The analytical framework of *con respeto y cariño* (with respect and in friendship) (Valdés, 1996: 13), referred to the context of the relationships between the researcher and the teacher and to finding a voice with which to write about findings. A core Latino value about the nature of relationships, *respeto* (Gonzalez, 2007; Hildebrand *et al.*, 2000; Souto-Manning, 2006), is the basis. It acknowledges that all people's social worth must be honored. It is operationalized as mutual and reciprocal deferential behavior that depends on status and roles actualized within a given situation. Social worth is rooted in the valuing of self and others and acting with dignity in relationships. Put another way, *respeto* is bidirectional. The social worth an individual holds in any given situation is a result of the relationships between status (social hierarchies based on educational achievement, socioeconomic status, age, etc.) and personal power (what the individual earns within the interaction based on character and behavior). The analysis of *respeto* is, thus, multilayered.

When Valdés (1996) speaks about *con respeto y cariño*, she was referring to the social relationships that she was able to establish with some of the parents throughout the course of her study. She adds to this the explicit need to find a voice with which to communicate such a relationship so that the social worth of those she studies come through in her writing. Nieto (1992) and Franquiz and Salazar (2004) both speak to the Latino students' articulation of their need to feel that they are being respected by the peers and adults in schools. *Respeto* brings the bonding needed for relationships that engage students in learning (Franquiz & Salazar, 2004).

The relationship Mrs Alvarez and I had was one of *con respeto y cariño*, but for this study the most important relationships established within the framework of *con respeto y cariño* was that of Mrs Alvarez and the students in her classroom. The nature of the relationships was critical because the students were bilingual. Within the broader social US context, being bilingual conjures up social stigmas that contextualize the pedagogical dilemma Mrs Alvarez faced when confronted with the need to move students academically and linguistically while ensuring respect and caring for the individual child and their community ways. The relationship between Mrs Alvarez and her students embodied the care she took in preparing for the Read Aloud prior to the actual event, the contagious excitement of the class when the teacher indicated it was time for Read Aloud, and the respect displayed by the teacher and the students as they engaged in the Read Aloud activity. The students' fondness of the teacher was visible in the eye contacts, facial expressions, tones of their voices, and the how, when and what was said in an interaction. Within, however, I will focus primarily on their speech. Thus, by design such analysis is incomplete and open to new interpretations.

Each of the interactions was selected as an instance reflecting the pattern of mutual respect observed throughout the year in this classroom. They were collected during a year-long study of Read Alouds in Mrs Alvarez's 5th grade classroom. The school district in which this study took place opted for a policy that promoted the enrichment of more than one language of instruction in schools for both minority and majority linguistic populations in the form of dual language education. This was in contrast and side by side to the increasing move towards restriction of other than English languages in the US language policy, as was seen in California, Arizona and Massachusetts. All three states repealed their bilingual education laws. Since education is a state right, it is at this level where the battle for and against bilingual education is taking place. Some state language policies have maintained the use of other than English languages for the purpose of instruction and New York has been one of them. The local educational agency, the school district and, ultimately the school, is also another place of affirmation or inhibition of non-English language use.

The students in this classroom were between the ages of nine and 10. Most of the students had been enrolled in dual language schooling since they were five years old; a few were recent immigrants. For a very small number of students, English was a native language. The majority of the children were learning English as a second or third language. For the hand-ful of Mixteca children, an indigenous immigrant group from Mexico, English was the third language in their repertoire. Their indigenous Mix-teca language was the first and Spanish the second language. The majority of the students in this inner-city US classroom, however, were not at the beginning stages of English language learning; nonetheless, they were from marked language minority groups (Lyon, 1968).

Read Aloud is a distinct instructional activity in which the teacher reads a book to the whole class; most of the time the text read is beyond the lis-teners' ability to read on their own. Thus, the reading requires mediation at various levels. In this classroom, the students were seated on a rug and the teacher sat on an adult chair. In addition to the management issues that were taken care of with this positioning of the teacher – she could see and address all the students and drew greater attention than any one student – her positioning facilitated showing illustrations in the text, if there were any. The researcher and research assistant observed from the back of the rug one morning a week; we videotaped 14 Read Aloud sessions.

To enact a social interaction *con respeto y cariño* meant that the social ten-sions around language required that the teacher take into account the dynamic interplay between the two language codes and the subtle and/or distinct referents and meanings in the each of the languages or storylines. While each of the segments of interactions selected posed different tensions and rendered different versions of appropriateness, they were all done *con respeto y cariño*. Within, we will use Gee's (1999) notion of cultural models, Nunan's (1990) analysis of types of listening, and Gibbons' (2002) notion of scaffolding to analyze the relational aspects of the actors with each other and in relation to the task.

Gee (1999) proposes that a cultural model is the tacit theory, an explana-tion, or an image in a person's mind that situates the meaning given to a par-ticular word. It reflects a 'pattern that a specific sociocultural group of people find significant' (Gee, 1999: 41). Gee's notion of cultural model served to identify the 'storyline' and the point of view the speaker was attempting to communicate and, thus, the relational identity between the speaker and the listener as well as their respective relationships with the storyline of the text.

Whether the listener is required to respond verbally or not is the first dis-tinctions in Nunan's (1990) analysis of listening. Nunan's second distinc-tion is the type of topic, whether it relies on the information of everyday events or if it requires more information. One can see it as the continuum of formality of language required by the response, where there is one required. Traditional Read Alouds are conceptualized as listening activities. In Mrs Alvarez' classroom, the Read Aloud was also interactive at times. While the teacher did the reading, the students shared in pairs before, during, and after the reading. It is within the teacher-guided reporting of pair share that the interactions analyzed within were chosen. This is when the students took turns reporting to the teacher and the whole class on the more private discussion that occurred within the designated pairs around a question posed by the teacher about the students' understanding of the reading. In the face-to-face pair share discussions, the individual student had the opportunity to try out and practice what s/he might want to say in the more public forum of the teacher guided reporting. For a student to participate actively as a listener, a receptive understanding of information beyond that used in every day situations is required. Thus, both teacher and students are listeners at different point in times.

Nunan (1990) does not address the speaking requirements and the element of audience that are important when the student is the producer of language. The teacher's mediation of productive language skills occurred most frequently on a one-to-one basis during the reporting back process. Gibbon's notion of scaffolding – 'a special kind of help that assists learners to move toward new skills, concepts, or levels of understanding' (Gibbons, 2002: 10) – was helpful in looking at what Mrs Alvarez did with students' responses and the care she took to respectfully guide and negotiate, with the students, their storylines and their language use. Gibbon points out that what a second language learner wishes to say and how they have to say it are two distinct processes that the teacher must attend to when the student is trying to produce an utterance. Within, there is a third interactional aspect that emerged – that is, turn taking. The teacher resolved turn taking by making it a non-issue and her responses to the students served to support them in their search for the language and information required and/or expected in the more formal and academic setting of the reporting back when the audience was both the teacher and the class.

Interactional Data

Appropriateness of ways of speaking and communicating

The specific social interactions selected for analysis occurred during the second semester of the academic year, when the teacher and, especially, the children were familiar with each other's ways. This is important in understanding that while one can identify patterns of interaction only over time, they are patterns because they are enacted repeatedly and systematically in the social interactions observed.

During all the interactions selected, Mrs Alvarez was reading William H. Armstrong's book, *Sounder*, an historical fiction chapter book about share-cropping that was beyond the students' reading level, providing the students a bit of a challenge. *Sounder* has an abundance of figurative speech and I was particularly intrigued by how the meanings seemed to flow through the words rather than contained by them. More practically, I was interested in how the teacher called attention to and dealt with both language use and the multiple meanings that emerge within the context of what was being read. Furthermore, I was interested in how the students interpreted and transformed what was being read in ways that made sense to them. While there were many opportunities for extended speech for the students in the interactive pair shares and teacher-guided reporting, I noticed that Mrs Alvarez entered into monologues. The teacher talk during these monologues could be characterized as teachable moments that generally focused on the development of students' academic vocabulary. Some of these teachable moments emerged spontaneously, from the student talk, or were skillfully contrived, as the reader will see within.

In Extract #1, Mrs Alvarez introduced *Sounder* as the new Read Aloud book. Prior to reading, she located the historical context of the story as a time between slavery and the 1960s' civil rights movement. The children had listened to other Read Alouds on different US historical periods. Mrs Alvarez reminded the students of an instructional activity they had previously engaged in where, based on the stories read, they developed multiple ways of describing what they imagined slavery was like. The purpose of the pair share was for them to remind each other of the words they had previously identified as descriptive of the lives of slaves. The following exchange occurred during the reporting back to the whole group.

Extract #1

01	T	Let's share some of your thought but I want you to explain a little bit. Don't worry about raising your hands. I'll hop around a bit. Cecilia, what did you say?
02	Ce	Sadness because you're taken away from your family.
03	T	OK, sadness because of that...{Teacher signals to student 2}
04	Ma	They were unhappy because they were in jail getting whipped and they couldn't even get time to sleep.
05	T	Unhappiness because they want to do what other people can do but they're tied down.
06	Ju	They don't have enough things so they can play.
07	T	They have nothing. They only have what the master would give them.
08	Ed	A prisoner. It's like a prison...
09	T	Over here, I'm reminded, Gerardo and Jaime, of a word they found today when they were reading about Harriet Tubman. And what was that word?
10	Ge	Neglected
11	T	Neglected. And what does that mean?
12	Ge	They ignored him.
13	T	Yeah they're totally ignored, they don't care about you.

The teacher, as she asked the students to share (01), gave cues on the standard for appropriateness of the use certain lexical and grammatical structures in the students' responses. Because the students would be taking the floor to speak as they reported back what the pairs had been discussing, the teacher also signaled what the appropriate rules for taking the floor would be. In doing so, she gently reminded the students that she would act as the dispenser of goods (taking the floor) and, thus, that they did not have to concentrate on vying (raise their hands) for it. Mrs Alvarez made the task simpler. While in control, Mrs Alvarez did not necessarily dominate the conversation. Instead, she moved the conversation, asked for clarification, and helped the students in their construction of responses.

The open ended questions Mrs Alvarez posed for the pair share also communicated that there were multiple acceptable ways of fulfilling the standard established by the teacher. The students were able to enter the conversation on their own terms. The first two students' responses included a descriptor of feelings (sadness, unhappy) with a conjunction (because) that connected to their causal explanations (02, 04). In the first case, the teacher repeated part of the student response, in an incomplete sentence, as a way of indicating that the response was appropriate and moved to the next student (03). In the second turn, the teacher rephrased the student's response to a more general level while structurally modeling appropriate English grammar (05). In the next turn, Juan Carlos deviated from the grammatical structure established by the first two respondents (06). The conjunction, 'so', served to connect to the explanation of his response. Mrs Alvarez rephrased (07) Juan Carlos' response to make the connections to slavery more specific. There was no teacher response (08) to the following student's contribution.

It appears that Mrs Alvarez's non-response occurred as she attempted to move proactively to expose the children to an academic word. She turned the floor to Gerardo or Jaime by stating, 'Over here, I'm reminded . . .' (09) and called out their names. She set up their contribution to the conversation about descriptors of slavery by reminding Gerardo and Jaime of a word they encountered in a previous literacy activity during the day. Gerardo espoused the word to which the teacher wanted to expose the children. The word was 'neglected' (10). The word did not seem to be part of the students' academic vocabulary yet. This was signaled by the one word response. Mrs Alvarez, nonetheless, made space for its use. The nature of the exchange here was similar to the traditional initiation–response–evaluation/feedback (IRE/IRF) exchange (Mehan, 1979; Wells, 1993). Ms Alvarez's feedback was a repetition of the word (11). She then probed, asking the student to provide the meaning of the word. Gerardo gave a parallelism, a more familiar word that had the same meaning (12), and the teacher elaborated further, thus, provided feedback on his response (13).

Of interest in these interactions was the use of the pronoun 'they' to refer to the slaves. Not once was the word slaves used. The use of the pronoun appears to have the effect of distancing the speaker with the status of slavery. There is one exception, when Cecilia spoke (02). In her response, some ambiguity in meaning was introduced by the use of 'you're' because she seemed to be implicating herself in the meaning. One of the interpretations could be that she was identifying with oppression of the slaves or expressing a fear of being separated from the family. From the structure of the sentence, it is unclear.

Overall, this interaction showed the pattern of interaction of the teacher-guided reporting of pair share during read aloud. The interaction was a two-way conversation focused on an information-based topic (Nunan, 1990). There were two levels of conversation when students report back. The students spoke to both the teacher and their fellow classmates. The productive requirements pushed the second language learners to rehearse in pairs and display in group a response that paid attention not only on what they wish to say but on how they are saying it (Gibbons, 2002) so that it could be understood by fellow classmates and the teacher. Thus, appropriateness was in part determined by the audience. It requires that the audience/listeners actively construct an interpretation of what was said, bringing in prior knowledge or experience to the meaning making, and attending to different aspects of the language system. Lastly, it requires that the teacher provide clear standards of appropriateness of responses, to ask questions that permitted students to enter the conversation on their own terms, to move the turn-taking amongst students while giving each enough space to articulate their point, to provide more academic models of speaking, to probe and ask for further clarification, and to mediate the learning of new vocabulary within the authentic context of student responses.

Appropriateness in meanings, points of view and identity

A few exchanges after the above interaction, on the same day, the teacher moved to set up an image of how big the plantations in the south of the United States were by connecting its size to that of Central Park, an image of dimension within the students' experience. Right after she introduced the size of the land, she again asked the students to think and partner share reasons they might believe slavery occurred.

Extract #2

01   T   You have to imagine a large place like that. Now we know that a lot of what they planted was cotton, tobacco. Now in those times, were there any machines to pick up this stuff? ((Students shake their heads)) So, that meant that humans had to be used. Why

didn't they hire a lot of people and pay them? Why did they go
out of their way to buy slaves to work in these giant plantations?
Why didn't they? Why didn't they?

02 Ju   They didn't want to hire people because they thought they'd be
wasting their money. They're greedy, selfish.

03 Xa   They didn't do it on the White people because that was from their
people.

04 T   And they would have to pay them, right?

05 Lu   Blacks were the kind that they needed so they could pick up the
cotton and plant stuff and they wouldn't have to pay them.

06 T   Right, so basically the slaves became the machines that they
would use.

07 Ed   Those people thought in those times that black people were animals but that was wrong (xxx) different colors.

08 T   So you're saying that in those times blacks were considered different from Whites so they could be treated as animals but you
consider that to be wrong.

09 An   They didn't want to lose the money. They didn't want to pay anybody because they had so {student hand motions indicate and
emphasize amount} much cotton. That means that they would
have to pay a lot of people to do the work for them. And since
they didn't want to pay, they wouldn't be able to afford that type
of pay without having to get frustrated of wasting so much
money. They just went to Africa and dragged the people, the
African Americans and make them work with no pay.

10 T   OK, I want to clear something up. A lot of you use the word waste
for spending money. Esto es porque en español, ustedes usan una
palabra como gastar *This is because in Spanish you use the word
waste/spend*. Gastar, waste. In English, waste means that you're
just throwing your money away {teacher makes hand movement
of throwing something away}. OK, when you waste your money.
In English, the word to use is spend. They didn't want to spend
their money in that kind of way. So, remember that from now on.
Now, Angel hit on a point. The plantation owners wanted to make
money and they knew that paying a lot of people would be very
expensive. So, it wasn't only that they were greedy. It's just that
they thought of the expense, that it was going to be too much
money so they ended up with slaves.

The interactions in this excerpt show that the way of talking and communicating was well established during read alouds teacher-guided reporting.
In this example, I would like to focus on the negotiation of the appropriateness of points of view by focusing on the clarification of meaning triggered

by the entire discussion. Specifically, I will focus the last two turns (09–10) as the student repeated and summarized the different students' contributions and the saliency of the negotiation of the storyline are also present.

In this exchange, the teacher and the student appeared to be co-constructing both identities and meaning, historically, institutionally, and socially. First, the dialogue was about the economic reasons for African slavery in the United States. Angel established the possible curtailment of profit as an economic reason for slavery. The growers of the cotton needed laborers to realize profit. There was also a construction of a proposition of intentionality – the growers were greedy. It was constructed through the use of negatives (didn't, wouldn't, no) and repeated four times: they didn't want to pay, they didn't want to pay, they wouldn't be able to afford, and make them work with no pay. Thus, the growers' participation in slavery was predicated on their willingness and ability to pay, their potential profit, and their greed. The word, 'wasting' brought forth some ambiguity and negotiating of meaning. It seemed to meaning squandering, or an unnecessary use of what might otherwise be profit.

By establishing the intentionality of greediness, which dominated his utterances, Angel seemed to be establishing his point of view – that is, a stance against (the use of negatives) oppression. Reaching into his historical understanding of slavery, Angel gave an image of whites going to far away lands, Africa, and 'dragging' the people (blacks) to work without pay. Here he seemed to be establishing a different relationship – that of injustice and racism. He seemed to be reiterating his stance with the oppressed. By inserting African American, inappropriately and ungrammatically within the sentence, Angel established the source of the unfairness of the power relationships that African Americans face today within the historical context of slavery. Angel reinforced through redundancy a stance for the oppressed and, in this utterance, identified not just with oppression of African American but also of other minorities, including the one from which he came.

Mrs Alvarez called attention to the entire class, not just the student that spoke, when stating 'OK, I want to clear something up. A lot of you.' The teacher moved to an issue of semantics and translation. The use of 'the word waste for spending money' had two possible intentions that she seemed to feel needed to be clarified. The English words 'waste' and 'spending' refer to the same Spanish word, *gastar*. *Gastar* refers to the act of spending but does not evaluate its appropriateness. Waste would require an adjective, *mal gastar* or literally, bad spending. The second possible intention in Angel's utterances was to clarify, and establish appropriateness, of the interpretations of his cultural model or point of view (Gee, 1999). Following Mrs Alvarez's moves might give us some clue as to her dilemma.

After Mrs Alvarez established who her audience was (the entire class); she moved to Spanish (in an act of *respeto*, an acknowledgement of the students' linguistic resource as well as an act of linguistic solidarity with the audience) to explain why she thought Angel might have used the word 'waste'. Her explanation was that Angel may have been literally translating, again acknowledging the native language as a resource. Then, she gave the two possible meanings of the word as misuse of money and spending. In clarifying these two words she may have also been bringing forth the different roles and identities she was embodying in the moment. They are what Gee (1999) calls the 'cultural models' that are being played out in the moment of speaking. They occur simultaneously. There are at least three different identities converging in this interaction for Mrs Alvarez. She was the teacher, a representative of the state, the governmental apparatus that responds to and construes the culture of the market economy, thus, the differentiation in storylines when making a distinction between the meanings of 'waste' and 'spend'. The farmers might have been greedy and felt that to pay for work was a waste, or the farmers might have been thinking of the expenses of production and the end profit. Mrs Alvarez was also the language teacher. She needed to move the children from Spanish to English and establish an appropriate context of use of the academic language involved. Moreover, she was a Latina, also a member of a minority community which Angel was making reference to at some level – that of speaking the same language and agreeing with a stance of social justice. She was, simultaneously, the teacher/institutional representative, the language teacher, and the Latina. Some of her moves were clearly one or the other, as we could see when she moved into Spanish, but overall the three identities were converging.

After clarifying the meaning of the words waste and spend, she signaled a transition by using 'now' to turn to the meanings of point of view. She foreshadowed an ideological affirmation of what the student had said by stating 'Angel hit on a point'. The teacher provided a gist of what Angel had said from an economic and historical perspective. In the way she verbalized the two inferences in Angel's construction, she wore all her identity hats – 'So, it wasn't only that they were greedy' referring to Angel's dominant view and the previous student's comment ('It's just that they thought of the expense, that it was going to be too much money, so they ended up with slaves'). The teacher ended by espousing a multiple factorial cultural model that agreed with Angel's point of view that the farmers were greedy but signaling that it may have been a bit more complex. The adverbs, 'so', 'only', and 'just', and the negative, 'wasn't', served to shift the emphasis away from identifying with the source of oppression as greed (the minority point of view) as only one factor to the less likely to be verbalized more academic socio-economic construction of slavery as the relationship between expenses and profit (the institutional/economic point of view) during a socio-historical period. Because she ended up agreeing with Angel, it is likely that her central purpose in this interaction was dominated by her language teaching identity.

Appropriateness in the co-construction of a response

Four chapters later and just before the reading of the fifth chapter of *Sounder*, the teacher set the students up for what they might encounter. She does so with a focused question that required the students to think about the character of the boy in the story. The boy had no name yet. Mrs Alvarez asked the students to tell her how the boy might have been feeling at the end of the fourth chapter. Students report on their pair share discussion.

Extract #3

01 Ja It also said that the boy was hungry but once the man was squishing the cake, he didn't feel like eating it.
02 T   Yeah, why?
03 Ja Because, he felt kind of scared of the man and he felt like the man was just doing it for fun, without respect.
04 T   So he felt he was disrespected right? The boy, there were so many things going on in the experience he was having. Let me ask you this, do you think this kind of experience is going to affect him?
05 Ss Yes!
06 T   Yes, as a matter of fact, he's already thinking revenge. He's already thinking revenge. I'm going to take 2 more comments and then we're going to begin reading because I do want to read all of Chapter 5 today because it's a very important chapter.

In this exchange, the teacher was setting up the appropriate listening for the Read Aloud of Chapter 5. In the story, the boy had gone to visit his father at the jailhouse. The boy's mother had made a cake for the father's birthday. The boy's feelings of happiness on his way to the jailhouse turned when the jailer destroyed the gift of love he had so carefully carried for the visit. Jasmine re-told and rephrased parts of the story (01). Mrs Alvarez asked Jasmine to clarify the reasons for the boy's feelings; it is a cognitive question, giving her the opportunity to further work out the intended meaning. Jasmine began with a conjunction (because) responding to the teacher's cue (03). In Jasmine's two sentence response, she tapped into feelings the boy might have been experiencing but was generally in a retelling detail mode until she reached the meaning she wanted to give to what occurred in the story, 'without respect'. Mrs Alvarez followed up with a comprehension check question (04) and by making more explicit the dilemma facing the character. With a strategic move (Let me ask you this . . .), the teacher gave a turnover signal, which shifted the conversation from Jasmine to the whole class. The students responded to her in chorus format (05). Thus, Mrs Alvarez skillfully moved to bring in the larger audience and provided the students with a gist of the chapter to come – 'he is already thinking revenge'. The teacher emphasized the gist by repeating it.

This exchange provides an example of how teacher-guided reading may serve to push the second language learner of English 'beyond what they are able to do alone in English' (Gibbons, 2002: 34); the kind of scaffolding and space the teacher might need to provide for the students to be able to think aloud until they found the exact word for the meaning they were intending; and the centrality of the concept of *respeto* Latino students zeroed in on to frame their talk about relationships.

Discussion

The instances of social interaction within were but a few of the many observed in this classroom. A *con respeto y cariño* framework guided both the interactions and their analysis. At the end of the year, in a Thank-you-for-participating-in-this-study pizza party, the students asked my assistant and me to share our findings. Betsy, my assistant, spoke about the findings related to the student interactions and I told them I had focused on how Mrs Alvarez had brought life into the readings. The children burst out in cheers and applause. They were agreeing with me and acknowledging Mrs Alvarez for the relationship of *respeto y cariño* that made it possible.

Appropriateness had many meanings within. It was established in this classroom as general social, cognitive, and linguistic behaviors within specific instructional activities and in very concrete interactions. In the first extract, the norms, roles and responsibilities for interacting in a teacher-guided reporting during a read aloud were identified in the classroom observed using Nunan's (1990) analysis of listening and the requirements of a two-way conversation focused on an information-based topic and Gibbson's (2002) notion of scaffolding to characterize the processes required by the productive language involved in speaking within pair shares and in a whole group situation. In the second extract, the dilemmas around identity and interpretation were explored through the use of Gee's (1999) notion of cultural models for creating meaning. Lastly, in the third interaction, the role of the teacher in assisting the students to make meaning in the second language was featured. As stated previously, Valdes' notion of *respeto y cariño* was extended to examine the teacher/student relationship in this classroom setting. The teacher of English language learners continuously faces the dilemma that the social, historical, and institutional tensions bring into the process of language learning/teaching in all classroom contexts. As Nieto (1992) and Franquiz and Salazar (2004) propose, the instructional negotiations are enhanced within the relational construct of a Latino value, *respeto*. Within, *con respeto y cariño* was seen in the patience the teacher exhibits in making spaces for students to articulate their point of view and in moving children beyond what they knew while acknowledging with dignity the value of their responses. Within bilingual settings, the teacher has a greater range of linguistic and cultural resources available with which to work. Within, we were able to see how different resources were used in one classroom in a dual language education program and how the teacher, Mrs Alvarez, did not miss any opportunity, by seizing on or creating them, in order to push on the students' capabilities while being respectful and communicating fondness to the student learners. Together the teacher and the students created a relationship of *respeto y cariño*. The concept of *respeto* can be useful in establishing teacher/student relationships within mono-lingual classrooms as well.

TAKE 2

In the following section, we interpret the data from the perspective of constructivism. First we provide a brief recapitulation of the salient features of constructivism and relate it to the co-construction of learning. Then we argue that meaning and knowledge are constructed in this classroom via active participation of the teacher and the students. We then compare this classroom interaction with that in a Malaysian classroom (see Chapter 7 of this volume).

The theoretical underpinning of constructivism is that knowledge is 'constructed' through interaction with others (Hendry *et al.*, 1999). During this process of interaction, knowledge is co-constructed. In order for knowledge to be co-constructed, conversation exchanges have to be highly interactive and collaborative (Sonnenmeier, 1993). A high degree of interpersonal connection between the individuals working in the process (Goldstein, 1999: 648) is also expected. Besides this, the process of co-construction takes place through inferencing (Sonnenmeier, 1993). From the constructivist paradigm, co-construction takes place in the classroom if the interactions are highly interactive in nature, whereby both the teacher and the students contribute actively towards the learning. Given this theoretical underpinning, the teacher's role in encouraging and promoting active interaction in the classroom is important. Besides acting as a source of curriculum knowledge, the teacher has to provide meaningful activities in which students are able to co-construct understanding.

The discussion that follows shows how meaning is co-constructed in the US classroom. The data clearly suggest that meaning and knowledge are verbally co-constructed through the 'active inferencing' (Sonnenmeier, 1993), and interpersonal connection (Goldstein, 1999) between the teacher and students. Where appropriate, comparisons are made with the Malaysian classroom.

Co-construction of knowledge

The construction of knowledge is a two-way communication. Students responded to the teacher's questions without inhibition, for example in

Extract #1, there was an alternation of teacher and student talk throughout. This is also evident in Extracts #2 and #3. Questions were used (e.g. Extract #1 09, 11; Extract #2 01, 04; Extract #3 02, 04) to elicit responses and this was done successfully. There are only two instances of extended teacher talk. The first occurred in Extract #2 where the teacher explained the scenario of the big plantations in the south of the United States and where a lot of labour was required to work these plantations (Extract #2 01). In the closing of Extract #2, the teacher's turn was extended as she went on to explain the English words *spend/waste* versus the word *gastar* in Spanish.

Students responded individually without being prompted most of the time. In the Malaysian data, students almost always answer as a group and the answers are a form of 'safetalk' (Chick, 1996) and more often than not, monosyllabic in nature. In the Malaysian data, students are prompted to respond to close-ended, display questions to which the answer is already known to the teacher. In the US data, learners respond to open-ended questions seeking new information and opinions. Thus, it can be said that the knowledge in the US classroom is co-constructed actively between the teacher and the learners as is evident in the length of student turns. Silence on the part of students is not evident at all in all the extracts. Learners talk freely without inhibition throughout and the relationship between the teacher and the learners is relaxed. Teacher talk and student responses are not the 'safetalk' evident in the Malaysian data. Here, the teacher's discourse is exploratory in that she elicits answers and the relationship built here is relaxed and friendly.

Teacher is not in authority

In comparison with the Malaysian classroom, the Western perspective of constructivism is clearly evident in this set of data from the United States: there is a high degree of explicit cognitive interaction between the teacher and the students. One distinct feature of the US data is that the teacher is not seen as the sole provider of knowledge in the classroom. The numerous exchanges clearly indicate that the students viewed themselves as important contributors of a learning community. In contrast, in the Malaysian classroom, the data clearly indicated a teacher-centered class where the students hardly contributed to the learning environment. The students only spoke when the teachers asked a question. Even when they spoke, it was in single word utterances. The reason for this behaviour of the Malaysian teacher and the students has its roots in religious and cultural norms which view the teacher as an authority, and one not to be lightly challenged by students. In the US classroom, the teacher does not come across as authoritarian like the Malaysian teachers; instead she is seen as a point of reference for the subject matter, *an* authority for the subject matter but not *in* authority like the Malaysian teachers.

Codeswitching

It is also in the closing of Extract #2 that there is the one and only instance of codeswitching on the part of the teacher. Codeswitching is necessary here to explain the difference in the use of the words *spend/waste* in English and *gastar* in Spanish. This strategy is similar to teachers in Malaysian primary classroom where codeswitching is used to facilitate students' understanding of the content of the lesson. The difference is that in the US data, codeswitching serves to explain a particular aspect of the language whereas in the Malaysian data, it is used to explain content concepts. Another motivation on the part of Malaysian teachers for using this strategy is that they and the learners are not competent in English while this not the case in the US data. The US learners generally do not have a linguistic deficit in English although the target language was their L2 or even L3, a characteristic shared with Malaysian learners. The fluency and proficiency of the US learners is perhaps not surprising since English is used as a medium of instruction across the curriculum, and not merely in one or two subjects. Thus codeswitching is used to compensate for linguistic deficiency in the Malaysian data, while in the American classroom it is used for linguistic enrichment.

Final points

There are some similarities between the students in both these environments: most of the students in both these classrooms were learning English as a second or third language. However, we find it extremely interesting to note that all the US students participate actively in the classroom interaction. In fact, the data clearly indicates that this is a student-centred class. The fact that they do not wait for the teacher to invite them to talk is probably based on the notion that they have both content and linguistic knowledge of the subject that is being discussed – and the freedom to express their views and developing understanding. On the contrary, in the Malaysian classroom, the teacher and students do not have the content knowledge (in English) of the subjects being taught and may be thus constrained from developing an interactive classroom discourse.

In conclusion, from our point of view, the US data supports the notion that knowledge is explicitly co-constructed in the classroom based on the highly interactive and collaborative nature of exchanges. In addition, the teacher plays the role of a facilitator who encourages and promotes the learners' active participation in the learning process.

TAKE 3

This segment is part of the introduction of the fifth chapter of *Sounder*, during the reporting back of pair share, from which the third excerpt in

Take 1 was taken. The teacher set the students up for what they might encounter in the following chapter with a focused question that required the students to think about the character of the boy in the story. The boy had no name yet.

01	T:	Talk to your partner for maybe 2 minutes, talk about how the boy changed. What were his feelings? What caused those feelings? Talk!
02	Er:	He went in sad and when he went out, he was angry.
03	An:	He went inside the jail afraid, scared of a lot of think that he had been dreaming about. When he came out, he changed totally, he became braver, more mature and he got angry at the white people.
04	Er:	No, not the white people...
05	An:	The red faced man.
06	T:	OK, let's hear some things. Don't put up your hands. I know everyone has been talking so I'm going to jump around. Vl, tell us. How did he change between the time that he went in and he came out?
07	Vl:	He changed, he become a little scared from what he sees.
08	T:	He was scared going in but you're saying he's getting even more afraid. What kinds of things made him so afraid?
09	Vl:	He saw the man on the bus looking at him.
10	T:	Ah, he gets more scared by inmates, right? (writing on chart) Is that what affected him the most? Is that what caused his biggest change? Ge, what do you think?
11	Ge:	I think that what caused him to be more scared is when he saw the red headed man.
12	T:	You mean the red faced man.
13	Ge:	crushing the cake. He thought there were something, tiro, the iron so he crushed the cake.
14	T:	You think that he got more scared because of the saw the red faced man.
15	Ge:	But he didn't think, he just wanted to mess up the cake.
16	T:	You don't think that the man did it because he thought there was something in the cake. You think the man treated the boy like that because he wanted to. Now how did the boy feel when the man did that?
17	Ge:	Angry!
18	T:	Angry. Actually, she has a great word. It wasn't angry, what was it? Furious. He was furious because of the treatment that he got from the red faced man. (writing on chart) OK, Da, go ahead
19	Da:	I think the boy felt even more than angry. I think he felt envy.
20	T:	He felt envy? Now envy means that he's jealous of something. So then, you mean, he's so furious... Tell me, what you mean.

21   Da: He felt madder than angry and furious because of the treatment they were giving his father and how they were treating him.

22   T: OK, so the treatment that he remembers how they treated his father when they came to get him and now the treatment that they gave him. So, more than angry and furious. (writing on chart) I mean he's so angry and furious, that what's happening in his head? What is he planning in his head? What is the word we were talking about? Ch?

23   Ch: Revenge

24   T: Yeah, he wanted basically, he wanted revenge but since he knew he couldn't take it, where was the revenge happening?

25   Ch: In his mind!

26   T: Yeah, revenge. He imagined all kinds of horrible things. OK, {teacher calls on another student}.

Guiding questions for Take 3

(1)   What are the norms of turn taking? Is it student-facilitated or teacher-facilitated?

(2)   How are different meanings of emotions (i.e. anger, fear, envy, vengeful) negotiated and understood in the classroom? How is the classroom discussion helping the students explore the meanings and implication of these emotions?

(3)   How is the teacher acknowledging and confirming each student's response?

Acknowledgement (by María E. Torres-Guzmán)

This study was made possible by the Teachers College Dean's Research Grant for Tenured Faculty that I received in AY2005–2006. I also want to acknowledge and express my appreciation to the teacher, Mrs Berta Alvarez, and her 2005–2006 classroom on which this paper is based. Mrs Alvarez has given permission to use her name. All student names are fictitious. I also want to acknowledge my research assistant, Elizabeth Crowell, and other student volunteers like Victor Quiñonez, Amber Trujillo, Thao Tran and Vanessa Handal-Raskin.

References

Chick, J.K. (1996) Safe-talk: Collusion in apartheid education. In H. Coleman (ed.) *Society and the Language Classroom* (pp. 21–39). Cambridge: Cambridge University Press.

Franquiz, M.E. and Salazar, M.C. (2004) The transformative potential of humanizing pedagogy: Addressing the diverse needs of Chicano/Mexicano students. *The High School Journal* 87 (4), 36–53.

Gee, J.P. (1999) *An Introduction to Discourse Analysis: Theory and Method*. New York: Routledge.

Gibbons, P. (2002) *Scaffolding Language, Scaffolding Learning: Teaching Second Language Learners in the Mainstream Classroom*. Portsmouth, NH: Heinemann.

Goldstein, L.S. (1999) The relational zone: The role of caring relationships in the co-construction of the mind. *American Educational Research Journal* 36 (3), 647–673.

Gonzalez, V. (2007) *El Camino Real*: Where culture and academia Meet. *Diversity Digest* 10 (2). On WWW at http://www.diversityweb.org/digest/vol10no2/gonzalez.cfm.

Hendry, G.D., Frommer, M. and Walker, R.A. (1999) Constructivism and problem-based learning. *Journal of Further and Higher Education* 23, 359–371.

Hildebrand, V., Phenice, L.A., Gray, M.M. and Hines, R.P. (2000) *Knowing and Serving Diverse Families* (2nd edn). Upper Saddle River, NJ: Prentice-Hall.

Lyons, J. (1968) *Introduction to Theoretical Linguistics*. London: Cambridge University Press.

Mehan, H. (1979) *Learning Lessons*. Cambridge, MA: Harvard University Press.

Nieto, S. (1992) *Affirming Diversity* (1st edn). White Plains, NY: Longman Press.

Nunan, D. (1990) Learning to listen in a second language. *Prospect* 5 (2), 7–23.

Sonnenmeier, R. (1993) Co-construction of messages during facilitated communication. *Facilitated Communication Digest* 1 (2), 7–9.

Souto-Manning, M. (2006) A Latina teacher's journal: Reflections on language, culture, literacy, and discourse practices. *Journal of Latinos and Education* 5 (4), 293–304.

Valdés, G. (1996) *Con Respeto: Bridging the Distances Between Culturally Diverse Families and Schools: An Ethnographic Portrait*. New York: Teachers College Press.

Wells, G. (1993) Reevaluating the IRF sequence: A proposal for the articulation of theories of activity and discourse for the analysis of teaching and learning in the classroom, *Linguistics and Education* 5, 1–37.

Chapter 5

Interaction in a Taiwanese Primary School English Classroom

TAKE 1: CHING-YI TIEN AND ROGER BARNARD
TAKE 2: FRED E. ANDERSON

TAKE 1

Introduction

In 2000, a proposal that English be declared to be an official language alongside Tai-yu and Mandarin (Scott & Tui, 2007) was eventually rejected. This move does however indicate the importance that the English language has in Taiwan, where government and many international companies now require certain proofs of English competence when hiring employees. The national drive to learn English has increased its importance as a requirement in the high-stake entrance examinations to universities and high schools; it has also led to an enormous amount of English courses being taught outside the national school system: English-speaking preschools, cram schools and private tutoring are very important growing private sectors in the domestic economy. However, the teaching of English is perceived to be not particularly effective. According to the latest available statistics from English Testing Service (ETS, 2005), the average Taiwanese test taker of the written TOEFL test (Test of English as a Foreign Language) scored 205. Taiwan was ranked 21st out of 29 Asian countries while Japan ranked 28th, Thailand 25th and Korea 14th. Statistics from the Cambridge ESOL (English for Speakers of Other Languages) Examinations reported a similar situation. Largely as a consequence of the perception of ineffectiveness, in 2006 the Ministry of Education (MOE) in Taiwan – like those in Japan, Korea and Thailand – decided to introduce English instruction from the third grade of primary schools. Thus, under the current education system, Taiwanese students finishing college education receive four years of basic English instruction in primary school, six years of more advanced English instruction in junior high and high school and at least six credit hours of English in college.

Confucian Attitudes Towards Teaching and Learning

Traditionally, a Confucian attitude towards education is based on political utilitarianism (Hui, 2005), which has been explained by Zhu (1992: 4) as 'its usefulness to those in power'. This is reflected in the emphasis placed on EFL (English as a Foreign Language) by the Taiwan Ministry of Education, and its introduction in primary schools. Formal examinations have always played a key role in Chinese education (Chu, 1997) and are today still seen as the main gateways for academic progress and social esteem. The pressure of examinations is particularly acute for entrance to higher education, but the effects percolate through the entire system, and teaching methods are closely geared to the competitive needs of examinations (Lin & Chen, 1995). Taiwanese schoolchildren like those everywhere else, are likely to have clear, if implicit, perceptions about the nature of learning and teaching. These include appropriate relationships between teacher and learner and the way that knowledge is constructed in the classroom. The typical Chinese learner has been characterised as having great respect for the teacher (Mezger, 1992) and formally addresses him or her as *lao shi* (teaching master). The high moral status ascribed to the teacher has led to an authoritarian didactic style, where he/she is expected to be responsible for initiating all classroom interactions (Hui, 2005). At a surface level, at least, the teacher is not seen as a facilitator of learning, but as a presenter of knowledge (Warden & Lin, 2000: 536). The learners, therefore, are accustomed to teacher-centred instruction (Gao, 1988) in which the learner's role is to be diligent and put great effort into achieving high grades (Hu, 2002). The learner must also demonstrate good memorisation skills whenever called upon (Hui, 2005). Typically, they show little initiative and appear to be passive and non-critical (Biggs, 1992; Cortazzi & Jin, 1996). To question a teacher would seem an impertinence and an implied criticism that the teacher has not made things clear (Chu, 1997); rather, they should be self-critical if failure to understand occurs (Hui, 2005).

Many of these general attributes of Chinese attitudes towards learning are consistent with the findings of a survey on motivational strategies carried out among 387 Taiwanese teachers of English (Cheng & Dörnyei, 2007), of whom 50 (11.2%) were working in national elementary schools. The importance of pencil-and-paper tests, and the backwash effect on pedagogy, led to the 'tendency to overemphasise learning outcomes at the expense of the learning process' (Cheng & Dörnyei, 2007: 170). Like those reported by Hu (2002), these teachers believed in the importance of motivating their students to make effortful engagement in the lessons. They did not consider it necessary to adopt interesting learning tasks to stimulate their students, and were reticent in allowing their learners to organise their learning process. They rated the promotion of learner autonomy the least important of all the macrostrategies covered in the survey; consequently, the authors infer that this strategy is virtually not used in Taiwanese EFL contexts (Cheng & Dörnyei, 2007: 168).

Context of the Research Site

This chapter intends to illustrate how teaching and learning are conducted in an EFL class in an urban primary school classroom in downtown Kaohsiung, the second largest city in Taiwan. Established in 1952, it is one of the top primary schools in the city and in 2006 there were a total of 47 classes consisting of 1552 students and 99 staff. The curriculum for the first two grades requires students to take 10 different subjects every school year; from the 3rd grade to the 6th grade students have to learn 14 different subjects, one of which is English.

The participants in this study are a 6th grade class of 27 students – 10 girls and 17 boys – all of whom are bilinguals speaking Mandarin and Taiwanese. The normal class size is around 35 to 40 students, but this class is smaller because it comprises students who were selected for their exceptional talent in music and arranged into a 'music class'. They are believed to be the top students in that school and, typically in Taiwan, such students have a higher financial status than their peers in regular classes. The English language teacher who participated in this study had taught this class for two months, relieving the regular teacher absent on maternity leave. She was doing an internship at this school, having recently graduated from one of the private universities in southern Taiwan as an English major. After one of the observed lessons, she said that this group of students had been spoiled by the school; they sometimes did not respect teachers and had some sort of arrogant attitude toward learning in all kind of subjects except in music.

The class was one of many observed by one of the authors of this chapter, and the audio-recorded interactional data were transcribed verbatim and supplemented by field notes written during the lessons and supplemented by reflective notes made afterwards. When all the data were analysed, it seemed that the Initiation-Response-Feedback (IRF) framework, originally proposed by Sinclair and Coulthard (1975), might yield some interesting interpretations about the construction of classroom understanding.

Analytical Framework

The IRF framework of discourse analysis (Coulthard 1986; Sinclair & Coulthard, 1975) has been shown to be one of the most common structures of language learning classroom discourse, at least in Western classrooms. Over the years, the basic structure and nomenclature has been amended (Cazden, 2001; Mehan, 1979; van Lier, 1988; Wells, 1993; see also Chapters 2 and 6 in this volume) but in this chapter, we apply the original framework. The structure of interactive exchanges between teacher and students typically has three parts: initiation, response and follow-up. Any turn in the exchange structure may consist of a number of separate acts, and the following options within IRF structure are those presented by Coulthard (1986: 127):

Initiation	Response	Follow-up
Informative	Acknowledge	–
Directive	Acknowledge (react)	Accept Evaluate
Elicitation	Reply	Comment

Generally speaking, it is the teacher who opens and closes each exchange. Although variations are of course possible, the discourse is thus dominated by teacher-talk, as two-thirds of the structure is generally spoken by the teacher who is 'unequivocally in charge' (van Lier, 2001: 95). When strictly adhered to, the IRF structure thus discourages student initiation and questioning, and there is also a tendency for the students' contributions – the response turn – to be limited in terms both of the amount of language uttered and the conceptual or cognitive quality of the utterance. This is due to the preponderance of 'display' questions – that is, questions to which the teacher (and very often the students) know the answer – posed in the initiation move. In its elemental form, IRF constrains the students' ability to verbally co-construct meaning with the teacher or each other, and thus reinforces inequality of participation and learner dependence.

However, the basic threefold structure could be extended to increase student verbal participation – thus, I–R–R–R–F would at least reduce the sheer amount of the teacher's talk because it would allow for more student turns. There could also be occasions when the exchange structure could be initiated by the students rather than the teacher, and in this way they could to some extent at least steer the direction, if not perhaps the substance, of the discourse. The exchange structure could also be taken beyond what Young (1992) refers to as GWTT(Guess What Teacher Thinks) to include opportunities for the teacher to probe deeper into the cognitive processes of the students by more open-ended and searching initiations; if this were done, the students would have scope for creating and expressing their thinking processes rather than merely drawing on rote memorisation. Drawing on principles of scaffolding explained in his earlier work

(1996: 195), van Lier (2001: 96) argues that the basic IRF structure can be used initially to draw on learners' previous learning to establish a platform upon which new knowledge and understanding can then be scaffolded, co-constructed and developed.

The interaction in the Taiwanese EFL classroom was therefore examined to see the extent to which the discourse was dominated by the IRF structure, and whether there were opportunities for the structure to be developed to allow for more active verbal co-construction of meaning among this teacher and her students.

Classroom Interaction

The lesson presented and discussed below occurred in the fourth week of the term, and began with a warm-up activity to revise the vocabulary presented in the previous lesson.

Extract #1

01 T   好，現在開始上課囉。*Right, now let's begin with our lesson.* OK, number 2. Who is number 2? {a student raises a hand} Please stand up. {student stands} OK. Can you tell me what this is? {with a flashcard of the picture pepper.}

02 Ss   Pepper.

03 T   Pepper, very good. 26. Where is 26? Ok, what is this?

04 SS   {silence}

05 T   OK, everyone stand up. 如果你可以保持安靜的話，請坐下。沒關　係，你想要　stand up 沒關係，我知道你想要講話，沒關係。我們的　規則就是，你想要講話，就站著講話。*If you keep quiet, please sit down. That's ok, if you want to stand up, it's all right. I know you want to chat. That's fine. Our rule is that, if you want to talk, you have to stand up.*

06 T   Ok, it's ok. 26. What is this?

07 Sa   (xxx)

08 T   In English. No Chinese.

09 Ss   Butter.

10 T   Ok, next one is one. Please number 1. What is this?

11 Sb   (xxx)

12 T   Ok, good. Next one is 22. Number 18. Ok, what is this?

13 T   Salt.

14 T   Next one is 23. Ok, 23.

15 Ss   不在。*Not here.*

16 T   去哪裡？*Where is he?*

17 Ss   23 24 不在。*No. 23 and 24 are not here.*

18 T   Ok, next one. Number 14. Where is number 14?

19　T　Yes, dates. Ok, 29. Who is 29? Loudly.
20　Sc　Vinegar.
21　T　Yes, vinegar. Ok, next one. Number 16. Who is number16? What is this?

This extract clearly shows the lesson following a standard IRF format. Thus, the first turn contains several initiating acts: the first is an informative (*Right, now let's begin with our lesson. OK*), the first and last words forming the boundary of the act, and to which no response is needed, or – in this case – sought. The next (*number 2,*) is a directive, followed by an elicitation (*who is number 2?*) and a directive (*Please stand up*), each of which received a non-verbal response; the latter was followed up by an acceptance (*OK*). The teacher's final elicitation in (01) calls for the students' choral response (02), which the teacher follows up (03) with a repetition (*Pepper,*) as a confirmation and a follow-up evaluation (*very good*) to close this brief exchange before starting, but not completing, another. The transaction ends with a simple set of IRF turns (19–21).

In these exchanges, the teacher is eliciting information already known by her, and there is no sense that the teacher is attempting to develop the students' linguistic performance in English beyond a minimal verbal response, nor to probe their cognitive processes beyond a declarative level. There are one or two interesting points that may be discussed here in terms of classroom conventions. First of all, the teacher refers to students by allocated number, not by name; while this might be explained by the fact that this is a relief teacher who has only taught the class for a matter of weeks, such numerical elicitation is nevertheless a typical feature of Taiwanese classrooms. Second, it is interesting that codeswitching is a regular feature in this classroom: the teacher uses Mandarin to maintain and reinforce classroom pragmatic conventions (04), and the students use it to inform the teacher of the absence of a student. Finally, as noted by Hui (2005), the teacher applies a typical authoritarian didactic style. In short, as van Lier (2001: 96) has noted, '[s]students' opportunities to exercise initiative . . . or develop a sense of control and self-regulation . . . are extremely restricted in an IRF format'.

The following extract occurred a few minutes later, when the teacher held up a flashcard with a picture of butter on it:

Extract #2

01　T　How about this?
02　Ss　**'Butter.'**
03　T　**'Butter.'** {repeat again trying to show the right way to pronounce the word} OK. 快一點把你的舌頭點下來。 *You should tip your tongue lower.* **'Butter.'** {repeat and emphasize the pronunciation again.}

04 T   Ketchup.
05 Ss   Ketchup.
06 T   Pepper.
07 Ss   Pepper.
08 T   Pepper. OK, look at here. 告訴我這個是上面這個，還是下面這
         個。 *Tell me, it's the one on top or the one under?*
09 Sa   上面的。 *The top one.*
10 T   那下面這個是什麼？這個是紙。怎麼唸？ *What is the one under
         it? This is paper. How do you say it?*
11 S   Pepper. Paper.
12 T   怎麼會一樣呢？誰會區別呢？ *How can they sound the same? Who
         knows the differences between them?* Please raise your hand.
         我給你加 分,記住如果你今天 - *I give you extra points. Remember,* if
         you did a good job, you can get a can of Coke。

Once again, the basic classroom IRF format of elicitation–reply–follow-up is
immediately evident (01–03) although the follow-up move is less positive
than those in the first extract; here, the teacher is recasting the student's
monosyllabic reply and correcting the mispronunciation. There follows a
brief form-focused episode, in which the teacher provides metalinguistic
advice on correct pronunciation, using Mandarin to do so. It may reasonably be assumed that the appropriate terminology in English would not
be comprehensible to the class. After a brief series of elicitation–response
moves (04–07), the teacher accepts the students' choral response,
and follows this up with a directive (*OK, look here*) and a display question
(08) to elicit whether the students had understood the correct placement
of the tongue in the pronunciation of /e/. The next exchanges (08–12)
follow the pattern I–R–I–R–I, but the teacher then moves into a limited
degree of explicit co-construction by soliciting a conceptual response
from the class (*Who knows the difference between them?*) and offering two
forms of reward for a good response. This form of extrinsic material motivation, that is, a can of coke, is unconventional in Taiwanese classrooms,
but one which appears to be gaining popularity in some quarters. In this
extract, we see the teacher's use of Mandarin extending beyond classroom
management to its use in brief informative moves of explanation and
concept checking, but the students' conceptual and linguistic contributions
are still very limited: the teacher dominated the content and progression of
the lesson.

After the warm-up activity the teacher turned to the topic of the day:

Extract #3

01 T   OK. So, now open your book. Turn to page 15.
02 St   老師今天不用考試。 *Teacher, we don't have a test today?*

03	T	我已經考完啦。誰表現得好，我都記在腦子裡，

不是說我們沒有考 試嗎。每一次上課我都在打分數。 *I have done, with the test. I have it all in my memory, about who did well. Didn't I say we don't have a test today? And I'm scoring each time we have class.*

04 St   老師你是耍人喔。 *Teacher, are you kidding us?*

05 St   老師，我都沒被抽到。 *Teacher, I didn't have my turn.* <Referring to the warm-up activity earlier>

06 Sa   你可以爭取機會阿。 *You could have won your own chance.*

07 T   Raise your hand. /// 給你 30 秒請你快速的把課文看一遍。 *You have 30 seconds to quickly read through the article in your textbook. /// So, are you ready?* {The teacher plays the audiotape of the lesson content}

08 CD   'Come with me. Now it's your turn. Repeat after me. Dinner is ready. Time for dinner.'

09 Ss: Dinner is ready. Time for dinner.

Clearly, in this extract the conventional teacher-dominated IRF pattern is less in evidence. The teacher's directive (01) is followed by a student initiation (02) and an informative response by the teacher (03) leading to another elicitation from the student (04). The exchange is then diverted by two student asides (05 and 06), before the teacher switched on the CD player and allowed the recorded voice to vicariously continue the lesson with a series of elicitations and replies.

The teacher's instruction to the class to open their books is immediately questioned by one of the students, an interesting example of a verbal challenge to the teacher's predetermined agenda. Surprisingly perhaps, the teacher's detailed explanation is then questioned (04), possibly rather colloquially, by the same student, asking whether the routine daily test was not to take place. What could be seen as a repeated challenge to the teacher's authority may indicate the 'arrogance' of these 'special' students referred to in the introduction, or else may be another indication that conventional Confucian attitudes of respect and deference to the teacher (Hui, 2005) may be weakening. Before the teacher could respond to this question, another student interrupted the planned sequence of events by referring back to the previous activity (05). This was then commented on by another student (06) and this time the teacher gave a directive in English 'Raise your hand' (07) to imply that students should bid for a turn, rather than initiate interactions, and followed this with a directive in Mandarin. Having thus reasserted her authority after this altercation, the teacher could proceed with her planned activities.

The following extract occurred later in the lesson presents on the start of a game, intended to be a communicative-like activity to reactivate the vocabulary previously learnt. The selected student covered his eyes and was given a small titbit to taste and provide the flavour in response to a question.

Extract #4

01	T	This is number 5. You ask him 'how does it taste?'
02	Ss	How does it taste?
03	Sa	Salty.
04	T	Salty? 你什麼時候會用到這個? *When will you use this item?*
05	Sa	不知道! *I don't know!*
06	T	你什麼時候會用到? 吃什麼的時候會用到? 告訴他們看吃什麼的時 候會用到? *When will you use this item? What things are eating when you see this item? Can you tell them what are you eating when you use this item?*
07	Sa	Bread.
08	T	Bread. 他吃 bread 的時候。{toward the class} *When he is eating bread.* OK! 你可以選人了, choose。*You can select the next person to taste, choose.*
09	Sb	(xxx)
10	T	You. So, the answer is? /
11	Sc	(xxx)
12	Sd	The answer is (xxx).
13	Se	Butter.
14	T	Butter. That's right? OK! This is butter. So, your number is? // Number 5. OK! Next one. OK! You want to try?
15	Ss	用抽的。*Let's draw the numbers.*
16	T	Come here. OK! One to ten.
17	S	Number 8.
18	T	OK! Number 8. Close your eyes. OK! Everyone ask him.
19	Ss	How does it taste?
20	T	OK! One more time.
21	Ss	How does it taste?
22	T	Clues. Some clues. How does it taste? How?
23	Sb	Salty.
24	T	He says "salty." What is salty?
25	Ss	鹽。*Salt.*
26	T	OK! You raise your hand if you know. You choose one.
27	Sf	Salt.
28	T	Salt? Is it salt?
29	Sf	Yes.
30	T	Yes, it is salt. Ok! Very good 8, and your number? 6.

31	Ss	老師你都叫男生。 *Teacher, why you always call on boys?*
32	T	等一下再一個女生。 *Please wait, I will call on girls later.*
33	Sg	Six.

After the teacher's directive (*You ask him*), the IRF exchange is initiated by a student (02) to which another responds (03). Typical of much classroom discourse, the response is not followed up by the initiating student but by the teacher (04) in the form of a clarification request – an implicit negative evaluation. Her elicitation (in Mandarin) in the same turn seems intended to probe the student's conceptual knowledge, but the student is unable to respond appropriately (05). The teacher's follow-up comprises three rapid elicitations (06), each slightly clarifying the intended meaning until the student responds monosyllabically, but correctly or at least acceptably – according to the teacher's next move (08). The next set of exchanges (09–15) might be interpreted as an attempt by the teacher to pass control of the discourse to the students, but is thwarted by her own interruptions (10 and 14). Her identification of another student to play the game (*You want to try?*) is countered by the students' suggestion that the player be chosen by lot. The teacher accepts this (*OK! One to ten*), and this may be seen as another, rare example of the students' and teacher co-constructing classroom procedures. The following exchanges show a pattern of teacher initiations (18, 20, 22) followed by choral responses (19, 21) until finally the selected student provides the desired response (23). Confirming the accuracy of his reply, the teacher begins another brief IRF exchange to elicit the class's understanding of the word 'salty' (24-26). This is followed by an equally brief exchange about salt. Interestingly, the students again try to co-construct the procedure of the lesson by questioning the teacher's preference for selecting boys (31), the teacher having presumably flouted the previous decision to allocate turn by lot.

In this extract, it may be seen that the IRF structure allowed for student initiatives, but was nevertheless tightly controlled by the teacher to maintain her dominance of the discourse. It may be significant that the teacher did so by using only English herself, and by eliciting monosyllabic or formulaic responses from her students – possibly at the expense of their conceptual learning.

A few minutes later, the teacher wished the students to continue practising the key adjectives:

Extract #5

01	T	Now, I ask you how does it taste? Delicious or bad?
02	Ss	好吃! *delicious!*
03	T	Great or bad?

04	Ss	Great.
05	T	Great. OK! Tasty is here. Let's see here. /// OK! Now, can you tell me how does the corn soup tasted? How? /// OK! Now, listen to me. OK! If you know the answer, raise your hand. /// OK! Please tell me how does the corn soup tasted?
06	Sa	(xxx)
07	T	Taste good, taste great. // What is your number?
08	Sa	24.
09	T	OK! 24. Very good. OK! Next one is- /// Can you tell me / does anyone need ketchup?
10	Ss	Yes.
11	T	Raise your hand. /// OK! One more time. Does anyone need ketchup?
12	Sb	Yes.

The basic teacher-dominated IRF exchange structure features here, with little opportunity given for the students to develop either linguistic or cognitive skills; their responses are entirely monosyllabic, whether in English or (once) in Mandarin, and the teacher solicited merely minimal declarative knowledge. Perhaps what is most interesting about this extract is the teacher's exclusive use of English; this was the longest stretch of discourse in the entire lesson conducted in the target language. The teacher's long turn (05) reveals perhaps her lack of control over the structure of the language, and the repetitions here – and later – may indicate her awareness of the learners' own need for comprehensible input.

The following extract concluded the lesson, when the teacher informed the students of the next week's test:

Extract #6

01	T	OK. Listen to me about our homework. 我只講一次喔。 *I will say only once.* /// OK. Next week, our homework is.../ / first one: review 'read with me.' 什麼是 review? *What is 'review'?*
02	Ss	複習。 *Review.*
03	T	Number 2 is 'Spell the New Words.' What are 'new words'?
04	Sa	老師這個要考嗎? *Teacher, will these be in the test?*
05	T	Yes! OK, we will have a test on new words. This is new words 8. And number 9 is 咖哩 *curry*, 怎麼講 *How do you say it?* OK. Curry, and next one // number 10 is- // 這些東西我們統稱什麼? *How do we name these things generally?*
06	Ss	調味料 *condiments.*
07	T	ment / How does it pronounce?
08	Ss	ment.

09   T   di [d], con / condiment / 重音在這裡 *The stress is on con.* // Ok
這些 統稱調味料。 *These are named condiment.* 全部坐下 ,
除了你之外 *All of you sit down, except you.* /// 來告訴 我 , 下次的
homework 是什 麼 ?/// *Come one, tell me. What is your next
homework?*

10   Ss   (unintelligible. Mandarin)

11   T   preview 是什麼習 ? {no replies from students} /// 預習 *What is
preview?* It's preview. / 我們的· *our* // Read with me. 再來第二個
then our second assignment, 我們要考喔 , 像我們上次考單字一樣
You are going to have a test, like you had on the vocabulary test. For
example, I say, number one, butter. BUTTER and you write
Chinese 奶 油 " *butter.* And number 9 is curry. What is curry?

12   Sb   咖哩 *curry.*

13   T   So you must spell **curry**. And number 10, condiment. What is
condiment? **condiment**. Just spell it. // Now, you write number
9 and No.10. 寫完就可以準備下課了。 *Once you have finished
writing it you can take a break.*

Once again, the IRF structure characterises the discourse, with the teacher's
voice and intentions dominating the discourse: the students' responses are
monosyllabic (other than 04) and in their first language – with the single
exception of the morpheme *-ment* (08). What is interesting here is the
teacher's codeswitching between English and Mandarin. She uses English
for basic information moves, such as in the first turn, when she assumes
that her students can understand the main message. Her warning (*I will say
only once*) indicates to the students that they should pay careful attention to
her spoken English. However, she feels that they need to understand the
meaning of a key term, 'review', so her elicitation is in Mandarin, as is the
response. She uses English for the next elicitation (*What are 'new words'*),
presumably assuming that they will understand the meaning of this from
the previous exchange. However, the students do not respond to this but
instead seek information about the content of the forthcoming test (04). The
teacher replies in English, but then reverts to Mandarin for concept checking, and this in turn receives a reply (06) also in Mandarin. Acknowledging
this response, the teacher seeks to elicit the pronunciation of the word,
obtains a minimal linguistic response, and accepts this, repeating elements
of the word. She follows this up (09) in Mandarin with a metalinguistic
explanation of correct pronunciation, a concept summary, two directives to
call the class to order and an elicitation intended to focus the students'
attention on the topic. Unable to obtain a satisfactory response from the students, the teacher provides more information about the test in Mandarin
before giving an example of a test item in English. The lesson ends with further instructions about the test and a final directive.

Discussion

The application of an IRF analysis to the above extracts has shown how the discourse was dominated by the teacher, in terms both of quantity of speech and in the content and direction of the lesson. Although the learners participated – to a limited extent – in the discourse of learning, there was very little evidence of any active co-construction of meaning; they merely responded between the teacher's lengthier turns at a monosyllabic level to display the subservient roles and memorisation skills normally expected of Chinese-speaking students (Hui, 2005) – in short, very little beyond Young's (1992) notion of 'guess what the teacher thinks'. To this extent, they were entirely prevented from participating in topic choice or development or – with very few exceptions – initiating exchanges or structuring the activity work. As noted generally in the literature, these Taiwanese students – also with rare exceptions – were non-critical and overtly respectful for the teacher. The relationship between teacher and students was, therefore, very hierarchical, distant and depersonalised (most clearly shown in the use of numbers rather than names to nominate individual student turns). This appears to be a very traditional, authoritarian approach to teaching through transmission of information rather than a transforming relationship between master and apprentice – the latter role being one of encouraging novices into a community of learning of which the teacher is an expert practitioner. As may be expected from the survey by Cheng and Dörnyei (2007), the teacher did not incorporate, within this lesson, any activity illustrative of leading her students towards autonomy. In summary, the extracts presented above suggest that dullness may be a characteristic of some Taiwanese language classrooms due to the rigidity or the limited interaction patterns and an overdependence on a pedagogy based on grammar–translation.

TAKE 2

I would like to approach this data from three perspectives. First, I will examine the overall structure of the interactions as related to the roles of the teacher and the students. Second, I will examine the use of the target language (English) vs. Mandarin, as reflected in teacher codeswitching and codemixing. Third, I will discuss teaching practices and issues of EFL methodology as related to the extracts, and considered within the cultural context. The first two perspectives draw primarily on my background as a researcher in sociolinguistics and applied linguistics, and the third incorporates my long experience as a teacher of EFL in the East Asian context.

Interactional Structure

The extracts presented here are striking in their close adherence to an IRE (Initiation-Response-Evaluation) participation structure similar to that characteristic of western primary school classrooms (Cazden, 1988; Mehan, 1979). Within this structure, the teacher initiates an interactional sequence by asking a question, and one student is called on to give a short response. Following the response, the teacher provides a brief evaluation – typically, 'Good,' 'OK,' 'Yes,' or a similar expression of positive reinforcement – then quickly moves ahead with a new question to the next student. The instructor's elicitations tend to be known answer questions, often referred to as *display questions*. They are analogous to the questions on written tests, in that students are expected primarily to display their knowledge of discrete facts rather than communicate new information or express opinions (Heath, 1982). While the IRE structure is found to some extent throughout the present data, it is particularly salient in Extracts #1, #2 and #5; here the teacher rarely deviates from IRE, except briefly to explain classroom procedures (e.g. Extract #1 [05]). Extract #6 is mainly centered around the teacher's explanation of homework and an upcoming test. Extract #3 includes somewhat more initiation on the part of the students, but this is largely in Mandarin and focuses on organizational concerns (e.g. the upcoming test) rather than on the content of the lesson itself. Extract #4 also allows some deviation from the IRE structure due to the game-like nature of the activity, and the teacher does ask students to question each other; but even so, the questions used in the 'game' are mainly display oriented ones. One thing that is not clear from examining the present data alone is whether the IRE mode of teaching is prevalent in Taiwan more generally, or employed here because this is an English lesson. My own investigations into Japanese primary school discourse (Chapter 1 in the present volume) suggest that other modes of teacher–student interaction are available in the East Asian context in native-language settings.

Codeswitching and Codemixing

What I find more revealing in the present data than the overall interactional patterns are the strategies by which the teacher moves back and forth between Mandarin, the students' native language, and English, the target language. This occurs primarily in the form of codeswitching (switches made between English and Mandarin across utterances) but sometimes also as codemixing (where a single lexical item from one language is integrated into the framework of the other language). To a large extent the teacher seems to be cognizant and in control of her switching; of course, interviews or other methods of research triangulation would be necessary to ascertain this.

Looking more specifically at the linguistic codes represented in the data, Mandarin seems to have two primary functions. For one, it is used as a tool for classroom management: either to scaffold lessons as a whole (as in Extract #1 [01], Extract #4 [32], Extract #6 [01]) or to direct student behavior within specific activities (Extract #1 [05], Extract #2 [08, 10, 12], Extract #3

[07]). In addition, Mandarin frequently has a metalinguistic function related to teaching English. For example, the teacher uses Mandarin to explain how to pronounce English words (Extract #2 [03, 12]), as well as to elicit vocabulary items (Extract #4 [06]). Codemixing – with an English word embedded within a Mandarin sentence – is also sometimes used for the purpose of vocabulary teaching, as in Extract #6 [01] where the teacher asks, 'What is 'review'?' although *review* is the only English item here.

The teacher's use of English in these extracts does not contrast with Mandarin so much as it complements it. Like Mandarin, English, on the utterance level, is used frequently for the purpose of classroom management. The main difference seems to be related to whether or not the students are familiar with (or judged by the teacher to be familiar with) the specific English phrases used. Some directives such as 'OK, stand up' (Extract #1 [05]), 'Who is number 16?' (Extract #1 [21]), or 'Please raise your hand' (Extract #2 [12]) are hence given in English. These, however, are relatively simple linguistically compared with the Mandarin directives discussed above.

Not surprisingly, a second major function of English in the data is presentation of the actual language to be taught. Hence throughout the extracts that incorporate language practice activities, English is the preferred medium for the teacher's questioning (initiation phase of IRE), the students' responses and the teacher's confirmation of their answers (evaluation phase).

As a general observation, based solely on the codeswitching and codemixing patterns, it would appear that the teacher was aiming to conduct as much of the lesson as possible in English. However she also seems to have felt it necessary to use Mandarin in order to manage the classroom and assure the pupils' comprehension. In other words, she was pushing her students toward the use of greater quantities of English, while simultaneously conducting reality checks based on her perception of their current level.

Discussion

Finally, I would like to slip into my persona as a classroom teacher and teacher educator, but not without a word of caution. It may be presumptuous of me to relate my experience from Japan – where I have taught (mostly at the university level) for around 25 years, and where I have also spent time in primary schools as a researcher – to the situation in Taiwan. Clearly Japan and Taiwan are different countries with different histories and cultures. Nevertheless, they do have cultural similarities that cannot be ignored, particularly those characteristics based on Confucianism (as discussed in Take 1). Confucian attitudes are influential throughout East Asia, and for this reason my background in Japan may have relevance to Taiwanese education as well.

My first impression of the Taiwanese English lesson was that it relied excessively on IRE structure and display questions. This pattern tends to discourage, or even disallow, students to participate actively in the construction of the lessons; which is equally true of Western classes that rely too heavily on it. To a detached observer, the pupils in this type of class often appear more like programmed automatons than human beings with original thoughts and developmental needs. In the present extracts, this impression is reinforced by the teacher's referring to the pupils by number rather than name. While I am aware of the difficulty of recalling student names in large classes, especially for a teacher who is a temporary intern, it did seem to me that she could have tried harder to call on students in a more humanizing way. For instance, their names could have been written on index cards and shuffled into a deck; individual cards could then be drawn, and students referred to by name, without burdening the teacher with actually having to remember them.

Examining the data a second time, more from the East Asian cultural perspective, I was able to see the teaching in a less negative light. If the purpose of English education in Taiwan, as suggested by the authors of Take 1, is indeed to prepare students for high-stakes entrance examinations, then an argument for a classroom approach based more on discrete answers to test-like questions than on communicating relevant information may be culturally justified. But even so, one wonders whether teaching explicitly to tests, rather than providing more general skills that would trickle down to tests, is the best strategy. For example, Guest (2000) has pointed out a gap between what is taught in Japanese high school English classes, where the alleged goal is to prepare students for college entrance tests, and the actual content of the national university examination. Guest's evidence suggests that the entrance exams are more progressive than high school teaching practices, and that teachers are in many ways prisoners of older paradigms. If one is permitted to extrapolate from Japan to Taiwan on the basis of similarities in the exam-driven systems, it would appear that entrance exams, TOEFL, and other testing devices may in the end be more of an excuse for retaining familiar teaching practices than a justification for them.

A third look at the data, focusing on the teacher's codeswitching strategies, led me to what I see as the most positive aspect of the lesson. In examining the extracts from the perspective of codeswitching, I realized that I myself often codeswitch between Japanese and English in university English classes; and that I do this quite consciously and without guilt. While I do believe that the target language is the ideal medium for a language class – and that the language use should gravitate toward this ideal, if not always attaining it – I also believe that codeswitching into the students' native tongue for specific purposes can be a productive strategy, especially at the lower proficiency levels. Without some use of the native language, comprehensibility may be an issue, which may in turn make it difficult to focus on the task at hand. It is here – in performing the balancing act between use of the target language and the native language – that the novice teacher of this lesson showed the most potential. Her push toward the target language (English), despite obvious weaknesses in her own English proficiency, is admirable. If I am allowed to make suggestions, I would say that her main shortcoming is not in using too little English, but in not encouraging her students to elicit information or ask questions through the target language. In other words there are no genuine uses for English outside of the testing/display-answer structure. Creating a framework within which students could feel comfortable expressing more than pre-packaged ideas in English would clearly add to the lesson. Such a framework does not have to conflict with traditional East Asian notions of the roles of teacher and student. My own data (Chapter 1 in this volume) may in fact represent one model of how self-expression and traditional roles can peacefully coexist in East Asian educational settings. Moreover, the shifting between informal and formal registers of Japanese, as shown in my original Japanese data but unfortunately lost in the English translations, is in many ways analogous to the Mandarin-English switching in the Taiwanese extracts.

TAKE 3

01　T　OK! So, open your book. 如果我們這邊做完，就可以做你想要做的事，所以把握時間唷! *If we finish it, you can do anything that you want to do. So you should control your time. ///* OK! Open your book to 24. 準備好了嗎? *Are you ready? ///* Please open your book to 24. 如果 有一個人沒有打開，我們就一直到下課。

你們耽誤的是你們的時 間，不是我的唷! 一樣老規距，我改完了，

你們就可以做自己的 事。還有人還沒有打開。還有兩個人沒有打開。 *If there is one person not to open the book, we will continue until the bell rings. You are wasting your time, not mine. As long as I read and finish your assignments, you can do anything you want. There are two people who haven't opened their books.* If you hear the answer, please check it. For example, first one is venues, please check it. Be quite!
{The teacher is waiting for the students to open their books.}

02　T　If you hear the answer, please check it. For example, first one is venues, please check it. Be quite!

03　CD　Listen and check. Example: Do you need some ketchup? Yes, please. Number 1: Please pass me the soup. Here you are.
{The CD player continues playing the lesson content for about 3 minutes.}

04　T　OK! One more time. 很多人都答錯。再一次唷 ! *Many people gave the wrong answers. One more time!*

05   CD   Listen and check. Example : Do you need some ketchup? Yes, please. Number 1: Please pass me the soup. Here you are. {The CD player continues playing the lesson content for about 3 minutes.}

06   T   OK! 來, 把你的課本放在桌上, 如果我還沒有改的話請你放在桌上 *OK! Put your book on the desk. If they are not corrected yet, please put them on your desk.* {Teacher is correcting students' books.}

07   T   {the teacher is talking to one student} 請你嘴巴閉上, 做你自己想做的事情 *Please shut your mouth, and do whatever you want to do.* {Teacher continues correcting students' books.}

08   T   {the teacher talks to another student} OK! You can take break.

09   T   要上課了喔 ! *Time is up.* // OK! 把握時間, 上課了喔! *watch out for your time, we are going to start the lesson.* // OK! Now, repeat the word again. OK! What is this one?

10   Ss   Chilly sauce.

11   T   Ok! Chilly sauce. What is this?

12   Ss   Ketchup.

13   T   What is this?

14   Ss   Pepper.

15   T   Pepper. OK! Very good.

16   Ss   Butter.

17   T   OK! Butter. Next one.

18   Ss   Salt.

19   T   Salt. How about this one?

20   Ss   Mayonnaise.
          (xxx)

21   T   OK! 現在我要你們做什麼？仔細聽喔! 我只講過一次。OK! 仔細聽喔! 等一下我會選人上來這裡。*Now, what I want you to do is- Listen carefully. I only speak one time. I will pick up someone up to here.* OK I can choose one what number I choose. Number14. OK! Come here and /// Ok! I have one to by 1, 2, 3, 4, 5, 6, 7, 8, 9, 10. Be quite! /// And you can choose one you like it. For example, you like number 3 and you tell me number 3. OK! And then, I choose number 3 hap. You use your close eyes and you use your first finger and taste it. And, everyone ask how does it taste? You can give them some clues. What is clues?

22   Ss   Clues 是提示。*Is clue.*
          {The teacher continues giving the activity instruction in Mandarin.}

Guiding Questions for Take 3:

(1)   The appearance of choice and mandate are interspersed in the transcript, what patterns would you construct if you were to look at each separately and if you were to analyze them as a relationship?

(2) Based only on what the teacher instructs, what would you say are his/her expectations? Are the teachers expectations met by the students? Why or why not?

(3) What is the role of the CD in this language lesson? How does the teacher integrate and/or reinforce the CD as part of the lesson?

References

Biggs, J.B. (1992) *Why and how to Hong Kong Students Learn? Using the Learning and Study Process Questionnaires. (Education Papers 14)*. Hong Kong: The Faculty of Education, University of Hong Kong.

Cazden, C. (2001) *Classroom Discourse: The Language of Teaching and Learning*. Portsmouth, NH: Heinemann.

Cheng, H-G. and Dörnyei, Z. (2007) The use of motivational strategies in language instruction: The case of EFL teaching in Taiwan. *Innovation in Language Learning and Teaching* 1 (1), 153–174.

Chu, M. (1997) Asian-Chinese students learning in New Zealand secondary schools. Unpublished PhD thesis, Hamilton, New Zealand: University of Waikato.

Cortazzi, M. and Jin, L. (1996) English teaching and learning in China. *Language Teaching* 29, 61–80.

Coulthard, R.M. (1986) *An Introduction to Discourse Analysis*. London: Longman.

ETS (2005) *2005 Annual Report*. On WWW at http://www.lttc.ntu.edu.tw/2006_annualreport/p26-33.pdf. Accessed June 2007.

Gao, L. (1988) Recent changes and expectations of science education in China. Unpublished MA thesis, Auckland, New Zealand: University of Auckland.

Guest, M. (2000) 'But I *have* to teach grammar!': An analysis of the role 'grammar' plays in Japanese university English entrance examinations. *The Language Teacher* 24 (3), 23–25, 27–29.

Heath, S.B. (1982) Questioning at home and at school: A comparative study. In G. Spindler (ed.) *Doing the Ethnography of Schooling* (pp. 102–127). New York: Holt, Rinehart and Winston.

Hu, G. (2002) Potential cultural resistance to pedagogical impacts: The case of communicative language teaching in China. *Language, Culture and Curriculum* 15 (2), 93–105.

Hui, L. (2005) Chinese cultural schema of education: Implications for communication between Chinese students and Australian educators. *Issues in Educational Research* 15 (1), 17–36.

Lin, J. and Chen, Q. (1995) Academic pressure and impact in students' development in China. *McGill Journal of Education* 30, 2.

Mehan, H. (1979) *Learning Lessons: Social Organisation in the Classroom*. Cambridge, MA: Harvard University Press.

Mezger, J. (1992) *Bridging the Intercultural Communication Gap. A Guide for TAFE Teachers of International Students*. Australia: National TAFE Overseas Network.

Scott, M. and Tiu, H.K. (2007) Mandarin-only to Mandarin-plus: Taiwan. *Language Policy* 6 (1), 53–67.

Sinclair, J.M. and Coulthard, R.M. (1975) *Towards an Analysis of Discourse*. Oxford: Oxford University Press.

van Lier, L. (1988) *The Classroom and the Language Learner; Ethnography and Second-Language Classroom Research*. London: Longman.

van Lier, L. (1996) *Interaction in the Language Curriculum: Awareness, Autonomy and Authenticity*. London: Longman.

van Lier, L. (2001) Constraints and resources in classroom talk: Issues of equality and symmetry. In C.N. Candlin and N. Mercer (eds) *English Language Teaching in its Social Context: A Reader* (pp. 90–107). London: Routledge.

Warden, C.A. and Lin, H.J. (2000) Existence of integrative motivation in an Asian EFL setting. *Foreign Language Annals* 33 (5), 535–544.

Wells, G. (1993) Reevaluating the IRF sequence: A proposal; for the articulation of theories of activity and discourse for the analysis of teaching and learning in the classroom. *Linguistics and Education* 5, 1–37.

Young, R. (1992) *Critical Theory and Classroom Talk*. Clevedon: Multilingual Matters.

Zhu, W. (1992) Confucius and traditional Chinese education: An assessment. In R. Hayhoe (ed.) *Education and Modernisation – The Chinese Experience* (pp. 3–22). Oxford: Pergamon Press.

Chapter 6

Learning Through Dialogue in a Primary School Classroom in England

TAKE 1: SYLVIA WOLFE
TAKE 2: CHING-YI TIEN AND MARÍA E. TORRES-GUZMÁN

TAKE 1

Introduction

Studies in the UK and the United States indicate that learning is particularly effective when pupils participate actively in classroom discourse with opportunities to build on the teacher's input and their own ideas (see, e.g. Chang-Wells & Wells, 1993; Mercer, 1996). This interactive/dialogic approach to knowledge construction underpins the National Literacy Strategy (DfEE, 1998) in England, although its pedagogic prescriptions have raised dilemmas for practitioners. In the absence of deep level understandings of the mechanics of interaction, how to invoke and sustain communicative exchanges likely to maximise learning, many teachers continue to be bound by 'traditional' ways of interacting in which pupils are 'positioned' as compliant supporters in the teaching-learning processes (Smith *et al.*, 2004).

The introduction of the Primary National Strategy (DfES, 2003) offered clarification in its first publication 'Speaking, Listening and Learning' (QCA/DfES, 2003). This outlined (1) strategies for promoting 'teacher talk' and (2) suggestions for collaborative practices intended to motivate and challenge students' thinking. Simultaneously, researchers in the field continued to focus on improving the quality of primary education by championing dialogic processes in schools and local authorities throughout England (Alexander, 2004; Burns & Myhill, 2004; Dawes *et al.*, 2000). Alexander (2004/2006) suggests that 'dialogic teaching' appears to be characterised by learning that is *purposeful* and *cumulative* (ideas build on and develop each other) and social relationships that are *mutual*, *collective* and *supportive*. These principles relate to lesson content and the dynamics of interaction: they are properties of a cultural milieu determined by a particular permutation of the 'routines, rules and rituals' (Alexander, 2001) that prevail in classroom settings and frame pedagogical activity.

It is in this context of changing practice and empirical research that my example is set. Extracts are taken from a video recording of a single lesson in which children are learning to reason through guided participation in the processes of historical argumentation. The lesson forms part of a larger study (Wolfe, 2006) in which I observed a range of lessons with a view to understanding the coincidence of circumstances that allows dialogue to flourish naturally during whole-class instruction, despite the constraints of a setting in which the teacher is required to control as well as teach large numbers of children, often without support. To protect the confidentiality of those involved in the study, pseudonyms have been used throughout.

In this chapter, I argue that 'dialogue' in educational settings is best understood not as a discrete pattern of communication but rather as a principled approach to pedagogy in which the potential for communicative variety owes much to conditions in the contexts of interaction and the nature of the relationships mediating the action.

Classroom Communication

The 'traditional' pedagogical relationship, in which teachers seek to check students' acquisition of knowledge through repeated questioning, is associated with a pattern of communication in which teachers initiate an exchange (I) a pupil responds (R) and the teacher follows up (F) usually with a simple evaluation or acknowledgement (Sinclair & Coulthard, 1975). In recent years, researchers (Alexander, 2004; Nystrand *et al.*, 1997; Wells, 1999) have challenged the notion that this pattern of exchange necessarily constrains students' participation in instructional discourses, arguing instead that Initiation–Response–Feedback (IRF) has considerable potential when the follow-up (F) move is used strategically to elaborate and probe students' medial responses (R). What then becomes of interest is the way in which the cycle of IRF is fragmented and/or sequenced in the production of educational meanings and the conditions that facilitate this. These include not only the way in which classrooms are resourced and organised for learning, physical aspects of the environment, but also the less visible signs and symbols (semiotic conditions) that mediate relationships and hence educational activity. These include the proximity and orientation of individuals to each other and their use of gaze and gesture.

Confusingly for many school children, the 'rules of participation', how individuals should position and conduct themselves effectively in their social interactions, often remain tacit or convey meanings at odds to those expressed verbally and usually by the teacher. Alexander (2001: 384) identifies themes that are regular targets for teacher deliberation and control: time, procedures, interpersonal relationships, rules of interaction, the linguistic structure of interaction and the kinds of contributions and ways of acting and knowing associated with particular disciplines. These can be inferred from the discourse and lend insights into the nature of classroom relationships and matters that are deemed of value or concern to those involved.

Given the embeddedness of social action in culturally perpetuated ways of thinking, behaving and valuing, how is it possible to conceptualise and explore the processes of classroom communication and evaluate the effectiveness of different forms of interaction for student learning, without attending to the conditions in the immediate settings and wider contexts of interaction influencing the discourse?

A Methodology for Exploring Dialogic Processes in Classroom Settings

Drawing on an activity theoretical perspective (Leont'ev, 1978) that extends the work of Vygotsky (1978) beyond his interests in language and communication to consideration of complex human activity, mediated by roles, relationships and objects, as the medium of development, I adopted an ethnomethodological approach to gathering data. This combines the methodologies of anthropology and ethnology (case studies using video observation and reflective dialogue with teachers) with Conversation Analysis (CA), fine-grained analysis of participants' 'talk whilst doing'.

Although the techniques of CA (Atkinson & Heritage, 1984), adapted to accommodate non-verbal behaviours, produced transcripts at the level of detail required for subsequent top-down analysis, my choice of 'tool' was not straightforward. The emphasis in CA, on examination of the turn-by-turn unfolding of *brief* conversational exchanges *in situ*, was ostensibly incompatible with the socio-cultural assumptions underlying my study. These call attention to the embeddedness of educational practices in social and historical contexts. Nevertheless, there are clear precedents for using CA as a *starting point* for studies of institutional discourse. Citing a seminal paper by analysts Sacks *et al.* (1974), Hutchby and Wooffitt (1998: 148) suggest that institutional interactions are characterised less by their social structures than by the particular discourse requirements (length of utterances, content, turn-taking rights) to which participants orientate in their 'conversational practices'. Everyday conversation is a 'bench-mark against which other forms of talk-in-interaction can be distinguished', a useful proposition given the conversation-like (dialogic) qualities that I was searching for in my analysis of classroom discourse.

In addition, the paper cited provides a strong rationale for my interest in examining the sequencing or structuring of classroom discourse rather than attending to discrete patterns (structures) of communication, such as IRF. Sacks *et al.* (1974: 728–729) argue that the 'turn-taking system' in conversation has a 'proof procedure' for the analysis of turns, which is 'intrinsic to the data' and a 'central methodological resource for investigation of conversation'. Since parties are 'obliged' to 'display their understanding' of the prior turn's talk, or other talk to which s/he is directed, by focusing on the meanings taken, the analyst becomes privy to the understandings of participants which are the bases for their next turns.

If we accept that learners are actively seeking to build and make sense of shared understandings, it follows that the processes of internalisation involve the 'appropriation of meaning' and 'semiotic uptake' on the part of the acquirer (Wertsch & Addison Stone, 1985). It therefore seems essential that researchers interested in tracking the processes of learning consider what follows a contribution or *sequence* of contributions, for only then might the meanings 'as taken' become clear. Alexander's (2004/2006: 25) suggestion that adoption of dialogic principles in classroom talk may shift the locus from the teacher's talk to the student's responses as the 'true centre of gravity' for a 'learning exchange', qualifies the notion of *sequence* in the context of the re-evaluation of pedagogic practices in England today.

I triangulated my research, and diagnoses of stretches of discourse as 'more' or 'less' dialogic, by coding the dynamics of interaction using Linell *et al.*'s (1988) Initiative-Response analysis (not to be confused with the IRF sequence). This symbolic scheme allowed me 'see', almost literally, abruptions and changes in classroom discourse and to explore the sequencing of discourse in terms of pedagogic purpose(s) at different points in the lesson (see Wolfe, 2006 for further discussion).

Drawing on Alexander's (2001) deconstruction of the activity of teaching extended through identification of some properties of 'dialogic teaching' (see above), I developed a Framework for Analysing Contextualised Episodes of Classroom Discourse (Wolfe, 2006) that allowed me to hold up for simultaneous inspection pedagogical goals, material and semiotic conditions in the settings, the structuring of discourse and progress in thematic content and student learning. This framework operated top down on the data and permitted (1) study of the evolution of classroom processes over time (an activity, lesson or curriculum unit), (2) evaluation of the consequences and outcomes for student learning of changes in the patterning of discourse, and (3) identification of communicative 'triggers' provoking more genuine stretches of dialogue. By focusing on regulatory aspects of classroom life (the semiotic conditions) it was possible to expose the nature and quality of pedagogic relationships: what is 'rewarded and valued' by teachers and students in their joint activities (Christie, 2002: 91). Factors in the wider sociocultural and historical contexts likely to enrich my understanding of events were woven into the explanatory narrative.

Pedagogical Goals and Learning Activities

The imperatives of the National Literacy Strategy for children in Year 5, Term 3 (UK 9–10-year-olds) require that students begin to identify with and adopt different perspectives in their reading and writing and develop the skills to persuade others of their own viewpoint. Teachers in Ashford School, a high achieving Church of England village school, treated the strategy as a guideline, which they adapted according to pedagogical purpose and the needs of learners in a particular class.

Ms Tate, an English graduate from an American university with experience of subject teaching in secondary schools, sought to integrate instruction in literacy and history by inviting children to 'become' representatives of indigenous tribes in America and construct a case, supported with reasons, against settlement of their lands by Europeans. Students were, in her words, expected to 'come up with arguments' 'supported by reasons' and to 'think about the kind of language likely to incite the emotions in the Indians'. In addition they were encouraged to use 'different actions' to 'drive home your case' and 'make sure everybody understands'.

The dual goals, acquisition of historical knowledge and development of linguistic skills required for effective argumentation, were to be realised solely through talk. By adopting the role of chief protagonist on behalf of the European settlers, Ms Tate created a situation in which her lone voice was likely to be challenged by children's multiple different perspectives. Seating arrangements in the classroom hinted at the potential for variation in participant roles and relationships when compared with more traditional whole-class settings in which students sit facing the teacher, compliant supporters of an educational 'game' in which they are often simply recipients of knowledge. In Ms Tate's class, 28 children sat at tables arranged in parallel rows facing each other across a narrow 'corridor'. This arrangement fulfilled a practical necessity (the positioning of whiteboard/interactive whiteboards on walls at either end of the classroom) and reduced the 'distance' between participants, physically and in terms of their status and authority.

Significantly for my interest in understanding the conditions supporting dialogic interactions, the seating plan had been negotiated with students, a practice embedded in the group psyche and reflecting Ms Tate's concern to promote collaborative practices underpinned by mutually agreed and clearly explicated ground rules. At the start of each school year Ms Tate invites children to consider (1) What is learning?, (2) What makes it difficult to learn? and (3) What helps? Class rules are framed positively and based on matters of importance to pupils but with an emphasis on enhancing communication and learning rather than enforcing procedures and desirable behaviours. Since this lesson occurred late in the third (summer) term we might reasonably assume that these rules and routines had become internalised and required little direct regulation. Indeed, according to Ms Tate students were accustomed to first listening and watching with opportunities to 'go do' later.

Classroom Interaction

Lesson structure, variations in discourse and cognition

Ms Tate begins the lesson with a brief question and answer exchange which functions to remind children of their past historical research and bring relevant information (the names of tribes) to the conversational floor, making these 'common knowledge' (Edwards & Mercer, 1987). In expository mode, she then sets the scene for the forthcoming lesson by presenting arguments on behalf of the settlers. The provocative statements (Indians are portrayed as 'wild animals' that need to be 'civilised', 'converted to Christianity' and 'contained') lack invitational qualities and students listen without interruption.

There follows a two-minute period in which children discuss their initial reactions to the proposals in pairs. Remaining in their seats, they turn to each other and talk animatedly. Ms Tate uses students' feedback to the whole-class to model the processes of argument and counter-argument.

Extract #1

01	T	So what I would like to hear is what your initial reactions are to the – to our proposed changes / thinking about what the person in front of you has said / whether you agree or disagree, whether you're adding to that or whether you are starting a completely new conversation. So we'll start off with Jack
02	Ja	Well, the new settlers can't boss us around. We we're – the Indians, the Indians were here first, it's **our** land so we, so we should really be in charge because we were here first.
03	T	But you don't have any fences. I don't know what part is your land. Where – how do you know which part is **your** land?
04	Ja	We – we roam free across the plains. The entire Continent is almost our land. We'll tell you what to do, this is our land, we roamed **it** / before you so (xxx)
05	T	Henry?
06	He	Um well I agree with Michael <a previous speaker> but I'm starting a new one <a new point> about, um, you taking our children and learning – and teaching them Christianity. I think it's a good idea but I don't really want them taken away from me. Why can't **I** come and join the – join in with them as well, like help, help you with them?

07 T   I'm so glad you see the importance of Christianity and that your ways are **wrong**. About worshipping God, erm, in particular ways. For, for someone like you who is open to new ideas that / that probably could be worked out but I'm not sure that everybody is going to share your idea of taking on Christianity quite so readily {Nods to girl, Fiona, with hand up}

08 Fi   Um, I think we should worship God, if we **want** to. We – as we worship animals we don't really **have** to worship God

09 T   Okay. So you disagree with Henry /

10 Fi   {nods}

11 T   Okay so here we go. Two Indians and even you don't agree but all Christians understand – the White Man understands the importance of worshipping one God, so we're all in agreement with that, okay / Sally?

12 Sa   Um, well my argument is, why um why should you just be able to come in and push us around? We were living perfectly before you came along and just told us what to do. Cos if we live in tribes, hunting buffalo and moving with the seasons, that's what we should do

13 T   You're saying you live **perfectly**. Do – what Indian tribe are you?

14 Sa   Um the Blood tribe

15 T   The Blood tribe. Ooh the name **blood** makes **me** think that, maybe you aren't peaceful? Did you not have problems with the tribes around you?

16 Sa   Well we might / we might have done but we're living fine we don't – this might disrupt our lives at home and away as well

17 T   Yes, well I'm fairly sure that your tribe is one of the one's that is pretty nasty to the people around you and you get a bit savage in the way you treat them and torture them / Andrew?

18 An   Well, adding onto Henry Um well if, if you're going to teach them Christianity, I don't want them to be teached Christianity because if I **believe** in – in my spirits, I want them um to learn about **my** spirits not about this **Christianity**

19 T   Exactly now there's a perfect case of somebody we need to civilise

20 Ss   He's disagreeing {laughter}

This approach, in which the teacher simultaneously participates in and offers a meta-commentary on the role play, is repeated when it becomes clear that children are struggling to support their opinions with reasons and factual evidence. Having generated ideas in pairs, students are required to talk in small groups to develop their cases before presenting them to the class. In an episode of contingent instruction following the first presentation, Ms Tate models how pupils might improve their performances.

Extract #2

01 T   Andrew?
02 An They have a head chief] /
03 T   [Okay
04 An [and, um, they um they obey his rules and um nearly every –
        every time a head chief dies they will elect a new one by his skills
        and by how, how much he believes in the tribes and if he can raise
        spirits
05 T   So you, you could use that as an argument about the fact that you
        are not like wild animals {extends arm} cos you do have some-
        body that's in charge, you do have somebody that makes rules
        and everybody follows them and they have a way in which they
        select a new one
06 An {nods}
07 T   So good evidence to support something that says 'No we're not
        like wild animals / we do have rules, we do have order in the
        way we do things.' So a good example of something that could
        be used. Anybody else think of something? Jack
08 Ja Um, well some of the Indians were um normads so um – nomads –
        so they liked to um / that means they travelled around, they
        don't live in homes, towns or cities um so it would be like err like
        really hard for them to settle in one / complete area, the isolated
        area that they were only allowed to stay in so it would be quite
        hard for them to stay in there
09 T   So you could use that as evidence of why that particular culture
        wouldn't work very well. Okay, another good example. Fiona
        you had one
10 Fi Um well they live in tepees and they and they travel around and
        (xxx)
11 T   Okay so what would you use that [for?
12 Fi [um, for the (xxx) cos you were saying that the Indians could
        make a house out of wood and then you said (xxx)
13 T   'kay. So you would – how would you use that to make your argu-
        ment better?
14 Fi Um / because it's about them / living in tents
15 T   Okay so they had a different style of living, are you saying? That
        it isn't wrong, it's just different. So you are living in homes, you're
        not sleeping out / sleeping under the stars at night, are you?
        They do have a shelter, and they do have an organisation in the
        way that they do things. They have a reason why they're living
        out. Okay you need to develop those points a bit more / Michael?
16 Mi Um, I know that a skilled hunter can catch a buffalo – can catch
        two buffalos on horseback.

17   T   Okay, so what would you use that for? // it's an interesting fact. Believe me, buffalos are not small animals to bring down so it's definitely a skill / What could you use that to support / in your / in an argument whether it was in yours or a different argument? What would that be used as evidence for?

Clearly, some students have accumulated and can recall a great deal of factual knowledge about the indigenous tribes and Ms Tate uses this intentionally to lead children into more complex ways of reasoning. Her turns (05 and 15) appear to function as a 'vicarious form of consciousness' (Bruner, 1985) as she draws inferences and elaborates on the facts proffered.

Let us pause to consider the significance of this observation for understanding the role of semiotic mediation in the enactment of teaching and learning. Bruner uses the notion of *vicarious consciousness* to explain the processes by which all those in a tutoring role assist learners through Vygotsky's 'zone of proximal (potential) development' (ZPD). By 'scaffolding' the learning task tutors 'make it possible for the child, in Vygotsky's word, to internalize external knowledge and convert it into a tool for conscious control' (Bruner, 1985: 24–25). Extracts #1 and 2 exemplify the 'scaffolding' process in action. By building on children's responses and articulating her own cognitive processes, Ms Tate affords students opportunities to participate actively in the target discourses and supports their understanding of the particular meaning-making (semiotic) game in which they are involved. Indeed, research suggests that this kind of 'apprenticeship in discourse' is an effective strategy for enhancing learning (Edwards & Mercer, 1987; Wells, 1999, 2003).

Demonstration of students' mastery of effective argumentation (Bruner's *'handover'*) obviously marks the goal of instruction but it is interesting to observe the different levels of student response at this stage. In Extract #2, Jack (08) is a reflective and skillful communicator and has represented his school in debate. He monitors his own communicative efforts, correcting the mispronunciation of 'nomad' and defining the term for others. In so doing, he demonstrates awareness of the obligation on participants in conversation to assist sense-making processes by giving sufficient information in an intelligible form (Grice, 1975). Jack then draws the inference that, given their roaming lifestyles, tribes would find it hard to settle. His words directly inter-animate Fiona's utterance (10). She also notes that the Indians 'travel around' and supplies information missing from Jack's contribution (tribes lived in 'tepees'). Unlike Jack however, Fiona and Michael struggle to manipulate and communicate 'what' they know in ways associated with higher levels of mental functioning.

Variations in discourse: Roles and relationships

The fruits of this scaffolding approach to instruction are evident in the third extract which takes place mid-way through the lesson. It reveals how students were able to hi-jack the interaction in an episode of problem-solving talk that originated in their own interests. As the lesson progressed, Ms Tate continued to challenge assumptions that the Indians were 'uncivilised' by drawing attention to their resourcefulness in utilising all parts of the buffalo. Many children found it difficult to conceive of a society without waste and Andrew asks 'What did they do with the bodies'?

Extract #3

01	T	An, we're going to look at that later this week, okay? Um, Hayden?
02	Ha	Well even um they um they probably want to eat everything up and stuff because they had nowhere to put the rubbish so they don't want – so, so they don't want any rubbish left (xxx) cos if they do put it somewhere, it's going to smell round there//
03	T	Okay. Those are all things and you've got some different ideas. So the next people who come up here have to think on their feet a little bit, rather like they had to when they went to the debate competition last week. It's nice to have everything all prepared and, ooh, I'm going to say this, but in fact when you get in debate or when you're arguing with your parents, your brother, your sister, your **teacher**] /
04	Ss	{laughter}
05	T	You're having an argument or disagreement in the classroom, when we're debating something, you have to think on your feet, you have to **draw** on other things you know] /
06	He	Ms T?
07	T	Okay so feel free to add little bits to what's not been rehearsed / (xxx)
08	Ro	Um, would they, uh it's just a guess really, but would they um dig the um buffalos' bodies um under the ground? [/
09	T	[They could have buried buffalos' bodies underneath the ground [but they used err almost / everything
10	Ro	um, and / yeah cos as they um haven't got any shovels, could they do it with their hands, or? /
11	T	Okay
12	St	They could use the buffalo's scalp [(xxx)
13	An	[They could use
14	T	[What could they have used for a shovel, they wouldn't have had one like ours? Do you think they ever dug anything in the earth? / I bet you they had tools to dig in the earth, 'kay. Don't have any pictures of them but [they would have had /
15	An	They had deer antlers. It's deer antlers, isn't it, to dig into the ground? It's deer antlers.

16 Ss   Yep]
17 St   [They used that at Stonehenge
18 T   Yeah, you're right. Okay so well done Andrew.
19 Ja   Um and they also used, what's the shoulder blades of / they might also have used shoulder blades of the buffalo as um, um the shoulder blades of buffalos as shovels.
20 T   Okay, so were they uncivilized?
21 Ss   No. No they were not
22 T   No, okay, and these are examples of things you need to add to your arguments.

It is interesting to observe in the above extract how the teacher and students collectively, and mischievously, acknowledge the potential of 'argument' to subvert authoritative roles and relationships (03–07) and their increasing mutuality is reflected in the discourse. Three aspects of this dynamic exchange merit attention. Firstly the fast-paced interaction, of which this is a small fragment, is characterised by incomplete and overlapping turns in which suggestions are made and ideas rebound. Children's conversational asides and interruptions, marked by a [, are frequently 'taken up' and woven into the flow of talk, revealing how students' interests, rather than the teacher's intentions, can at times divert the pedagogic agenda. Secondly, the tone of the discourse is provisional and speculative, tentativeness reflected in the level of modality, 'could' 'would' and 'probably', and Robert's declaration that his idea is 'just a guess' (08). The teacher's locution 'I bet you ...' (14) functions as a 'modal adjunct' that entertains the possibility of alternative viewpoints and uncertainty in discourse (Halliday & Matthieson, 2004: 147). Finally, students are speculating and reasoning (02), problem-solving (10, 12) and, crucial to their effectiveness as learners, asking questions.

Children continue to co-construct ideas across the floor drawing on prior knowledge (the construction of Stonehenge) and with minimal intervention from the teacher until eventually the dialogue gathers momentum and participants' thinking begins to transcend the confines of the lesson. This exchange sequence appears to support Edwards and Mercer's (1987: 70, 165) proposition that 'abstract' thinking, the alleged goal of education in literate societies, originates in concrete activity and is distinguished by individuals' reflective capabilities rather than actual 'disembeddedness' from material contexts.

Focus on the teaching–learning interaction

There is much to be learned about the mechanics of interaction from close scrutiny of the communicative devices through which stretches of dialogic discourse were triggered and sustained. Let us return to an excerpt from Extract #2.

09	T	So you could use that as evidence of why that particular culture wouldn't work very well. Okay, another good example. Fiona you had one
10	Fi	Um well they live in tepees and they and they travel around and (xxx)
11	T	Okay so what would you use that [for?
12	Fi	[um, for the (xxx) cos you were saying that the Indians could make a house out of wood and then you said (xxx)
13	T	'kay. So you would – how would you use that to make your argument better?
14	Fi	Um / because it's about them / living in tents
15	T	Okay so they had a different style of living, are you saying? That it isn't wrong, it's just different. So you are living in homes, you're not sleeping out / sleeping under the stars at night, are you? They do have a shelter, and they do have an organisation in the way that they do things. They have a reason why they're living out. Okay you need to develop those points a bit more / Michael?

Fiona's barely intelligible utterance is her first contribution in a dyadic exchange consisting of seven conversational turns in which the teacher probes her response (11) and requires her to explain how she could use it to strengthen her argument (13). It is interesting to observe how Ms Tate consciously monitors and adjusts her use of language. By substituting a potentially finalising move – 'So you would ...' with a question 'how would you ...?' – she keeps the dialogue open and passes the responsibility for thinking firmly to the student. Fiona is given time to explain: her next contribution (14) is punctuated by pauses /, as she struggles to express herself. Finally, whilst deferring again to Fiona's own meanings – '... are you saying?' – Ms Tate offers a possible reason, an injection of 'new information' (15). In her closing comments, she offers some constructive feedback, suggesting that Fiona needs to focus on developing her arguments. Of course, this brief example is fertile ground for debate since it appears to be little more than manifestation of the traditional IRF script. Nevertheless, there is much in the wider contexts of interaction to support an alternative interpretation: that IRF might be viewed as a one pattern of communication in a repertoire of discourse formats selected according to pedagogic purpose (Alexander, 2006; Cazden, 2005).

Supportive discourses at class and school level

We have seen how learning in this lesson is structured through the discourse, Ms Tate matching form and function as pedagogic purpose dictates. The opening sequence is didactic with few opportunities for students' active participation as the teacher sets the scene, imparting information and encouraging recall of relevant historical facts. As the lesson progresses children are given opportunities to discuss ideas and construct their arguments in pairs and groups. These stretches of collaborative talk are interspersed with episodes of contingent instruction in which Ms Tate challenges and probes children's utterances. Whilst closely resembling the traditional IRF sequence of questioning, characteristically Ms Tate's responses build on students' responses, rather than her own agenda, as she models the processes of argumentation. Having established a degree of 'common knowledge' the discourse becomes more spontaneously dialogic as participants strive to build new understandings together.

The communicative episode represented in this chapter captures not only the plethora of (talk) activities in which teacher and students were jointly engaged but also the quality of relationships mediating the action. The lesson was conducted in a climate of respect with ground-rules that encouraged reciprocity and collaborative construction of knowledge. Ms Tate maintained an unswerving focus on (1) developing children's historical understanding and (2) externalising the processes of reasoning and argumentation for their benefit. Confident in her own subject knowledge, she was free to focus on the mechanics of interaction: how best to engage and advance pupil learning. All these factors exemplify Alexander's principles of 'dialogic teaching' (2004/2006) at the classroom level. Nevertheless, whilst Ms Tate clearly subscribed to a reciprocal pedagogy, students (the other side of the dialogic equation) also understood how to contribute relevantly and constructively.

There are factors at institutional level, the wider systems of human relationships in which pedagogic activity is embedded, that perhaps help to explain the potential for more dialogic interactions in Ms Tate's classroom. Drama and public speaking were highly prized in Ashford School. In fortnightly assemblies children were expected to talk about their learning, often without scripts, and many members of the class I observed, expressed themselves confidently using a wide-ranging vocabulary. Moreover, the children had recent experience of participation in an inter-schools debate. Finally, however, although pupils came from many different social backgrounds, the school's Christian status bound all students to the wider local and religious communities. The school day ended with a prayer and children and adults treated each other courteously and with respect.

TAKE 2

This transcript shows the teacher enhancing the students' communication skills through guided practice. In Extract #1, the teacher gives clear instruction on what she would like students to do in the debate (01) and then starts off by calling on a particular student to give his/her viewpoint. The students' perspectives, shown in this extract, also demonstrate their understanding of the task: they are able to take on a role in the European/ Indigenous exchange and express what they imagine might be a perspective within the interaction. Jack (02) makes a firm statement on the issues of protecting the original inhabitants' rights and territories. However, the teacher questions Jack's argument with a potential comeback from the 'other side' of the argument and – in her role as teacher – requests stronger supporting evidence. Jack attempts to restate (04) his position, but ends with an unfinished utterance potentially indicating that he is still thinking about how to make the land claim when there was no sense of possession within the indigenous ways and how to turn it into a way of life argument. Henry raises a new point (06), following the instruction that if the response was on another subject they ought to indicate so. He moves on to the issue of religious belief, bringing to the dialogue an important point in the encounter between the European and the Indigenous people. It seems that Henry is unable to put himself into the indigenous role and speaks to the issue from the perspective of self-as-student by accepting the imposition of the Christian education by the Europeans because Christianity is inherently good. Ms Tate reminds the students about the role they are playing when she states that not everyone can change his/her religious beliefs easily. The teacher seems to be making reference to religious tolerance in the present. Fiona (08) picks up this cue and expresses the belief more explicitly - people have the freedom to choose whatever they want to worship and, furthermore, the nature of the worship can be very different from our own.

The last item partially picks up where Jack left off – why no one should be able to push others around – an item of basic human respect. Sally (12) opens up the argument of the prior students by centering her argument on cultural traditions – which incorporate religion and ways of living. The teacher's comeback here (13) is in her role of the European settler – 'blood' brings up the stereotype of the Native American as nasty, as a savage and as capable of the barbarities of war – and putting the student within the Native American role on the defensive. Andrew then takes a stance (16) within his indigenous role making a claim about the right to decide on what his/her children learn: it is a statement of fact, not an argument. The statement is met with another by the teacher within her role of European settler – completing the role assumption game. Relief occurs in the form of laughter (20).

This accomplishment illustrates that the students had previously been given enough background information about the Native Americans in order to participate fully in the discussion.

In Extract #2, the goal seems to have shifted a bit in that the teacher is no longer requesting that the student to take a particular role; she is now trying to assist the students in articulating the arguments. The students are bringing in different facts and Ms Tate extends their argument by putting the facts within the context of their significance as an argument.

Andrew's back-channelling 'um' (04) suggests that, when called upon by the teacher, he is not so sure of how to extend the argument, and subsequently makes a statement about the selection of new chiefs. The teacher elaborates (05) by differentiating wild animals from a civilized society that establishes and obeys community norms. The student's nod (06) seems to be a thinking gesture. Jack then reminds the participants of the conversation that while there were community norms there were internal variations in the norms as different Native American groups had different traditions. Jack goes back to his argument on land claims. He is tentative in his argument (08) as there is back-channelling (*um* and *err*) noise throughout the utterance.

By paraphrasing and elaborating on the students' arguments, Ms Tate is assisting the students to not just be in the shoes of the speaker but also how to elaborate the storyline in the message they want to communicate by bringing in the details they have learned about the Native Americans. When Michael adds to the conversation (16) the role of hunting buffalos, he is providing a detail that he remembers as an aspect of the way of life of the Native Americans. In the final turn in this extract, Ms Tate acknowledges this comment and channels it back by raising questions that further guides the students' thinking about building the argument rather than just adding facts.

In Extract # 3, the reader gets the cues for establishing the context of the instructional activity – a debate competition – as important in the lives of the students and a context for being careful in building arguments. It also illustrates how the teacher is incorporating the skills of argument and thinking on your feet as part of the academic and the personal project of the students – as she makes reference to everyday arguing situations (05). The students, in turn, bring into the discussion their concern with whether the buffalo is consumed in its entirety and how they could use body remains such as shoulder blades as digging tools. To make this claim the students use prior knowledge when they make reference to the deer antlers used at Stonehenge. It is in this excerpt as well that we can see the teacher constantly complimenting and encouraging students to talk freely.

The key in the dialogue occurs as the teacher sums up the conversation (20) and points the students to the meaning of their message 'Okay, so were they uncivilised?' It is a question that helps the students create community in their stance in their collective response – 'No, no they were not' (21) – that while Indians might not have modern facilities, this did not mean that they were uncultured.

Discussion

What can we learn about Ms Tate's classroom through these excerpts? Can we take away something useful for teachers in classrooms? There are four distinct learning issues that popped out at us. First, that through language we can get at the social norms of a community, in this case the learning community in Ms Tate's classroom. In this classroom, for example, both students and the teacher are active participants in constructing arguments that will serve them within another context – the debate competition. It is not a social studies class in which the topic is Native Americans and where facts are learned. Second, there are connections made between the academic and personal/social projects at various levels. Learning of the topic is organized in a purposeful way – for what occurs in the classroom has a purpose beyond the classroom and there is motivation beyond the learning of the topic itself. And there is reference to other situations in daily life where the value of the skills and the knowledge of arguing are referenced. The third understanding is related to how the teacher plays a role in extending the content learning through language. This is related to how the learning of facts is presented. The learning of facts is not presented in isolation as the facts are channelled into an argument – students are asked to think about the connections between the facts they have presented with the argument being made. The last understanding is the intricate relationships between language and action – it is through language that we make our world as Ms Tate illustrates when she establishes the safety of the relationships with students that permit them to say what they feel, even when it is wrong.

TAKE 3

The following extract occurs towards the end of the same lesson as above:

01	T	What do you like best about your argument? ////
02	St	I like arguing about // Toby's, cos he / he's got a really good point / about just living how he wants to live
03	T	Okay. Jack what do you like best about / your argument?]
04	Ja	I like // I quite like Toby's. He had a lot of expression / he used a lot of expression and actions to give it emphasis.
05	T	'kay. Kenneth?
06	Ke	(xxx) <Contribution masked by playground noise >
07	T	'kay. Toby?
08	To	Um I like Jack's part because it / cos um he he had some really um main points and um it was clear and um I could understand and um, um I couldn't really argue myself.
09	T	Uh hm. Okay, so the rest of you <addresses class> Okay. Couple of things you liked that they did really well, couple of things they could improve next time remembering that we haven't had long preparation and rehearsal so the forgetting and things like that / we don't want to focus on. Andrew?

10   An   Um I thought it was really good but maybe Fiona got stuck because she said that we need our farming land, we // um the Indians don't need farming land, they don't do farming.

11   T   Okay. Some Indians actually did a little bit of farming. They didn't do it quite to the extent that White Man did when they cleared acres and acres so they would have small plots that they did do a bit of farming / 'kay. Was that what you were referring to, Fiona, or not?

12   Fi   I said 'we need farming land'

13   T   Okay. What do you need farming land for?

14   Fi   Um to grow vegetables

15   T   'kay. Are you saying that your tribe currently does that or is that for learning to farm?

16   Fi   Um / {looks around uncertainly}

17   T   'kay. I guess what Andrew's saying is that it wasn't clear. Okay?

18   Fi   {Nods and smiles}

19   T   So it's just defining that a bit more /Okay Hilary?]

20   Hi   Well um I liked Jack's and Toby's actions cos I liked it how '**You** {points} cannot barge {sweeps hand across chest} in with our ways' cos it's like you're trying to / to was trying to push you out {pushes hands forwards} but you <White Man> were just sort of coming in {brings hands together} That's why // I thought that was quite good actually

21   T   Okay, one last one, Norman

22   No   Well um it was really good but Fiona was agreeing instead of dis-agreeing because /

23   T   Okay so you / so she didn't come across real strongly that she was disagreeing, okay. <to Steven> So that just means that you have to develop that a bit more and explain a bit more, Okay, cos in your head it's probably real clear how you're feeling]

24   St   {Nods}

25   T   But you need to make sure that these ideas come out here {touches lips}

26   St   Yeah, it's really hard to put them into words

Guiding questions for Take 3

(1) How does the structure of this interaction differ from the IRF cycle characteristic of traditional pedagogic exchanges?

(2) What might the teacher hope to achieve by asking students to evaluate each other? Whose meanings were developed in this extract, and how were they expressed?

(3) What kind of relationship can be inferred from the extract? What aspects of pupil behaviour are targets for teacher regulation? How are these manifest in the discourse?

References

Alexander, R. (2001) *Culture and Pedagogy: International Comparisons in Primary Education.* Oxford: Blackwell Publishers.

Alexander, R. (2004, revised and reprinted 2006) *Towards Dialogic Teaching. Rethinking Classroom Talk.* York: Dialogos.

Atkinson, J.M. and Heritage, J. (eds) (1984) *Structures of Social Action: Studies in Conversation Analysis.* Cambridge: Cambridge University Press.

Bruner, J. (1985) Vygotsky: A historical and conceptual perspective. In J.V. Wertsch (ed.) *Culture, Communication and Cognition: Vygotskian Perspectives* (pp. 21–34). Cambridge: Cambridge University Press.

Burns, C. and Myhill, D. (2004) Interactive or inactive? A consideration of the nature of interaction in whole class teaching. *Cambridge Journal of Education* 34 (1), 35–48.

Cazden, C.B. (2005) *The Value of Eclecticism in Education Reform, 1965–2005.* AERA Annual Meeting, Montreal.

Chang-Wells, G.L. and Wells, G. (1993) Dynamics of discourse. In A.E. Forman, N. Minick and C.A. Stone (eds) *Contexts for Learning: Sociocultural Dynamics in Children's Development* (pp. 58–90). New York: Oxford University Press.

Christie, F. (2002) *Classroom Discourse Analysis: A Functional Perspective.* London: Continuum.

Dawes, L., Mercer, N. and Wegerif, R. (2000) *Thinking Together: A Programme of Activities for Developing Thinking Skills at KS2.* Birmingham: Questions Publishing Co.

Department for Education and Employment (DfEE) (1998) *The National Literacy Strategy: Framework for Teaching.* London: DfEE.

Department for Education and Skills (DfES) (2003) *Excellence and Enjoyment: A Strategy for Primary Schools.* London: DfES.

Edwards, D. and Mercer, N. (1987) *Common Knowledge: The Development of Understanding in the Classroom.* London: Falmer Press.

Grice, H.P. (1975) Logic and conversation. In P. Cole and J.L. Morgan (eds) *Speech Acts* (pp. 41–58). New York: Academic Press.

Halliday, M.A.K. and Matthiessen, M.I.M. (2004) *An Introduction to Functional Grammar.* London: Arnold.

Hutchby, I. and Wooffitt, R. (1998) *Conversation Analysis.* Cambridge: Polity Press.

Leont'ev, A.N. (1978) *Activity, Consciousness, and Personality.* Englewood Cliffs, NJ: Prentice-Hall, Inc.

Linell, P., Gustavsson, L. and Paivi, J. (1988) Interactional dominance in dyadic communication: A presentation of initiative-response analysis. *Linguistics* 26 (3), 415–442.

Mercer, N. (1996) The quality of talk in children's collaborative activity in the classroom. *Learning and Instruction* 6 (4), 359–377.

Nystrand, M. with Gamoran, A., Kachur, R. and Prendergast, C. (1997) *Opening Dialogue: Understanding the Dynamics of Language and Learning in the English Classroom.* New York: Teachers College Press.

Qualifications and Curriculum Authority/Department for Education and Employment (QCA/DfES) (2003) *Speaking, Listening, Learning: Working with Children in KS1 and 2.* London: QCA/DfES.

Sacks, H., Schegloff, E.A. and Jefferson, G. (1974) A simplest systematics for the organization of turn-taking for conversation. *Language* 50 (4), 696–735.

Sinclair, J.M. and Coulthard, R.M. (1975) *Towards an Analysis of Discourse.* Oxford: Oxford University Press.

Smith, F., Hardman, F., Wall, K. and Mroz, M. (2004) Interactive whole class teaching in the National Literacy and Numeracy Strategies. *British Educational Research Journal* 30 (3), 403–419.

Vygotsky, L.S. (1978) *Mind in Society: The Development of Higher Psychological Processes*. London: Harvard University Press.

Wells, G. (1999) *Dialogic Inquiry: Towards a Sociocultural Practice and Theory of Education*. Cambridge: Cambridge University Press.

Wells, G. (2003) Children talk their way into literacy: Published as 'Los ninõs se alfabetizan hablando'. In J.R. Garcia (ed.) *Enseñar a escriber sin prisas ... pero con sentindo*. Sevilla: Publicaciones M.C.E.P. On WWW at http://people.ucsc.edu/~gwells. Accessed April 2006.

Wertsch, J.V. and Addison Stone, C. (1985) The concept of internalization in Vygotsky's account of the genesis of higher mental functions. In J.V. Wertsch (ed.) *Culture, Communication and Cognition: Vygotskian Perspectives* (pp. 162–179). Cambridge: Cambridge University Press.

Wolfe, S. (2006) Teaching and learning through dialogue in primary classrooms in England. Unpublished PhD thesis, The University of Cambridge.

Chapter 7

Constructing Meaning in a Bilingual Learning Environment: Two Primary Classrooms in Malaysia

TAKE 1: WONG BEE ENG AND VIJAY KUMAR
TAKE 2: ROGER BARNARD

TAKE 1

Introduction

In the Malaysian education system, there are two types of government-run primary schools: national schools and national type schools. National schools use Malay as the medium of instruction while national type vernacular schools use either Chinese or Tamil. English is the second most important language in the Malaysian school curriculum and a compulsory subject at all levels of schooling; it is taught from the first year in all primary schools. All subjects with the exception of English were taught either in Malay or in the vernacular language until a change in policy in 2002. Since then, all primary schools are required to teach Science and Mathematics in English. However, exceptions were allowed for Chinese vernacular schools to teach Mathematics and Science in both Chinese and English. The classes in Mandarin are conducted during normal school hours while the ones in English are conducted after school.

The change in language policy has led to linguistic complexities in Malaysian classrooms. Many teachers studied Mathematics and Science in Malay when they themselves were in school, while others would have studied these subjects in Tamil or Chinese in primary school and in Malay in secondary school. Although most of these teachers had been trained to teach in Malay or one of the vernacular languages, and had no exposure to these subjects in English prior to 2002, they are now expected to teach these subjects in English. It should be noted here that in order to provide support for these teachers, the Ministry of Education provides in-service training in the form of a three-week course (ETeMS) for the teaching of Mathematics and Science through the medium of English. Many of these teachers, who are from the younger generation, do not have the content knowledge of these subjects in English to teach effectively.

The School Settings

In order to understand the linguistic complexities in the classroom, this study focuses on the micro analysis of classroom dialogues. Data for this study were collected from two schools (see Table 7.1). The first school chosen for this study, a national school, is located at the fringe of the federal capital, Kuala Lumpur. The teacher in this school taught a Mathematics Year 4 class which is expected to be taught only in English. The teacher in this case is an ethnic Malay who was initially trained to teach both subjects in Malay. The second setting was a Science Year 4 class in a National Type Chinese school located in an urban area in the Klang Valley. In this school, Science is taught in both languages each week. The teacher is an ethnic Chinese and was trained to teach Mathematics and Science in Mandarin. However, she is also fluent in Malay as she was schooled at the secondary level in Malay.

Ethical approval and official permission were obtained from the school authorities and students prior to the study. The teacher in each case assisted in the collection of data by audio-taping classroom teaching and conversations. In the former, the teacher recorded her teaching and the students' reactions and interactions as the class was going on. A recorder was placed at a strategic location in the classroom to ensure that voices from all

Table 7.1 Summary of the two school settings in the present study

	School A *National School*	*School B* *National type* *Chinese school*
Medium of instruction	Malay	Chinese
Class	Mathematics Year 4	Science Year 4
Maths and Science	Taught only in English	Taught in Mandarin and English
Teacher	Ethnic Malay (female)	Ethnic Chinese (female)
Teacher's own schooling	Malay	Chinese and Malay
Initial teacher training	Malay	Mandarin Chinese
English medium training at the point of data collection	Three weeks intensive course	Three weeks intensive course

corners of the classroom were recorded. The researchers were not present during the audio recording of the classes. The reason for this was the teachers felt that they would be very uncomfortable with other adults in the classroom.

Conceptual Framework

The data for this study is analyzed from the perspective of constructivism. Constructivism is based on the fundamental assertion that knowledge cannot exist outside our minds (Hendry *et al.*, 1999) but rather it is 'constructed' in interaction with others. What this means is that, knowledge is socially negotiated within a community. When one negotiates, conversation exchanges take place. Co-construction has been said to take place when conversational exchanges are highly interactive and collaborative (Sonnenmeier, 1993). Additionally, co-construction is said to take place during conversation through inferencing (Sonnenmeier, 1993). Inferencing is an active conversational skill which contributes to the understanding of a conversation. Inferencing also depends on the nature of the relationship. Another view of co-construction is that there must be a high degree of interpersonal connection between the individuals working in the process (Goldstein, 1999: 648).

From the constructivist paradigm, a classroom provides opportunities for knowledge to be co-constructed. The teacher plays a number of important roles in the knowledge construction process. First, the teacher plays the role as a facilitator who encourages and promotes active interaction. Second, the teacher acts as a source of curriculum knowledge. Finally, the teacher is the provider of meaningful activities in which students are able to co-construct understanding.

The 'Western' constructivist approach could be contrasted with Chinese schema of education. Hui (2005), for example, provides useful understanding of the philosophy behind Chinese culture which is grounded in Confucian teaching. Among the pinnacles of Confucian teaching is that teachers are regarded as transmitters of moral virtues and harmony. Based on this Confucian philosophy, teaching encompasses moral cultivation as this is seen as the ultimate means to mould learners to become appropriate members of an established society. As such, teachers command a high degree of respect. In fact, generic honorifics are used to show respect to the teacher. As a result of this, students 'are not supposed to interact freely with teachers on the basis of equal status' (Hui, 2005: 22; see also Chapter 5 of this volume).

The Malay schema of education is strongly shaped by Islamic teaching. Islamic teachings encourage learners to seek knowledge as it is believed that 'one will earn God's pleasure when one seeks knowledge' (Mohd-Asraf, 2005: 117). A good learner from the Islamic perspective is one who has a positive attitude towards learning and is able to associate the learning with 'race, religion and nation' (Washima *et al.*, 1996: 233). From the Islamic point of view, the teacher is considered to be a person of equal standing as parents. In other words, the teacher is regarded very highly. As such, a good student is one who is receptive of the teacher's knowledge and wisdom.

Given the multiple linguistic and cultural complexities in the education system, one wonders if a good learner in a Malaysian primary school can be considered as one who is able to participate actively in language mediated activities in the classroom. Indeed, as will be seen in the following lesson extracts, the extent to which the students in these classrooms are verbally active co-constructive participants in a community of learning is limited; their speech, and that of the teacher may be characterized by what Chick (1996) has termed 'safe talk'. The features of this form of classroom discourse are summarized as follows:

> [t]he talk between teachers and pupils becomes something of a cooperative venture or game played according to local rules; pupils do not expect to be given long turns at speaking or to be asked many open questions, and teachers are content to meet these expectations. (Cath & McLellan, 1993: 14; see also Chapter 3 in this volume)

Interactional Data

The first set of transcripts is from a recording of a mathematics lesson conducted in a Year 4 classroom in a national (Malay) primary school, the main objective of which was to teach the operation of division. The students had just returned from the two-week break between semesters.

Extract #1

01   T   Today, I want to continue errr, the lesson, ok? Open your textbook, page one hundred and forty-three, ok? Open your textbook page one hundred and forty- two, er three. Are you ready? Are you ready? One hundred and forty-three, ok? ok, divide unit of land, ok? How to divide? Same, same with another past lesson yang kita pernah belajar yang dulu-dulu. *that we had learned the last time.* Cuma *only* the difference is unit, ok? Errr the last lesson divide for what unit, for time **kan?** *right?* ok, now continue with land, ok, look at example number one, ok? Forty-two millimeters divide ok?, forty-two millimeters divide, ok?/ I want to show, I **don't** want to show you how to divide it because the step how to divide. The difference is unit, selalu awak buat tak ada unit atau unit masa kan? *normally do you have unit or timeunit, right?* ok, unit unit land, tetapi

but the step cara dia tak [sa] sama, *the method is not the same* ok? I want to, ok F, come here! ok, don't forget ah, if you get any question, you **must** do, ok, I want you to do / I want you to try, do in your textbook.

The authoritative tone and stance of the teacher is obvious from the start of the lesson. Her frequent use of imperatives ('Open your text book'), deontic modals ('you must . . .') and baldly stated demands ('I want you to . . .') clearly indicate her expectation that learners will follow instructions and directions in order to complete the tasks she prescribes. A good learner in the Malaysian classroom must also abide by the rules of the school, one of which is that a student has to stand in order to answer a question. The teacher's instruction (11) in the next extract illustrates this point.

The following extract occurred a few minutes later, after the teacher had been trying to elicit whether a smaller number can be divided by a larger:

Extract #2

01	T	So, four cannot divide by
02	Ss	By six
03	T	Ok, if cannot divide, so you take two number. Forty?
04	Ss	Two
05	T	Forty-two, ok? Forty-two divide by?
06	Ss	Six
07	T	Ok, can or not? Forty-two divide by six?
08	Ss	Can
09	T	Why can, Hanif? Why can? Why forty-two can divide by six?
10	Ss	((silence))
11	T	Please stand up. Saya tadi awak cakap empat tak boleh dibahagi dengan enam kan? *Just now I told you that four can't be divided with six right?* Sebab empat ini lebih kecil daripada enam. *Because four is smaller than six* So, sekarang *now* forty-two can divide by six, **Why?** Sebab apa empat puluh dua boleh dibahagi dengan enam? *Why is it that forty-two can be divided by six?* **Why?** Because forty-two is bigger number than?
12	Ss	Six.
13	T	Than six, ok so, benda yang besar, awak boleh bahagi dengan benda yang *the bigger number, you can divide it with numbers which are?* /
14	Ss	Kecil *small*
15	T	Kecil *small*. Kalau benda itu awak ada sikit, memang tak cukup bahagi kepada benda yang banyak, jadi awak tak boleh bahagi. *If the numbers are small, it's not enough to be divided by the bigger numbers, so you can't divide,* Ok, . . .

The imposition of the teacher's authority is here reflected in her elicitation technique, (01–09) which follows a standard Initiation–Response–Follow-up structure (Coulthard, 1986), where the students' responses are sandwiched between somewhat longer turns by the teacher. The students make very limited conceptual and linguistic contribution to verbal co-construction and negotiation of meaning, and there is no evidence of 'active inferencing' (Sonnenmeier, 1993); rather, what it means to be a good learner seems to be giving correct answers to the teacher's questions by a display of monosyllabic declarative knowledge. In both these extracts, the teacher relies on code switching to make her meaning clear. The reason for the use of Malay in the first extract may be simply to draw the students' attention to the structure of the lesson. In Extract #2, it may be because she feels that her students do not have sufficient competence in English to grasp the essential conceptual content – in this case, the operations of division and multiplication. It is also possible that the teacher herself is not too fluent in English, or at least in the ability to formulate or reformulate conceptual information accurately and spontaneously.

In fact, as will be shown below, the teacher engages in code-switching monologues throughout the lesson.

Extract #3:

01 T Cikgu pernah ajarkan macammana? *Teacher has taught you how?* Mana satu nak darab, mana satu nak bahagi? *Which number to multiply, which number to divide?* Which number to multiply? Which number to divide? Ok what you have, Amirah?
02 Ss (xxx)
03 T Ok, Hamid /// Right or wrong?
04 Ss Right
05 T Right or wrong?
06 Ss Right
07 T Right or wrong?
08 Ss Right
09 T Who said right? Please put up your hand! Who said **right?** Ok, who said right? Please put up your hand! **ok,** who said **wrong?** Ok, never mind. Ah, Salima, do the correction/// Ikut kawan, kawan cakap salah, awak pun angkat salah. *Follow friend, friend said the wrong thing, you also raised your hand wrongly.* Buat sini sini sini. *Do it here, here here.* Jangan padam *Don't erase, no no,* kenapa? *Why?* Semua dah lupa huh? *All forgotten, huh?* Cuti lama tak ingat? *After long holidays, can't remember?*

The teacher's initial repeated questions (01) are received in silence, the students presumably accepting them as reprimands for their lack of effort to understand what she has taught them about multiplication and division. The exchanges that follow (02–08) are best characterized as 'safe talk', with neither teacher nor students making excessive linguistic or cognitive demands on the other in what is only superficially a pedagogic dialogue. In her final turn (09), the teacher reprimands students who did not answer correctly and implies that they have neglected their studies. On the whole, the teacher in this lesson seems more interested in delivering short bits of mathematical knowledge and eliciting a limited amount of declarative knowledge from her learners than helping them to contribute meaningfully to the co-construction of understanding. There is a lack of the interpersonal connection between her and the students that Goldstein (1999) considers essential for active co-construction to take place.

The next set of data is taken from a recording of a science lesson conducted in a year four national type primary Chinese classroom.

Extract #4

01	S?	Class stand /
02	Ss	Good morning teacher
03	T	Ok, sit down
04	Ss	Thank you, teacher
05	T	Ok, good morning to you all, ok, erm, / how are you feeling today?
06	Ss	(xxx)
07	T	Fine, ok, I would like to see everyone is happy. Ok, now, teacher is going to teach you about, objects are materials made of different. Objects are made of different materials. Now you turn to your text book / to page seventy-six, ok? Alright? Properties of material. Have you found the page, seventy-six?

Here we see the traditional Chinese protocol in the way the teacher is greeted when she enters the class. The class monitor stands and tells the whole class to do the same (01). Then they all greet the teacher together, and thank her when she responds by asking them to sit. This is exactly what they do for all their lessons, whether conducted in Mandarin or English. In Chinese, the term of address for a teacher is the surname of the teacher followed by the term *lao shi* (Hui, 2005: 25). In this particular extract, the teacher's surname is not referred to as learners do not do so in an English or Malay lesson (04). The teacher seems polite as she asks the students how they are feeling (5) and in her comment that she wants to see everybody happy (07). Although these could be genuine attempts at sociability, perhaps even of attempting to increase the interpersonal connection between her and her students, it is also possible that they are merely formulaic. Before they are required to teach Mathematics and Science through the medium of English, primary school teachers attend short language improvement courses. Included in the syllabus are expressions used in greetings; given the teachers' lack of English communicative competence in English, these expressions would have to be memorized. It is also very common for a teacher in the Malaysian primary classroom to refer to herself in the third person (07), although it sounds odd in English. The teacher's clear explanation of the focus of the lesson is not unusual in a Chinese primary classroom; teachers are expected to be well-prepared for their lessons. In this case, the teacher might have memorized her lesson notes, as her tone of voice suggested that she was reading aloud from her lesson plan.

The following segment occurs only a few minutes after Extract #4. The teacher and the students are clicking pictures on computer screens as they go through the lesson:

Extract #5

01	T	We want to know what are the properties of the materials, ok? Next, click on the picture and try to find out. Would you like to find out?
02	Ss	Yes//
03	Tape	These objects are made of metal. Metal is shiny. It can be bent but cannot be stretched easily.
04	T	Ok, now you see these objects, the spoons and the forks, are made of //
05	Ss	Metal
06	T	Ok, metal is //
07	S?	Shiny
08	Ss	<in chorus> Shiny]
09	T	What are] the properties of metal? One more time//
10	Ss	Shiny
11	T	Yes, Metal's / one more time / Metal is shiny...

In the extract above, it is clear that no self-initiated talk was forthcoming from the students, and the interaction between teacher and students cannot be said to be academically or conceptually collaborative, although the participants were indeed cooperative in the routine classroom behaviour. Here, and indeed throughout the lesson, the teacher asked display questions where either a yes or no answer is required (e.g. 01) or simple *wh*-questions (e.g. 09) where a single word answer is sought, usually in chorus. The whole episode can be viewed as one example among very many in this lesson of 'safe-talk' (Chick, 1996), where neither party makes excessive linguistic (or conceptual) demands of the other.

To the extent that knowledge and understanding is co-constructed knowledge in the Malaysian classroom, it occurs in such safe talk, as may be seen in the following:

Extract #6

01	T	Ok, You can see there are so many kind of material here. Can you name it?
02	Ss	(xxx)
03	T	No, the material is... Metal / louder]....
04	Ss	Metal / Metal
05	T	Rubber]
06	Ss	Rubber, plastic, glass, wood, cloth, leather
07	T	Ok, now you see, what are the properties of metal? Can you tell teacher?
08	Ss	Shiny// can be bent
09	T	Ok, good, and what about rubber? Rubber is //
10	Ss	Tough / Can be stretched
11	T	Good, rubber is tough but it can be stretched. What about this one?
12	Ss	Light / Plastic]
13	T	Plastic is /
14	Ss	Light //
15	T	Glass?
16	Ss	Can be easily broken.
17	T	Glass is easily broken. Ok, What, what, what about wood?
18	Ss	Hard
19	T	Wood is, wood is, very hard. Ok? What about this one? Cloth //
20	Ss	Cloth]
21	T	Cloth] is soft. Can you feel the cloth on your body?
22	Ss	Yes]
23	T	Is it soft?
24	Ss	Yes
25	T	The last one is leather. What are the properties of leather?
26	Ss	Tough

In the exchange above, the response to the teacher's initial question (01) is silence. This is very common in the Malaysian primary classroom because of fear of giving the incorrect answer. The teacher expects the correct answers, if possible, all the time. The teacher then prompts the learners by allowing them to complete her sentences (03, 09). Thereafter, she cues other types of material which the learners repeat in chorus, with little room for expanding their simple declarative knowledge. This sort of repetitive, mechanical drill is commonly found in many English language classes in

Malaysia – as elsewhere – but is perhaps inappropriate to the development of conceptual learning in subjects like science. It is also not conducive to the development of a high degree if interpersonal connection (Goldstein, 1999) is needed for effective co-construction.

The following extract, which occurred about 15 minutes later, closed the lesson.

Extract #7

01 T We have some, activity for you to do, at home, you see plastic, leather, and cloth. You group the, object, ok? You group the object according to the material they are made of. And you written / what are the properties of the materials use. Ok? Teacher will distribute some of the work sheet for you all, you take it, you you bring it back to, at home, do it at home. ok? And you pass it tomorrow. Ok? And / That's the end for today's lesson and I hope all of you all enjoy the lesson. Do you enjoy the lesson?
02 Ss Yes
03 T Thank you very much.
04 Ss Thank you teacher.

Just as she began the lesson by stating the focus of the lesson, here she ends by structuring the students' after-class work, referring to herself again in the third person and making an attempt to be sociable. It is apparent that she had prepared her lesson well, and had attempted to make the conceptual input comprehensible to her class, making a very conscious effort not to speak in either Chinese or Malay. However, the extent of the students' conceptual development in this lesson was probably very limited not only by their own lack of linguistic competence but also by the fact that the teacher's own mastery of academic English appears to be so tenuous. As in the math lesson in the National (Malay) school, the above transcripts of the science lesson show evidence that the teacher's voice dominates the discourse; the construction of knowledge occurs by the teacher transmitting elementary conceptual information which the students echo, apparently uncritically.

Discussion

The discussion that follows suggests that meaning and knowledge are not verbally co-constructed through the 'active inferencing' suggested by Sonnenmeier (1993) nor that there is a high degree of interpersonal connection (Goldstein, 1999) between teachers and students.

The teacher is *an* authority

Although a student-centered approach is officially promoted in the curriculum, this was obviously not the case in these classrooms. Mathematics and Science classes in the Malaysian primary schools seem more teacher-directed than student-centered. In the typical Malaysian classroom, the teacher is the authority on the knowledge being imparted, and rarely is there a co-construction of knowledge as it is viewed in the western world. This does not mean that learning does not take place, only that conventions of teaching and learning are different. These are the traditional ways known in the Chinese culture and Islamic Malay communities, which hold teachers in high regard as dispensers of knowledge and wisdom. For the former, this notion is transmitted from generation to generation and this is evident in the philosophy of the Chinese diaspora, particularly descendants of immigrants. The Islamic Malay community regards the teaching profession as a noble one due to their religious belief. Thus it is obvious that culture and religion pervades the construction of what it means to be a good teacher, as well as a good learner, in the Malaysian primary classroom.

The teacher is *in* authority

This study clearly indicates the authoritarian voice of the teachers in the classroom, who were always in control both of the content and the discourse of learning. The teachers' frequent use in the transcript data of deontic modals and imperatives shows that the learners had no overt control over their learning in the classroom. In some instances, the teacher spoke harshly, and there seemed to be a lack of caring about interpersonal relationship which is deemed essential – at least in the west – for co-construction to take place in the classroom. A comparison of the recordings saw the teacher in the national classroom speaking in a harsher tone than the Chinese teacher, who seemed more patient and tolerant. However, Malaysians of Chinese and Malay origin typically do not express their emotions overtly, and teachers carry this attitude into their classrooms. Thus, even if they do care, this is not manifested in the way the westerners are used to.

The role of silence

In all the transcripts, there was not a single case of utterance which was initiated by the student other than the normal salutation when the teacher entered the class. This seems to indicate that co-construction is not verbally expressed equally by both the teacher and the students. This may be due to a combination of three influences. Firstly, Malaysian teachers expect good learners, at least in the primary classroom, to be obedient and to listen attentively in the classroom and to respond appropriately with the correct answers; it would certainly be considered impertinent to question the teacher. It may be said that both sides have reached mutual understanding of what it means to be a good learner based on their common cultural background. Students have not been encouraged to think that one can be a good learner by being actively involved in the verbal co-construction of meaning and knowledge, nor indeed, that they could construct knowledge in a more effective manner by thinking critically. Secondly, silence in these classrooms occurred when the learners did not know the answer to questions posed by the teachers – although most of these elicitation were display questions intended to reactivate the students' memorization skills rather than to seek new information or probe the students' knowledge. Here, it seems culturally more appropriate not to offer a response than to give a wrong answer. This seems to be a result of the perpetuation of the traditional notion that good learners, should as far as possible, provide only the correct answers in the classroom as wrong ones are more likely not tolerated. However, although they were noncommunicative, the students seemed respectfully attentive to the teacher's discourse. A third reason for their silence may be due to the students' limited competence in using English for academic purposes. Most students in these schools do not use English in school outside these subject areas and in English language classes. There are also limited opportunities to use English out of school as either Malay or one of the Chinese varieties is the language of communication at home.

Codeswitching

Like many other teachers, the teachers in these classes resorted to the use of either Chinese or Malay as a simplification strategy to help students understand the content. There is no official policy on the *exclusive* use of English to teach Mathematics and Science, and even if there were, it would be difficult to monitor the teachers in their classrooms. Thus, it is an acceptable practice for teachers to codeswitch, perhaps as a form of 'safe talk' (Chick, 1996), while teaching these subjects. This situation reflects the general Malaysian linguistic scene; that is, within the largely bilingual community, codeswitching during conversations is very common. Another possible reason for the teachers' codeswitching is their own lack of competence in English. The teachers themselves are struggling with the language and are therefore unable to cope with the mammoth task of using the language across the curriculum. It can be noted that the Malayan teacher in the national school classroom switched codes frequently and extensively while there was no evidence in the transcript data of such alternation by the Chinese teacher. However, other data collected by the researchers indicate there is some codemixing and switching in the Chinese teacher's lessons although the extent is still a lot less than that observed in the Malay classroom. This state of affairs could be explained by the fact that teachers in the national type Chinese classroom have the 'luxury' of teaching the same subject matter in two sessions, firstly in Mandarin and then in English, and so the students already have a conceptual grasp of the topic before they encounter it in the English-medium classroom. Another reason could be due to the insistence of the headmistress of the school that teachers should use English in the second session at all costs.

The medium of instruction

The medium of instruction is still a controversial issue, particularly among the Chinese and Malay communities. The Chinese community believes that Mandarin is adequate for the teaching of the two subjects while most Malay linguists (e.g. Awang Sarian, a Professor of Malay linguistics) do not agree with the use of English to teach them. With such limited English repertoires, both on the part of the teacher and the students, it is not entirely clear how it is possible to verbally co-construct a harmonious and effective community of learning in the Malaysian primary classroom. In fact, this so-called innovation of using English as the medium of instruction has resulted in incessant complaints that children were already overburdened by the tight school schedule and heavy curriculum which existed even before the policy change (Chan *et al.*, 2007). Moreover, the additional hours required to carry out the dual-language formulation in the national type Chinese schools could be a burden to the teachers and children as well as to the detriment of extra-curricular activities which are deemed crucial in a holistic approach to education (Chan *et al.*, 2007). However, according to Chan *et al.* (2007) the time allocated for the learning of English is seen as the right move towards addressing the need to improve English proficiency of Chinese school children although some teachers might consider the implementation a meaningless practice of translating and repeating lessons, wasting valuable human resources which can be put to better use.

In summary, the data suggest that co-construction of learning and meaning according to the definitions proposed by Sonnenmeier (1993) and Goldstein (1999) is sorely lacking. The manner in which knowledge is negotiated is not in line with what normally happens in the broader social ways of interacting where interlocuters take turns in almost equal proportions to construct meaning. Cultural schema for learning (Hui, 2005) and religious norms (Mohd-Asraf, 2005), added to the implications of changing language policies, hinder a Western type of learning experiences and construction of knowledge in these bilingual classrooms.

Having said this, one can safely say that the learners in these classrooms did learn something, but this was not due to active co-construction but rather perhaps to the uncritical reception of transmitted knowledge.

TAKE 2

Set A maths lesson in a Year 4 (Malay) classroom

In this class, we see the teacher attempting to activate her students' knowledge of division, with possibly a new element being the operation of division to produce improper fractions. The first thing that strikes me is the teacher's frequent codeswitching. This may be seen as a coping strategy to compensate for her insecure grasp of English syntax and vocabulary, but it is also likely that the teacher uses the common first language because the students' competence in English is insufficient to enable them to grasp the conceptual information of the maths lesson.

In her first turn in Extract 1, for example, the teacher is able to give elementary instructions in English ('Open your textbook', etc.), but her inability to use the language to relate the present lesson to the students' previous learning experience ('Same, same with another past lesson') pushes her to codeswitch to get her meaning across. Similarly, a little later in the same turn, she wishes to get the students to think about dividing different units, but after starting to explain in English ('The difference is unit'), she resorts to the Malay language to ask a concept question and then to give a short explanation (translated as: 'the method is not the same') in order to facilitate their understanding.

The second extract begins with an exchange between teacher and the students, and although the latter are verbally participating in the classroom discourse, the interaction seems to be along the lines of Young's (1992: 111) 'Guess what the teacher thinks' (GWTT) rather than any real attempt to co-construct new knowledge or understanding. The silence following the teacher's elicitation ('Why forty-two can divide by six?') is indicative of the students' inability to express their understanding, at least in English, by anything other than monosyllabic choral repetition. Probably realising this, the teacher uses the common first language with some English interjections to repeat, and hopefully clarify, the information previously given. Another short GWTT exchange follows, which the teacher concludes with another explanation in Malay to summarise the key point.

The final extract from this school shows a recurrence of the same interaction pattern. The teacher has switched to Malay as the matrix language to remind the class of what she has said, and she then seeks to elicit a response, repeating the cue – somewhat unnecessarily – in English ('which number to multiply? Which number to divide?'). Once again, there is a GWTT exchange terminating in a long turn by the teacher. Here, she uses the common first language apparently to criticise some of the students for their failure to provide the correct answer to a simple polar question.

Taken as a whole, the extracts indicate a rather distant atmosphere in the classroom, the teacher transmitting a limited amount of conceptual information, mostly in the common first language, and expecting little from the students but monosyllabic responses to her cues – and criticizing students when they failed to provide the expected answers. At no point in these extracts do the students initiate an exchange to ask questions, make comments or add to the common store of knowledge.

Set B science lesson in a year four Chinese classroom

The tone of the second set of extracts appears to be very different. The lesson begins (Extract #4) with a student instruction for the class to stand – possibly a ritual occurrence. The teacher's initial sociable comments, asking after the students' health and happiness, may also be formulaic, but they nevertheless contrast with the more distant relationship that is apparent in the Malay classroom. Like her ethnic Malay colleague, this teacher begins the lesson with an overview of the topic and instructions to open the book. She appears to be more competent in her use of English, with a wider range of syntactic structures and less need to repeat herself, and no need to switch codes – perhaps confident that her students would not need this form of linguistic support. Her use of 'we' in the initial comment in Extract #2 ('We want to know what are the properties of the materials, ok') implies that she intends for the topic to be collectively co-constructed in an exploratory mode, and this is reinforced by the, again sociable, enquiry ('Would you like to find out?'). However, the collaborative intention – if it is that – is not followed through; instead, the extract continues with a GWTT routine, with the teacher cuing the students to produce choral one-word responses, as can be seen in the following exchange taken from Extract #5:

04 T Ok, now you see these objects, the spoons and the forks, are made of
05 Ss Metal
06 T Ok, metal is /
07 S? Shiny
08 Ss (in chorus) Shiny]

This routine is very similar to that in the Malay maths lesson, and the transcript gives no indication of the voice quality of the teacher. It would have been interesting to compare the intonation patterns of the two teachers in these extracts to see if the Chinese teacher has a lighter touch than the other. The sociable comments at the start of this lesson might lead one to suppose this, but the interaction in Extract #6 continues in the same vein, for example:

07 T … what are the properties of metal? Can you tell teacher?
08 Ss Shiny // can be bent
09 T Ok, good, and what about rubber? Rubber is //
10 Ss Tough / Can be stretched
11 T Good, rubber is tough but it can be stretched. What about this one?
12 Ss Light/ Plastic]
13 T Plastic is /
14 Ss Light //
15 T Glass?
16 Ss Can be easily broken.
17 T Glass is easily broken. ok,

There is, however, a slight difference in the discourse structure here. In Extract #2, the exchange structure was binary: teacher elicitation and student response. In the extract above, three-part structure occurs: initiation–response–follow-up (Coulthard, 1986). At this later stage of the lesson the teacher was apparently asking her students to recall information from their long term memory, rather than (in Extract #2) merely echo words they had immediately before heard (on tape). This may be seen as a limited form of co-construction, and the follow-up moves – for example, 'Ok. Good' (09), 'Good' (11) and 'Glass is easily broken, ok' (17) are not merely confirmation that the students are correctly contributing to the building of knowledge but also positive evaluation of their efforts. If this is so, it again marks an attitudinal difference between the two teachers; the Malay teacher's evaluation of her students tended to be negative.

The final extract in the Chinese classroom sees the teacher carefully structuring the students' out-of-class assignment. Her command of English, though at times faltering, is still more assured than that of her colleague in the Malay classroom and she concludes the lesson on a positive note:

01   T   That's the end for today's lesson and I hope all of you all enjoy the lesson. Do you enjoy the lesson?
02   Ss   Yes
03   T   Thank you very much.

This may be contrasted with the Malay classroom, where the other teacher ended her maths lesson on a negative and perhaps sarcastic note (translated as: 'All forgotten, huh. After long holidays, can't remember').

Both classrooms

While these two lessons have much in common, there are some differences. The most obvious one is that the maths teacher resorted frequently to codeswitching to make points – whether informational or instructional – comprehensible to her students (and perhaps to maintain control in the classroom). The science teacher in the Chinese school used only English; this may be due to her own greater competence in English and/or that of her students; it also needs to be remembered that the content of this lesson had previously been delivered in Mandarin, in the dual language programme operating in this typical Chinese school. I have also detected a warmer emotional and social climate in the latter school, which may have encouraged a greater level of oral co-construction by the students.

However, even if this is the case I think it needs to be acknowledged that neither teacher sought, or perhaps was able, to create in their respective classrooms a community of learning in terms of encouraging their students to think creatively and critically in co-constructed instructional conversations (Tharp & Gallimore, 1991). The discourse of these classrooms was shown to be unidirectional, with the students making very limited linguistic responses to the teacher's elicitations; their contribution to shared conceptual understanding was minimal, and little else was expected of them. Both teachers tended to take an authoritarian stance, and maintain a marked distance between themselves and their students (the Chinese teacher's reference to herself in the third person may indicate this). They did not assume, by example or precept, a transformative role which intentionally and transparently guided their 'apprentices' towards eventual full participation in an inclusive community of academic practice. It may be argued that the Malaysian students in these classes were too young, too immature, for even peripheral participation. However, there are examples in the present book of other learning contexts where the teachers seek to, and to a reasonable extent manage to, involve learners of the same age in the verbal co-construction of shared understanding. However, in terms of Lave and Wenger's (1991) understanding of participation in socially situated practices, it may well be argued that the teachers were indeed inducting their learners into attitudes and behaviours that are culturally appropriate to the wider sociocultural environment in which these schools and classrooms were located; the teachers were most likely conforming to conventional expectations of their role, and those required of their learners. Here, however, lies a paradox. The choice of which language should be the medium of instruction is important not only in terms of the eventual ability of students to communicate in that language, but also because the medium of instruction will inevitably influence their ability to conceptualise the world in general, and the curriculum subjects in particular. The extracts of classroom interaction presented in this chapter have shown that the conceptual development of the students seems almost negligible. To a large extent this may be due to a lack of Cognitive Academic Language Proficiency – or even Basic Interactional Conversation Skills – (Cummins, 1980) not only on their part but possibly also on their teachers'. If these extracts are representative of the rest of the lessons, or are typical of other lessons in these and similar schools, questions must arise about the value of teaching content subjects such as maths and science through the medium of English.

TAKE 3

The following exchanges occurred a few minutes before the extracts in the Malay Year 4 mathematics lesson discussed in Take 1 above.

01   T   Ok, look here class. Insya-Allah, *God willing* every**time**, every**day**, I told you **how** to **do**. Awak ini lupa tak?, huh, tak ingat, tak? *You forget or you don't remember, no?* Ada tiga cara saya dah ajar dekat awak. *There are three methods which I've taught you* Berapa **cara?** *How many methods?*

02   Ss   Tiga *Three*

03 T How many steps?

04 Ss Three

05 T **Three. Satu** pun tak **ingat!** *One also you can't remember!* // Buka buku tak? *Did you open the book?* Cuti lama sangat! *The holidays are too lengthy!* B, look here, H, (xxx) The answer is **wrong**. So why you times **again?** H, buat darab itu salah. *You did the multiplication wrongly.* Jadi, kenapa awak buat darab lagi? *So, why do you multiply again?* K, A pun sama. *Also the same.* You look here, one cm equal to ten milimetre, inilah masalah awak. *this is the problem.* Masalah awak nak *The problem is you want to* convert. You don't know **how** to convert. If you **want** to convert cm to millimeter, **apa? what?** times? If you want to convert millimeter to centimeter

06 Ss Divide, divide ten

07 T Divide

08 Ss Ten

09 T Ini dia kamu perlu ingat. *This is it you must remember.* Kalau awak tahu, awak tahu sajalah. *If you know, you'll know.* Step one, ada tiga cara. *There are three methods.* Yang pertama, *the first* twenty-eight milimetre, **ok**, so now you want to convert milimetre to centimeter. So, you **must** divide ten, divide by ten. Ok, twenty-eight millimeter divide ten. **ok,** how many zero are they? One. One zero. Ok, I want to ask you? Ok, which point in this number twenty-eight, which point? Which the, decimal point for this number, for twenty-eight? (xxx) Di mana? *Where* **Sini? Here?**

10 Ss No

11 T **Sini? Here?**

12 Ss Yes

13 T **Sini? Here?**

15 Ss No

16 T Eh// look here. If two, twenty-eight. OK, you ask the decimal point here. Awak tak sebut dia *You didn't say it.* twenty-eight. Awak sebut dia *You say it* two point eight, eight. Sini *Here* twenty-eight nombor bulat dimana dia *Where is the even number's* decimal point? **Di mana?** *Where?* Di mana? *Where?* Di mana, *Where's* A? Sini juga, **Mari!** *Here too, **come!*** /// Show me. Where is the decimal point. **ah, dekat mana?** *At where?*

17 Ss Sini *Here*

Guiding questions for Take 3

(1) The constant switching between Malay and English can be an indicator of a variety of sociolinguistic arrangements. What do you think may be happening here?

(2) The teacher repeats that the students do not remember (Turns 1, 5, and 9). Is the teacher referring to the content or the language? Can it be both and what evidence can you find for each?

(3)   What do the students' responses indicate about their English language levels?

References

Cath, A. and McLellan, J. (1993) 'Right. Let's do some ah, mm, speaking': Patterns of classroom interaction in Brunei Darussalam. Paper presented at *BAAL Seminar on Bilingual Classroom Discourse*, Lancaster University, July 1993.

Chan, S.H., Wong, B.E. and Abdullah, A.N. (2007) Taking stock of the viability of the Malaysian language policy innovation. In Proceedings of *International Conference on Globalization in Education: Opportunities, Challenges, and Implications for Vietnam and the Region* (pp. 239–258). Southeast Asian Ministers of Education Organization (SEAMEO) Regional Training Center in Vietnam.

Chick, K. (1996) Safe-talk: Collusion in apartheid education. In H. Coleman (ed.) *Society and the Language Classroom* (pp. 21–39). Cambridge: Cambridge University Press.

Coulthard, M. (1986) *An Introduction to Discourse Analysis*. London: Longman.

Cummins, J. (1980) The cross-lingual dimensions of language proficiency: Implications for bilingual education and the optimal age issue. *TESOL Quarterly* 14, 175–187.

Goldstein, L.S. (1999) The relational zone: The role of caring relationships in the co-construction of the mind. *American Educational Research Journal* 36 (3), 647–673.

Hendry, G.D., Frommer, M. and Walker, R.A. (1999) Constructivism and problem-based learning. *Journal of Further and Higher Education*, 23, 359–371.

Hui, L. (2005) Chinese cultural schema of education: Implications for communication between Chinese students and Australian educator. *Issues in Educational Research* 15 (1), 17–36.

Lave, J. and Wenger, E. (1991) *Situated Learning: Legitimate Peripheral Participation*. New York: Cambridge University Press.

Mohd-Asraf, R. (2005) English and Islam: A class of civilizations? *Journal of Language and Education* 4 (2), 103–118.

Sonnenmeier, R. (1993) Co-construction of messages during facilitated communication. *Facilitated Communication Digest* 1 (2), 7–9.

Tharp, R. and Gallimore, R. (1991) A theory of teaching as assisted performance. In P. Light, S. Sheldon and M. Woodhead (eds) *Learning to Think: Child Development in Social Context 2* (pp. 42–61). London: Routledge.

Washima, C.D., Harshita, A.H. and Naysmith, J. (1996) English and Islam in Malaysia: Resolving the tension. *World Englishes* 15 (2), 225–234.

Young, R. (1992) *Critical Theory and Classroom Talk*. Clevedon: Multilingual Matters.

Chapter 8

Creating a Community of Learning in New Zealand: A Case Study of Students in a New School

TAKE 1: ROGER BARNARD
TAKE 2: JAMES McLELLAN

TAKE 1

Introduction

At the time the data for this chapter were being collected and analysed, the New Zealand national curriculum had been in place since 1994, and was undergoing review (Ministry of Education, 2002). Since then, a new national curriculum was instituted in 2008 in which many of the core values of the status quo were reinforced, among them that students should develop the following learning skills and attitudes:

- creative and innovative thinking;
- participation and contribution in communities;
- relating to others;
- reflecting on learning;
- developing self-knowledge; and
- making meaning from information.

(Ministry of Education, 2002: executive summary)

The review went on to reinforce the point that the curriculum statements were flexible enough to allow teachers to meet the needs of their students in a variety of ways. In an earlier Ministry report, the following statement was made about the desirable quality of teachers:

Teachers find their role moving away from the traditional approach to one where the teacher facilitates and mediates students' learning. Equally importantly, teachers need to diagnose individual learning and other needs and address these collaboratively with the student. Together with the challenges of greater social diversity, it is desirable that teachers possess a broad range of relationship management skills. (Ministry of Education, 1997: 20)

Thus, teachers in New Zealand primary schools are encouraged to seek their own solutions to pedagogic issues, devise their own teaching plans, and run the classes in the way they think best for their students to achieve the national curriculum goals.

Dimensions of Classroom Learning

The classroom data in this chapter will be considered in terms of three dimensions of classroom learning: interactional, instructional task performance and cognitive/academic (Richards & Hurley, 1990). The first of these – the interactional dimension – refers to conventions about who communicates to whom, when and how. This dimension embraces issues such as initiating, sustaining and terminating interactions, bidding for turns, asking questions, and so on. Such conventions apply also to various forms of nonverbal communication, such as eye contact, gesture and movement around the classroom. The point of the interactional dimension is that it is the social basis upon which classroom learning occurs; unless the conventions are adhered to, at least in large part, the other two dimensions of classroom learning will not be effective.

With regard to the second dimension of classroom learning – instructional task performance – Richards and Hurley point out that much of the primary school curriculum can be considered as a collection of various tasks through which learning is operationalised. Such tasks include copying, note-taking, symbolic manipulation (such as arithmetic calculation, adding punctuation to texts), information-extraction, comprehension of explicitly stated details, inferring implicit information, making summaries, comments, evaluation, and so forth. These tasks have widely different operational procedures (e.g. whether they are to be performed individually, in pairs, or in groups), apply a range of resources (such as print, visual, electronic) and specify various outcomes, which may be represented orally, visually or in writing.

By following the interactional conventions and carrying out the instructional tasks, primary school students are expected to make conceptual gains – and thus move into the third, academic/cognitive, dimension. Thus they learn technical terminology, comprehend new concepts, acquire new modes of enquiry, absorb the underlying discourse structures and modes of enquiry of the school subjects, and develop new learning strategies. Learners are also encouraged to develop metacognitive skills: they learn how to become good learners.

Setting

'Rosegarden' school was an intermediate school which enrolled students for the final two years (Years 7 and 8) of primary education from local feeder schools. (The names of the school and all the participants in this chapter are pseudonyms.) The class taught by 'Ms Wilkins' was typical of many such classrooms in that it was co-educational and included students of various levels of abilities. It was also ethnically diverse; although most of the thirty students were of European descent, the following other ethnic-ities were represented: two students each from mainland China, Fiji and Somalia, and one each from Kiribati, Tuvalu, Papua New Guinea and Syria. All of these students had previously attended local feeder schools. Ms Wilkins began the year armed with her knowledge of the national cur-riculum requirements, some 12 years teaching experience at this and other levels, a wide repertoire of pedagogic skills, and a somewhat scanty knowl-edge of the students' backgrounds (provided by enrolment forms for new students and one-page reports from feeding schools). Although the process of co-constructing the learning environment continued throughout the year, the first few weeks were crucial in establishing the ground rules for effective classroom learning. During this period, interactions among the students were audio-recorded via lapel microphones; these were tran-scribed and supplemented by field notes and reflective notes made by the researcher acting as participant observer.

Classroom Interaction

The interactional dimension

Much classroom discourse in the first few weeks focused on establish-ing how the students were expected to behave in the classroom, around the school, and even outside the school. The following extract, which occurred first thing in the morning on the fourth day after the start of school, is an example:

Extract #1a

```
02  Ss   Good Morning Ms Wilkins
03  T    Right. We have two people who are new today – Jill, and Jed
          (xxx). You'll soon get to know who's who. // Nathan, was it you
          I saw on my way to school this morning?
04  Na   Yes
05  T    It was. Thank you. I really enjoyed the wave and the smile. There
          was one thing I didn't like. Know what it was?
06  S1   (...) <indicates he does not get the point>
```

07 T It's actually against the law. Not just, you know we don't just say it here at Rosegarden. You know what it was?

08 S1 (...) <this time he has got the point>

09 T Good one. OK. So you won't ride on the footpath again, will you. Glad you had your helmet on though. Right. So, <starts to call register> Harry...

In this exchange with Nathan, the teacher wished to make a general behavioural point based on an out-of-school incident. The interaction might be interpreted in various ways. Ostensibly directed to one student, it might be regarded as a simple conversational exchange between two individuals. However, the classroom context – and the teacher's volume, tone and wide-ranging eye-contact – suggests that she was addressing the whole class. The explicit connection made (07) between the law and school rules reinforces that this was not merely a social exchange but that it served an underlying pedagogical purpose. The somewhat oblique question by the teacher (05) might suggest a stereotypical didacticism by which a student is supposed to guess what is in the teacher's mind (Young, 1992: 111) with few, if any clues as to what this might be. However, the structure of the entire exchange more likely suggests that Ms Wilkins was engaging with the class as a whole, who participated in the dialogue as active if silent auditors. Ms Wilkins' final assumption (09) about Nathan's future action might be seen as extending Nathan's understanding – and that of the class – from the specific to the general, and she closed the exchange with a final compliment.

In the above extract, the teacher may be seen to be inculcating, or reinforcing, the values of wider society with an implication of the school's expectations in this area: an example of socialisation *through* language (Schieffelin & Ochs, 1986). The tactful way in which it was done also suggests an intention to socialise the students *in* language – the use of appropriate forms of language for social regulation. The interaction continued with Ms Wilkins calling the register, with an explicit focus on socialisation *in* language use:

Extract #1b

09 T ....Right. So, <starts to call register> Harry...

10 Ha Yep

11 T Pardon <sharply>

12. Ha Ah - yes!

13 T Pardon <sharply>

14. Ha Yes Mrs. Wilkins

15 T **Ms** Wilkins

16 Ha **Ms** Wilkins

17 T Thank you, Harry. Yorin

18 Yo Yes Ms Wilkins

19	T	Trevor
20	Tr	Yes, Mrs. Wilkins
21	T	**Ms** Wilkins
22	Tr	Ms Wilkins
23	T	Thank you. The first day I told you that if I had the courtesy to address you by name, you have the courtesy to address me by my name. {Continues to call the register; all students respond appropriately.} Good.

Again, it is reasonable to infer that the exchange between the teacher and Harry (09–17) was intended to be attended to by the whole class; this may be borne out by the way that most of the class, except Trevor (20), subsequently responded appropriately. As in the previous exchange, the teacher chose not to explicitly correct the individual's solecisms (10, 12), but rather implied that he should think the matter through for himself with minimal interactive clues (11, 13). Harry accurately interpreted the illocutionary intent of Ms Wilkins' laconic elicitations, and gave an approximately appropriate response (14), which was corrected (15) and echoed by him (16) – indicating his uptake of the point. Typically, Ms Wilkins thanked him for his attention before passing on to another student. Here it is interesting to note not only the teacher's insistence on being properly addressed with her preferred social title but also the decision to make explicit her rationale for this (23), once the required responses were made.

The next extract, which occurred after the register had been called, shows that students were expected to follow instructions, or face the consequences.

Extract #2

01	T	Good. Hands up people who are **not** swimming today. **Not** swimming. Apart from Jane, who I know about. OK – and I'll excuse you too Jake, cos you didn't know. OK. {to David who raised his hand}. Why are you not swimming?
02	Da	Oh I forgot my]
03	T	You forgot? Oh dear. {Writes David's name on AD-Assertive Discipline-list} Detention after school. Why is that?
04	Da	For not bringing my togs
05	T	You didn't follow the instruction first time, and I did actually give you a reminder. Who else?
06	Al	{raises hand}
07	T	You too. OK Ali. Why are you not swimming?
08	Lo	{quietly, to another student} He's gonna be in trouble.
09	Al	(xxx)
10	T	True. (xxx) Have you been given your timetable?
11	Al	No

12   T   No? I'll make that an excuse. But each time we have PE you bring your togs. / Starting tomorrow.

One of the interesting points in this exchange occurs between 03 and 05. After telling David that he had a detention, the teacher immediately asked if he knew why; the student responded with a specific reason (04), which Ms Wilkins extended to the need to follow all instructions. Her regretful use of 'Oh dear' (03) may suggest that she, like the students, was bound by the school's discipline code. A few moments later, despite Lonnie's prediction (08), Ali was reprieved because he had an excuse. In this way, Ms Wilkins was inducting the class into the consequences of inattention or disobedience, but also that the sanctions might be waived in some circumstances.

Classroom interaction involves physical factors, such as zones of movement and the placement of students. Generally, the teacher expected students to sit where she wanted, but seating was sometimes negotiable – as the following exchange shows when Ms Wilkins was monitoring individual tasks.

Extract # 3

01   T   Good boy! // You might be able to carry on with that // {then to Mohammed} You can't (xxx). How about you move to Buna's desk, cos Buna's over there? // Buna, can he come and sit here?
02   Mo   No, (xxx) just (xxx) sit there]
03   T   Or move Buna's desk up - that might be better / You'll need that. You're working on that. That's right. // Put your desk in the middle. How about // {Mohammed goes and sits on the floor} Oh, you want to move on the floor? OK.

Ms Wilkins suggested Mohammed should sit beside Buna, typically seeking the latter's assent (01) before telling him to move desks – an example of socialisation through language. Initially, she overrode the boy's quiet verbal noncompliance (02) but in the middle of her utterance, Mohammed silently decided to take independent action. Without enquiring into his reasons for not wanting to sit beside the Polynesian girl, Ms Wilkins accepted his decision and moved away.

The instructional task dimension

For the first two weeks, the classroom discourse included much discussion about how learning tasks should be carried out. There is clearly a link between conduct required in social interaction in the classroom, and that required for instructional task performance – the former being a prerequisite for the latter. Ms Wilkins was keen to ensure that appropriate standards were understood and applied in both dimensions. In this extract from a handwriting lesson during the second week, she was revising the formation of letters, which she had introduced in previous lessons. She began with how work should be set out in the students' books:

Extract #4a

```
01   T    Trevor, where does the date go please?
02   Tr   In the top left hand corner
03   T    Good, thank you. Underlined in what colour?
04   P    (xxx)]
05   T    Good]
06   Na   Red!]
07   T    Good. / Thank you.
```

As illustrated above, the discourse of learning progressed by dialogue between the teacher and the class, using individual members as representative interlocutors. The intersubjective rules of speaker privilege and listener commitment apply, although – as can be seen above (04–07) – some degree of overlapping was permitted, as it would in out-of-class social conversation. Ms Wilkins continued by eliciting how certain letters should be formed and linked:

Extract #4b

```
07   T    Good... Thank you. {Shows OHT with handwriting task} What's
          this left letter, Calum?
08   Ca   'u'
09   T    Good. Where does it start? {Refers to pen movement for the
          letter 'u'.}
10   Na   From the top
11   T    Well, lower case 'u'...
12   S?   (xxx)
13   T    Good. OK. Now it's in the middle. And where does it go? Roger?
14   Ro   Oh. Down, and then it goes round and]
15   T     Where does it go down to? Down to / what?
16   Ro   (xxx) start at the bottom and then it goes up
17   T    Down to the line / there / Is that right down to the line? There /
          and // then]
17   Ro   Then go around and then you go down and then]
18   T    And then flick. / Good. OK. Starts in the middle, down to the
          line, up, around, down // over there again and flick / Good //
          Well done / /OK. Half way down to the line, up, down over /
          that, and a flick. Someone describe that flick to me please.
```

This extract shows how the teacher worked with language to co-construct understanding with the class. While it is clear that certain standards were expected, instead of simply transmitting the information, Ms Wilkins engaged in an instructional conversation (Tharp & Gallimore, 1990) to encourage active, if vicarious, participation by the class as a whole. The students' responses enabled her to gauge their existing abilities and promote their 'buds of development' (Vygotsky, 1978: 86) by a series of questions, such as illustrated in the exchange with Roger (13–17). At this point (18), she summarised and repeated the information before passing on to the next stage.

Extract #4c

18	T	Someone describe that flick to me please // <sharply> Nathan, describe that flick to me
19	Na	(xxx)
20	T	No. Put that pen down! / And **focus**. Describe what it looks like. How do you form that flick?
21	Na	It just comes (xxx) flick {gestures with hand}
22	T	Yes, and can we liken it something to? // So it's a nice, straight one. Not a curly thing. Right? /Good. // Now, if you want to join these two letters – what are they please? {gestures to a student}
23	S?	(xxx)
24	T	And..?
25	S?	Oh, 'u' and 'a'
26	T	Good.

Ms Wilkins nominated Nathan to describe a flick (18) because she perceived that he was not paying attention, and thereby flouting the classroom conventions associated with active listening. His response (19) appeared to confirm her assumption, and she sharply rebuked him. The illocutionary intent of her directive to focus (20) was that he should look at her, it being commonly understood in most New Zealand classrooms that visual engagement with a speaker implied listener commitment. Nathan's response (21) was accompanied by a gesture, which the teacher interpreted as indicating that he had grasped the point. Her tone of voice and positive language 'Yes … nice … good … please' (22) addressed partly to Nathan and partly to the rest of the class may have repaired any disequilibrium caused by her earlier rebuke, and the lesson proceeded smoothly.

In the above extract, the class was expected to follow the teacher's instructions literally to the letter, and not to add variations of their own. Soon, however, the students began to influence the way that tasks were carried out. In the third week of term, the following exchange took place as the students were working on a task associated with pond life for which they had to cut and paste a worksheet:

Extract #5

01	T	Just like those ones up there. Are there any questions. I think we have / right there over the back
02	S?	Erm / Do we have to cut every piece of white paper out?
03	T	You sure do. No / what I mean / by cutting them out / like a bubble, a circle, you don't have to cut right round the wheels, and // nope, just a bubble. Next question.
04	Gl	Can we colour them in?
05	T	Can you colour them in? I'd love you to colour them in. Ye-es. Not in felt tip, though – pencil – that gives them a nice colour. Felt tip for the outline, maybe, and fill in with pencil the rest.
06	Me	(Can) we move the paper round?
07	T	That's a very good idea. Right. When you're ready to start cutting you may /// Don't lose any pieces of paper – and I will give you your cartridge when you're ready. Put it on the table and I'll know your ready for the cartridge paper.

In this extract, three students made specific suggestions which the teacher positively evaluated and shared with the class as a whole by echoing, expanding and qualifying their contributions. She also implied (03) that one of them had anticipated her own thinking; whether that was the case or not, there is evidence here of explicit intersubjectivity – learners and teacher exchanging roles of speaker and listener – and actively working both with and through language (Mercer, 1995) to co-construct understanding within the dimension of instructional task performance. The teacher made consistent efforts to encourage a positive social and working environment by explicitly praising her students' efforts; a little later in the same lesson, the following exchanges occurred:

Extract #6

01	Me	<loudly, to T> What are you supposed to cut out? Just the words?
02	T	(to class) Just trim // Nancy./ hold yours up please. Everybody / look at Nancy's piece of paper. She's cut it out beautifully. Turn it round so the others can see. / Now that's]
03	S?	<quietly> What a stupid (...)]
04	T	[going to fit perfectly. Not going to stick out of the edges of the book. // That's going to go in here really well. / Look at that[

05   Na   [Yeah – that's what I'm doing, man].
06   T   That's really beautiful]
07   Na   <quietly> Yeah / I think that's just the best.

In this exchange, the teacher held up Nancy's work as a model for others to emulate. It is not easy to interpret the boy's whispered utterance (03). It might have been addressed to another student as a subversive comment on the teacher's appraisal. Alternatively, it might have been the externalisation of private speech referring either to what the teacher said, or to something completely different – such as his own work. Either the teacher did not hear him or else she ignored the remark and – except possibly for those nearest to him – the general discourse was not disrupted by the boy's remark. The teacher's next turn (04) – a continuation of her previous statement – was not intended to refer to anyone in particular, but to the class as a whole. It is not possible to tell whether Nathan's comments (05, 06) were social speech addressed to the teacher or another student, or externalised self-regulating private speech acts (Vygotsky, 1986: 218) – or indeed a shift from one to the other. What the extract does suggest is that the teacher's dialogue with the class was being internalised by the learners to create their own personal meaning – what Bakhtin (1981) refers to as 'appropriation' – from what is said on the social plane.

The cognitive dimension

As with learning in the two other dimensions, the favoured approach to the presentation of conceptual knowledge was that of an instructional dialogue between teacher and the class: 'education proceeds by the development of shared understanding' (Mercer, 1994: 90). The following extract occurred in the third week of term a day or so before the two extracts immediately above. The teacher addressed the class:

Extract # 7

01   T: Put your hand up if you can tell me what a habitat is. // A habitat /
              {Ja raises his hand} James, tell everybody what a habitat is.
02   Ja   A place where something lives.
03   T   Exactly right. A place where something lives]
04   S?   This is **my** habit]
05   T   This is / where is **your** habitat?
06   Ss   Hamilton
07   T   Exactly, yeah.

The teacher might well have introduced the topic by defining the key concept herself. Typically, however, she sought to involve the class by eliciting their ideas. James' definition was so close to what the teacher herself might have said that she promptly appropriated it for use in the rest of the lesson The general response (06) to her concept question (05) gave assurance that the concept was more generally understood. A few minutes later, the following exchange occurred:

Extract #8

01	T	We're actually looking at the dragonfly // so I really would like these first four questions filled out really importantly, and then we'll work through on the others today and tomorrow. // So / I'm going to read out what it says up here {refers to overhead projector slide}. You're going to read with me, cos you can all see that. Dragon fly. {reading aloud the first sentence of the slide}. 'New Zealand has eleven species of dragonfly'. Hands up if you knew there were more than one species of dragon fly // {a number of hands raised} Wow! Gene, how many did you think there was?
02	Ge	Three
03	T	How many do *you* think there was / Walt?
04	Wa	Seven
05	T	Only seven. Did you know, Lonnie, that there were eleven species?
06	Lo	I know <brightly>/ cos you just told me that there were eleven! {laughter}
07	T	Mnaa. {smiles wryly and recommences reading the text to the class} 'These insects have two pairs...'

Again, the teacher sought to involve the students by eliciting their pre-existing knowledge of the topic. Lonnie, who by now had established himself as the class humourist, responded cheekily which gave rise to general laughter. It is an indication of the relaxed atmosphere in the class that the teacher accepted it with good grace and continued.

On the first morning of the following week, a new unit of work was started in the area of Language Arts. Ms Wilkins wished to introduce the concept of a 'biopoem' by which she meant a poem about somebody's life. However, rather than tell the class what she meant, she first elicited their own ideas:

Extract #9a

01	T	Right {writes BIO on whiteboard}. // Who can tell me what this word means? // Should have a big clue from what I've just said
02	Ss	Bio!
03	T	Bio. I know that's what it reads. / But what does it **mean**?
04	Me	Bio[
05	T	Without calling out. / Without calling out. Yes, Melanie?

06	Me	Erm / it's about animals and insects and things
07	T	Ye-es. / That's a big part of it, sure // More about it
08	S?	Nature.
09	T	Yes.
10	S?	(xxx)
11	T	Pardon?
12	S?	Plant life.
13	T	Plant life / Oh, we're getting really close there.
14	Ge	Horticulture?
15	T	Sorry?
16	Ge	Horticulture?
17	T	Culture / yes, yes, that comes into it, sure // <to previous student> What did you say again? Plant life. OK – so just plant life? Cos we have something about animals here.
18	S?	Yeah.
19	T	Just plants? Or?
20	Na	(Animals)
21	T	Animal life? Yes]
22	Tr	(xxx) making a cleaner environment for animals and plants[
23	Da	Like two (xx)]
24	T	The word 'bio' (xxx). So / therefore, if 'bio' has got something to do with plants, animals, and life and a cleaner environment, / what then is a bio**poem**?

The clues Ms Wilkins mentioned (01) referred to an immediately previous conversation about the biotechnology room: this hint misled the class down a natural history path from which she was not immediately able to draw them back to the notion of 'bio' implying life in general. Although she verbally drew attention (05) to the by-now well established interactional rule of raising hands before speaking, she actually struck a balance between the need for order and the spontaneous generation of ideas – an attempt to co-construct conceptual knowledge – by as many students as possible. Thus she provided positive feedback to all suggestions, making a few probing moves (07, 13, 17) to develop the ideas she felt most relevant. Evidently, in the flow of the discourse, she slightly misheard Gene's contribution (14, 16) despite its repetition, possibly because she wished to steer the dialogue in the direction of the key word 'life'. Having involved the class in this way, she focused their attention on the key issue (24), and perhaps aroused their interest and then moved on to the next step:

Extract #9b

24	T	...what then is a bio**poem**? {adds POEM to BIO on board} / What's a biopoem? Cos we all know what a poem is[
25	Ss	Oh (xxx)[

26 Me (Is it) a poem about yourself?
27 T   Yes. / Does it have to be about yourself? / Does it have to be
         about you?
28 Ss No, no]
29 S? [It could be about someone]
30 T   It could be about anybody, or anything. Cos we can give life to
         other things...

Once again, the teacher elicited the students' ideas by open questions (24)
and eventually by rhetorical repetition of a leading question (28) to get to
the point she wanted. Then, wishing to broaden the concept beyond this
initial level, she gave an illustration of what she meant by relating what a
previous student had done:

Extract #9c

30 T: Cos we can give life to other things. One of the best biopoems
        I have ever read was written by a child in this room about three
        years ago. And we had done a study on New Zealand disasters,
        and she did hers on // <volume and pitch of voice drops> the
        Tangiwai disaster – the great train crash <almost whispering.
31 Ps Oh! <also quietly>
32 S? Cool!]
33 T   She wrote her biopoem, using a mountain – the life that came
        from a mountain. OK <sharp raising of volume, and pitch to a
        higher key> // So, essentially we're looking // {turns over wall
        chart on whiteboard} /A biopoem / isn't necessarily a self-
        portrait – it normally is, OK. / It doesn't have to be. / It could be
        about the mountains. It could be about the weather. / It could be
        about **somebody** else who you're going to do a biopoem on. OK?
        /// So it's a self portrait in words. You're going to write a
        biopoem about a person

It is significant that Ms Wilkins' anecdote related to a previous student in
the class, implying perhaps that its present occupants could emulate such
excellent work. The dramatic effect of the story was heightened both by setting the poem in the context of a well-known railway disaster and by the
teacher's voice quality. That this was effective is indicated by students'
breathless backchannelling (32). The sharp raising of the voice at the end of
the anecdote and using 'OK' as a boundary marker (34) clearly indicated a
shift of focus. Ms Wilkins moved from narrative to concept clarification by
providing examples, and reinforced the point by rhetorical repetition of
syntactic elements. At the same time, she referred the class to a wall chart
on which were written the specific task requirements; the teacher thereby

sought to convey understanding by both visual and auditory means. She then mentioned that there was a specific task involved: the first time that one had been specified, although it probably did not come as a surprise to the class. She summarised the concept of a biopoem in a terse, four-word definition (34): 'a self-portrait in words' and reiterated the aim of the subsequent task.

The route taken by the teacher to attain her objective might appear time-consuming: in fact, the entire dialogue about the biopoem took less than seven minutes. It might also appear imprecise, perhaps inchoate. Conceptual understanding might have been more rapidly achieved if the teacher had initially stated the definition of a biopoem – 'a (self) portrait in words', shown the class the instruction on the wall chart, and told them to write a biopoem, and perhaps given a formal concept check afterwards. It is, however, irrelevant to consider whether other strategies might have been more appropriate. The point is that a detailed analysis of this episode – and the others above – shows how the teacher used language as an interpsychological tool in an attempt to co-construct understanding with her class.

Discussion

The extracts presented above have been interpreted to provide plausible explanations of how learning occurred in a specific context, with a particular teacher and a particular group of students. Undoubtedly, other interpretations and explanations – equally or more plausible – are likely.

However, it seems to me that the teacher adopted a deliberate and consistent strategy of engaging her students in Tharp and Gallimore's (1990) 'instructional conversations' in order to co-construct with them appropriate attitudes and behaviour in the three dimensions of classroom learning under consideration. Rather than directly transmit instructions, task requirements and conceptual constructs, Ms Wilkins generally preferred to encourage the active – if often vicarious – participation of the class by sharing understanding with and among her students in give-and-take dialogue.

According to the new national curriculum (Ministry of Education, 2007: 12), New Zealand students should develop five key areas of competence: (1) thinking, (2) using language, symbols and texts, (3) managing self, (4) relating to others, and (5) participating and contributing.

The following may be seen as a summary of the main elements of these competencies. The first is about using creative, critical, metacognitive and reflective processes to make sense of and question information, experiences and ideas. The second is that students should be able to interpret and use words, numbers, images, movement, metaphor and technologies in a number of ways. The third is for students to establish their own goals, make plans and set high standards for themselves. Students also need to be able to relate to others, which includes the ability to listen actively, recognise different points of view, negotiate, and share ideas. Finally, they should have a capacity to respond appropriately as a group member, to make connections to others, and create opportunities by including people in group activity.

As was pointed out in the introduction, the data for this chapter were collected before the new national curriculum was introduced. However, the extracts presented here show that the teacher and her students were working together to co-construct what it means to be a 'good learners' in the spirit of the competencies subsequently formulated by the Ministry of Education.

TAKE 2

Reviewing this set of nine extracts from a New Zealand Intermediate school classroom, I would like to focus on issues of pupil participation and teacher feedback. What are the ground rules? Are they made explicit in these extracts? Or is it for the pupils to guess and find out by trial and error? Are the rules variable, according to the different transactions that occur in these extracts? We would expect lower tolerance of interruptions and strict adherence to behavioural norms when the register is being called, as this is a legal and managerial requirement. But during the 'biopoem' extracts (#9a, #9b and #9c), the objective and the desired 'outcome' of the unit of work, according to the curriculum documents cited in the introduction to the data extracts, is (presumably) the production by pupils of 'biopoems'. Here the teacher should be encouraging more student output, hence she decides to elicit understanding of the concept of a biopoem using a synthetic bottom-up approach, through asking about the meaning of the prefix 'bio'.

In this series of nine extracts, taken from different times during the first month of the school year, there is a pattern of progression from near-total teacher control of the interaction, to greater tolerance and encouragement of student participation and initiation. The series of extracts reflects the traditional wisdom imparted to teachers in training by lecturers and by mentors in schools, using clichés such as 'Don't smile till April'.

In Extracts #1a and #1b the teacher exerts rigid control, as she does in the management episodes in Extracts #2 and #3, and in the pedagogically-focused Extracts #4a, #4b and #4c where the focus is on accurate handwriting. Extract #5 shows students requesting clarification of the teacher's expectations in response to her prompt 'Are there any questions . . .' (5.01). Three questions are asked relating to the task in hand, by different students, in turns 5.02, 5.04 and 5.06.

Extract #6 begins with what is presumably a student-initiated clarification request, 'What are you supposed to cut out? Just the words?': the previous turn is not recorded. Students' comments occur in turns 6.03, 6.05 and 6.07. These are relevant to the task they are engaged in, but do not fully conform to the teacher's expectations at this point. She wants Nancy to show her work to the class as a good model, which she singles out for praise in turn 6.06. Turn 6.03, presumably an 'aside' picked up by the recording equipment, is ignored. Since this is a practical hands-on task, one can assume that at this teacher is not encouraging any student talk: she just wants them to get on with their cutting and pasting.

In Extract #7 the teacher is pre-teaching the concept 'habitat', which is evidently important for the later part of her lesson plan, and tries to elicit the level of comprehension of this notion. In turn 7.04 a student feels able to comment on the definition given in another's student's response (in 7.02) and repeated approvingly in the teacher's feedback move 7.03. Instead of censuring this as an interruption, the teacher recognises that this student is expressing understanding of the concept through applying it to herself, and in 7.05 she turns this into a question for the whole class, who respond collectively. Extract #8, taken from later in the same lesson, has an instance where a student (Lonnie) makes a cheeky comment, 'I know, 'cos you just told me there were eleven!'. This is also allowed to pass without censure by the teacher, who then returns to the main reading task. The interaction, especially the teacher's feedback, in these two extracts show a greater tolerance for students' exploratory talk.

Extracts #9a, #9b and #9c also involve foregrounding and preteaching, partly as a comprehension check but also as part of a pre-task explanation. The teacher's lesson plan is for the students to write a 'biopoem'. For this it is a prerequisite that they should understand the meaning of the prefix 'bio', which she writes on the whiteboard. Then she uses the elicitation 'Who can tell me what this word means?' in turn 9.01. After a pause she adds a prompt, 'Should have a big clue from what I've just said'. We have no transcript for what has gone immediately before, so cannot estimate how helpful this is for the class. The students predictably chorus the word as written on the whiteboard, and the teacher has to re-establish control by rephrasing her question in turn 9.03. After a reminder about the ground rules for turn-taking in her classroom in 9.05, 'Without calling out', she nominates Melanie, presumably in response to a bid expressed by a raising of the hand. Although Melanie's response, 'it's about animals and insects and things', is accurate and relevant, it receives only a luke-warm evaluation from the teacher in turn 9.07. The extended 'ye-es' and the use of the expression 'That's a big part of it, sure', immediately followed by the next initiating move 'More about it', are likely to make Melanie feel that she would have done better to keep quiet and not volunteer an answer.

The unidentified student in turn 9.12 who responds 'plant life', receives more positive feedback in the comment 'we're getting really close there'. This student has supplied the target word 'life', but the teacher is unable to accept it fully because the concept of 'plant life' is too restricted for what she wants to explain about the biopoem task. Encouraged by the teacher's positive evaluation of 'plant life', the student Gene volunteers the response 'Horticulture'. At first this is not heard or understood by the teacher, so he repeats it (turns 9.14 – 9.16). Perhaps deliberately, the teacher chooses to only repeat the second part of the word, 'culture', to which she gives another lukewarm evaluation, in turn 9.17, 'that comes into it, sure'. Surely this contribution, being a specialised technical term, deserves more praise than it receives.

Fearing that she has got the students thinking that 'bio' is only connected with plant life, she turns back to the student who had responded 'plant life', repeating his response in turn 9.17, and recycling Melanie's earlier mention of 'animals'. The teacher's evaluation of the student's turn 9.22 is also lukewarm, as her main concern is to return to the original key notion of 'bio', to prevent students from going off at tangents. This response is once again highly relevant, well-expressed and praiseworthy. In her evaluation in turn 9.24 she reiterates the topics 'plants' and 'animals' and includes a repetition of the phrase 'a cleaner environment', thereby showing a degree of approval for the turn 9.22 response.

In Extracts #9b and #9c the teacher appears uncertain as to whether she wants students to write a biopoem about themselves or about other people. Her evaluation of Melanie's tenuous but relevant response in turn 9.26, '(Is it) a poem about yourself?' begins positively ('Yes', in 9.27*), but then the teacher appears to be having a dialogue within herself as well as with the class, as to whether a biopoem should biographical or autobiographical. The final utterances in Extract #9c, turn 34, demonstrate the uncertainty: 'So it's a self-portrait in words. You're going to write a biopoem about a person'.

Throughout Extract #9a–c it is clear that a teacher has a fixed lexical target which she is trying to elicit from the students, the word 'life' as a synonym for the prefix 'bio' in the compound word 'biopoem', so that she can explain that a biopoem means a poem about a person's life experiences. This leads her to reject and even ignore some valuable and pertinent student contributions which are worthy of more positive evaluation: The students are trying to play the classroom interaction 'game' by her rules, but they are not always rewarded for this cooperative behaviour through positive feedback. There is a risk that, if they do not receive sufficient positive feedback for their on-task, relevant contributions, the students will prefer to remain silent and not volunteer answers unless they are sure that they know the teacher's exact target word or phrase.

This tendency on the part of teachers is well-attested in the literature on classroom interaction. Over 40 years ago Barnes noted that:

> [t]he teacher teaches within his frame of reference; the pupils learn in theirs, taking in his words, which 'mean' something different to them, and struggling to incorporate this meaning into their own frames

of reference. The language which is an essential instrument to him is a barrier to them. (Barnes, 1967: 29)

It has also been referred to as 'Guess what teacher thinks' (GWTT; Young, 1992: 111). The issue of whether this type of 'pseudo-questioning' promotes learning is raised by Stables (2003), who critiques the critical position adopted by Young, suggesting that this type of episode can promote learning through students' inner speech which occurs simultaneously with the audible and recordable interaction.

TAKE 3

The following interaction occurred immediately after Extract #4c above.

27	T	Good. So . . . in the middle, down to the line, up, down, now flick, which goes into making our /a/ – up, down and – what next?
28	P	(xxx)
29	T	Good. What shape are the letters? The letter. The general shape is what?
30	P	xxx
31	T	Mmmm. Sort of. Think about some shapes. <Draws some circles of different size on whiteboard>. What general shape are they? We used the word last week.
32	P	(xxx)
33	T	The size is right. What about the shape?
34	P	Oval?
35	T	Good girl. Thank you. Oval. We don't want to see big fat things. We won't want to see /u/s looking like this. We want to see some ovals. . . . OK? . . . What's this word?
36	Ps	Ruapehu.
37:	T	What's Ruapehu? Louis?
38	Lo	Erm Mount Ruapehu is a mountain on the er Desert Road?
39	T	Very good. Yes. When you get to the bottom, if you've still got time and xxx write the opposite of these word using un as your prefix, for example happy, *un*happy. lucky would become...? The opposite?
40	Ps	Unlucky
41	T	Good. That's if you've got time. OK. Sitting comfortably.

Guiding questions for Take 3
(1) What are some of the established routines and norms of writing in this classroom?
(2) How does the teacher introduce and extend the students' understanding of descriptive words?

(3)   What may have been the intention of the student in responding
      Ruapehu in line 36? What connection may the student have been
      making with the previous exchange about the shape of letters?

References

Bakhtin, M. (1981) *The Dialogic Imagination.* In M. Holquist and C. Emerson (eds)
   (M Holquist, trans.). Austin, TX: University of Texas Press.
Barnes, D. (1967) Language in the secondary classroom. In D. Barnes, J. Britton and
   H. Rosen (eds) *Language, the Learner and the School* (pp. 9–77). Harmondsworth:
   Penguin.
Mercer, N. (1994) Language in educational practice. In J. Bourne (ed.) *Thinking
   Through Primary Practice* (pp. 85 – 98). London: Routledge.
Mercer, N. (1995) *The Guided Construction of Knowledge: Talk Amongst Teachers and
   Learners.* Clevedon: Multilingual Matters.
Ministry of Education (1997) *Quality Teachers for Quality Learning: A Review of Teacher
   Education. Green Paper.* Wellington, New Zealand: Ministry of Education.
Ministry of Education (2002) *Curriculkum Stocktake: Report to the Minister of
   Education, September, 2002.* On WWW at http://minedu.govt.nz/index.cfm?
   layout=document&documentid=7823&data. Accessed 6 April 2005.
Ministry of Education (2007) *The New Zealand Curriculum.* Wellington, New
   Zealand: Learning Media.
Richards, J.C. and Hurley, D. (1990) Language and content: Approaches to curricu-
   lum alignment. In J.C. Richards (ed.) *The Language Teaching Matrix* (pp. 144–162).
   Cambridge: Cambridge University Press.
Schieffelin, B.B. and Ochs, E. (eds) (1986) *Language Socialization Across Cultures.*
   Cambridge: Cambridge University Press.
Stables, A. (2003) Target language teaching and the ISS: Why Robert Young was
   wrong about questioning genres. *Westminster Studies in Education* 26 (2), 99–105.
Tharp, R. and Gallimore, R. (1990) A theory of teaching as assisted performance. In
   P. Light, S. Sheldon and M. Woodhead (eds) *Learning to Think: Child Development
   in Social Context 2* (pp. 42–61). London: Routledge.
Vygotsky, L.S. (1978) *Mind in Society: The Development of Higher Psychological
   Processes.* Cambridge, MA: Harvard University Press.
Vygotsky, L.S. (1986) *Thought and Language.* Cambridge, MA: MIT Press.
Young, R. (1992) *Critical Theory and Classroom Talk.* Clevedon: Multilingual Matters.

Chapter 9

Language Socialization in a Canadian Secondary School Course: Talking About Current Events

TAKE 1: PATRICIA A. DUFF
TAKE 2: RHONDA OLIVER

TAKE 1

Introduction

Learning to make educational presentations to classes or other audiences is an aspect of communicative competence and academic preparation that often begins at a very young age in English-speaking settings. Show-and-tell sessions, oral reports and speech contests frequently occur in primary school, continuing in secondary and postsecondary contexts with presentations of projects, critiques of published research, discussions of current events; and, later, for those in graduate degree programs, with thesis defenses and sometimes conference presentations as well. In many professions, too, giving presentations is a fairly routine practice. Thus, it is an activity that traverses educational and professional life throughout the lifespan for many people.

In North American and other settings, moreover, oral presentations, group project work, and oral communication skills are now being stressed and assessed to a greater extent than in the past, reflecting, in part, the amount and quality of collaboration and communication – and not just text-book knowledge or theory – currently required in real-world knowledge-building and knowledge-sharing in a variety of professional, vocational and academic fields. Oral academic discourse has not received as much attention in applied linguistics research on academic discourse as writing (e.g. composition, genre studies) has to date, but new research demonstrates just how pervasive, yet socially, cognitively, and discursively complex and variable, a standard oral activity such as 'the oral presentation' can be (Duff, 1995, 2007; Kobayashi, 2003; Morita, 2000; Morita & Kobayashi, 2008; Zappa-Hollman, 2007). A single presentation also typically involves multiple sorts of texts (e.g. a written script, a primary source, posters or slides, a written report), and variable forms and lengths of interaction with the teacher and audience.

Giving an oral presentation and leading a related discussion might be considered a very familiar, straightforward and commonplace activity that poses few difficulties for students raised in such an academic culture. However, learning to present material to a group effectively often involves a great deal of mentoring, observation and practice and may still be very challenging for speakers, especially for English-language learners coming from a culture where in-class discussion and presentations are atypical occurrences (e.g. Duff, 1995, 2007, 2008; Morita, 2000; Kobayashi, 2003; Zappa-Hollman, 2007).

How, then, are students socialized into making effective presentations and leading classroom discussions? What are the criteria by which student presentations are evaluated and what kinds of difficulties do they encounter? What additional difficulties do (or might) English language learners from other linguistic and cultural backgrounds face when learning to perform and engage in these frequently required modes of discourse that might be alien to them?

This chapter draws on research conducted in a Canadian social studies classroom in which a number of immigrant English language learners were being mainstreamed for the first time (Duff, 2001, 2002, 2004). It is framed theoretically in terms of *language socialization*, a linguistic and anthropological view of how newcomers to a culture or community are inducted into the tacit knowledge, perspectives, ideologies and practices of that group, a process that is mediated by language and by social interaction, and that also results in the acquisition of communicative competence as well as content knowledge (Duff & Hornberger, 2008; Ochs & Schieffelin, 2008).

The research site was a large secondary school in Western Canada (teaching Grades 8 through 12), with a population of 1300 students, of whom approximately 50% were recent Asian immigrants. Given recent demographic changes in the city and school district, teachers and administrators were grappling with how best to integrate and support immigrant newcomers into mainstream content areas effectively. One of the social studies teachers' abiding concerns in this school was, furthermore, why English language learners participated so little in class discussions and what teachers might do to increase their participation (see Duff, 2002). The larger study was an *ethnography of communication*, examining classroom interactions in relation to a particular speech event over an extended period and then seeking participants' perspectives on both observable and unobservable teaching/learning processes and their own roles and behaviors (Duff, 1995, 2002). The classroom was studied over the period of an academic year, although excerpts from just four lessons are included here, from the second half of the two-semester course.

All students in the class examined in this chapter were required to make at least one short presentation of a news-related current event and then to be part of a related discussion afterward, while still standing at the front of the class. As a result, they had many opportunities to observe others' presentations and note the teacher's feedback. Excerpted from a larger study spanning two years at the same school, the data for this chapter include audio- and video-taped lessons with one experienced social studies teacher and his students, the latter representing a mixture of English language learners and native English speakers (see e.g. Duff, 2001, 2004). I deconstruct the focal speech event, *current events presentations (and related discussions)* and consider the implications for both old-timer (local) students and newcomers (recent Asian immigrants to Canada) in this academic culture.

Talking about Current Events: A Form of Language Socialization and Citizenship Education

The content of the Grade 10 social studies curriculum in British Columbia, Canada, is 18th to early 20th century Canadian history, the development of Western Canada and contemporary national and provincial economics, social and political issues. But in social studies curricula in Canada and the United States, the emphasis has shifted from simply learning historical 'facts' to understanding historical events and controversies from multiple perspectives, often reflecting a critical awareness of social justice issues and the differing experiences, viewpoints, voices, interests, and representations of historical figures or groups (e.g. First Nations or Aboriginal people vs. whites; males vs. females; see Case & Clark, 1997; Duff, 2001). Increasingly, students are also expected to engage with everyday media regarding current events taking place in the world around them. Discussing 'current events' is therefore a major component of the official British Columbia Grade 10 social studies (SS10) curriculum and was embraced by this teacher as an important means of educating students and making them more interesting, conversant Canadians.

In the class examined here, taught by an experienced and respected 30-year-old European-Canadian teacher named Mr Jones, one 80 minute lesson per week – or nearly a third of the course – was devoted to current events. One student was scheduled each week to bring in a topic with an accompanying newspaper headline and clipping, and a short written summary and statement of their personal opinion about the topic. They then presented it, often reading from their prepared text (despite admonitions not to read), and then fielded questions from the teacher and from students. Both oral and written components were graded by the teacher, although we will consider only their transcribed oral texts here. The topics were supposed to be important issues and controversies and 'not just tragedies' (like car or airplane crashes) that would generate an extended, free-ranging and compelling discussion afterward, which in most cases continued to the end of the class period. Most students enjoyed the discussion of current events but were nervous when it came to giving their own presentations. However, if local students felt anxious about their presentations, English language learners in the class were all the more so because of concerns about their ability to communicate well – and, especially, comprehensibly – in this public forum and their ability to understand the seemingly rapid-fire questions and comments of their peers and teachers about topics with which they often had little personal connection. Learning to become competent in another language and culture after having already been socialized into one's primary languages/cultures is, indeed, very challenging (e.g. Duff, 2003; Zuengler & Cole, 2005).

Classroom Interaction

Takes 1 and 2 will examine the socialization of students into this routine activity with local native-speakers of English in the role of presenter. Take 3 will then present some data from a Taiwanese English-language learner (new immigrant Canadian) in the class, later in the term, for readers to analyze.

Part 1: Structuring, managing, delivering and assessing 'current events'

Presentation 1

Extract #1a is a presentation by a local male student about the murder of a high school girl in the same city. Before Duncan (a pseudonym), the local male student assigned that day's current events presentation, can proceed, the teacher insists that everyone must pay attention and be 'a good member of the audience' (Turns 01–03). The teacher (hereafter Mr Jones) therefore calls on Susan, a local female student who is talking to a friend, to pay attention (01–03). Following that initial classroom management, Duncan begins to narrate the story about the murder victim's funeral, the ongoing police investigation, details about the victim's history with the murder suspect, and then his own opinion about the case. When Duncan finishes, after his extended Turn 04, the class applauds (06) and Mr Jones makes some evaluative comments about the presentation (06 and 08) and also opens the discussion up to class members, asserting that 'a lot of people know quite a bit about this' (08).

Extract #1a

01 T   Sooh, we're **finally** ready for current events /// so when Dean
           is paying attention // and when Susan]
02 Su   [Yeah.
03 T   is a good member of the audience, then we'll start / Yep.
04 Du   Uh / my article is on the, girl uh /(Poonan Rhandawa) who was
           shot last week, uh by / the guy named (Nindirjit Singh) well's it
           about her funeral, and uh / well the article gives details about her
           uh funeral? Uh honor- she was an honor student at CH
           Secondary {School} uhhh a lot of people liked her, and / she had
           like uh including staff and students / and uh they all gave
           speeches and her brother or not brother a couple of cousins wrote
           her poems / but anyway. Um police are looking for the / guy
           who shot her (Nindirjit Singh?). They uh / they say he's been
           stalking her for a few years / and / wanting wanting her to be his
           girlfriend and all that, 'cause he really liked her? But she just (xx)
           switched schools and then uh / but it didn't stop so // he fol-
           lowed her to CH {Secondary School} / and that's where it ended?
           Um my opinion is this guy was really stupid 'cause you don't go
           and kill someone you really like // like it's not right. You can find
           someone else. There is (xxx) who might like you back if // she
           doesn't like you.
05 Ss   {Applause by class}
06 T   Okay. Great. That was a nice uh conversational manner you have
           when you- it's not like you're reading. That's excellent 'cause
           you're **not** reading. Nice job there. Uh / there may be- What?
07 S2   (Nothing?)
08 T   There m- no I mean I'm encouraging that's good / public speak-
           ing. There, there may be a couple other things I want to know /
           but it's your chance first. Any / a lot of people know quite a bit
           about this. Uh Susan

What, then, are the criteria for a good presentation in this context? What are
the phases or components of a presentation, expectations regarding topic
selection, perspectivity, turn-taking and other interactional, affective or
epistemic aspects?

Based on the discourse in Excerpt #1a and then Mr Jones' explicit comments in Turns 06–08, it is clear that students must first indicate what news
item they are discussing, provide some background or details about the
incident, and express a personal opinion about the topic – thereby displaying
some affective engagement with the topic and the ability to take a stance or
articulate a perspective (Morita, 2000). To do these things of course,
presenters must have earlier consulted a recent, local English-medium

newspaper to make a selection that would appeal both to them and to the
class. They then need to summarize the main issue and take a position.
Although perhaps not the most insightful or eloquent way of expressing
his view, Duncan commented in Extract #1a that the alleged murderer/
stalker was 'really stupid' and 'it's not right [to kill someone you really
like, i.e. an unrequited love interest]'. Presenters – and many audience
members – must also be able to participate in an extended discussion or
question period about the presentation, and defend their views, as suggested by the teacher in 08 and demonstrated in the following section. Then
there is a public assessment of the presentation (06), a form of socialization
for this student and others, which occurred after every presentation. In this
particular extract, Mr Jones remarks that it was 'great', that Duncan used a
'nice conversational manner' and he was especially satisfied (it was 'excellent') that Duncan was not reading his script (08), which was an indication
of 'good public speaking'. This presenter, a local aboriginal student, was in
fact very shy and the register of his presentation was quite informal (e.g.
saying 'the guy's really stupid', when summing up his view of the alleged
murderer). However, rather than drawing attention to his register and the
content of his presentation, Mr Jones gave him credit for having spoken to
the class without reading.

Yet later in the same speech event, shown in Extract #1b, Mr Jones commented further on the choice of topic and the way it was taken up.

Extract #1b

58   T   I'm to give Duncan credit / for this being a bit different... uh
         Duncan chose a murder that's a little out of the ordinary. First of
         all it's very close to home for us right? Um / and I guess
         I wouldn't have minded- it would have been nice if Duncan in his
         opinion had also maybe / considered some broader topics. 'Cause
         an individual murder- it's important but it's / a tragedy. We're all
         we're all saddened by an event like that. What broader topics
         could this be tied into just for anyone doing current events. What
         are / some broader themes that come up that this is an example
         of / that are societal concerns.
59   S1 Stalking.
60   T   Stalking. Thank you. Right? Stalking. So we might have a few
         things to say about stalking. Teen violence? Is it worse? Is it is it
         a myth or is it a reality? So always you can think of those kind of
         things to flesh out / on opinions and tie it into bigger / topics.
         So what do we want to say about stalking. I saw Susan, Carol
         {indicating students who want to say something}. Susan.
         <Discussion continues for a few more turns, about stalking,
         restraining orders, etc.>

Thus, although acknowledging this choice of topic as being 'a bit different' or 'a little out of the ordinary' and 'close to home', all potentially positive descriptors, Mr Jones also noted that Duncan, and the ensuing discussion, had not broached broader social issues transcending this particular news event (a murder by a spurned, obsessed admirer). The teacher expressed his dismay very gently and indirectly though, stating that he 'wouldn't have minded' or 'it would have been nice' if Duncan's position and topic had been more developed (58). The teacher's explanation of this shortcoming in Turn 58 then triggers examples of appropriate related topics, such as stalking and teen violence (59–60). Therefore, he is socializing students into a genre of discourse that involves communicating about the news, expressing an opinion, and then considering the broader ramifications or wider societal issues or consequences.

Presentation 2

Extract #2a features an excerpt from another presentation, also by a local male student, Dean, on a different day, again validating and extending criteria introduced in Extracts #1a and #1b. This presentation focused on conflict between the United States and Iraq in February 1999. An additional preliminary structuring move opens the speech event, with Mr Jones telling Dean to write the title of his news item on the board (01) (which was required each time) and advising him not to speak too quickly (03). As in Extracts #1a and 1b, Mr Jones also emphasizes the need to have everyone's attention before starting (05). The student again concludes his short presentation of approximately five sentences with an opinion: 'Personally I agree with the US Department because they have to protect their allies and they have to, they have to contain Saddam Hussein from threatening anyway his neighbors. And I think the Americans should bomb Iraq' (12). As in other excerpts, the presentation phase ends with applause and shouts of 'Yeah! Yes' from the class (13–15).

Extract #2a

01	T	Um Dean come on up. We'll get started with current events quickly. Put your title on the board.
02	De	Okay.
		<approx 25 turns about absent students are deleted here>
03	T	So /// Dean, remember to **not** talk too fast because / then it'll last longer {some laughter}. No that's not the reason. So that
04	S1	(xxx)
05	T	remember that **no** one has heard your story before so don't feel you have to rush through / and uh / it seems like / you do have everyone's attention so you can / start.
06	De	Okay.

07   T   Whenever you're ready.

08   De   Okay this article ex // is explaining how Iraq is preparing for a
            major assault by / the US Air Force because Baghdad has been
            carrying out threats / towards Saudi Arabia and Kuwat Kuwait,
            Saddam Hussein himself has threatened both of them with /
            with attack and // uh

09   T   Who has?

010   De   Saddam Hussein.

011   T   Okay right.

012   De   And / and uh / the / for you for letting for um letting
            the Americans and British war planes use Kuwait and Saudi
            Arabia's air base. /And he's trying to enforce a no fly zone
            over / southern Iraq. And the US Defense Department has
            warned / any attack by Iraq against any of their allies / would
            be a severe mistake and would be met / with a swift and sure
            response. And air patrols of the northern and southern Iraq have
            / triggered several clashes since / December in which the Amer-
            ican war planes have targeted Iraq's air defense / and other /
            installations. Personally I agree with the US Department because
            they have to / protect their allies / and they have to they have
            to contain Saddam Hussein from threatening / anyway his
            neighbors. And I think the Americans should bomb Iraq.

013   S1   Yeah!

014   S2   Yes.

015   Ss   <Applause for about 4 seconds>

This applause then triggers a humorous or ironic comment by Mr Jones (16)
explaining that this applause is not actually related to Dean's position on
the issue (enthusiasm for bombing Iraq), for which there might be
differing perspectives, but to mark the conclusion of his presentation.
The teacher then opens the floor to further questions and discussion in
Extract #2b (20), with the preface that 'I hope it's not as simple as that' (18),
meaning that the United States shouldn't simply bomb another country
because of unheeded warnings.

Extract #2b

016   T   That's uh I'm sure there'll be different opinions but that's clap-
            ping for your / presentation. **Bomb Iraq / Yay! Bomb Iraq.**
            {mock clapping} No. No. I hope that's not](xxx)

017   De   ]Well they- they gave them too many warnings]

018   T   ]So sim- I hope it's not as simple as that (xxx). Sorry. You were
            saying Dean?

019   De   Well they've gave them too many warnings.

020   T   Okay so, are there questions? // I have a few questions but are there questions from you / today / for Dean <spoken in an announcer's voice>.

Thus, immediately following Dean's presentation, and prior to the discussion phase, there is no public assessment of the quality of the presentation or choice of topic. Only much later (in Turn 195, shown below in Extract #2c), does the teacher conclude the lengthy and heated discussion phase and acknowledge the 'good choice of article', with 'a lot of interest for people' and that Dean had done a 'nice job'.

Extract #2c

195   T   So I don't know how long this / problem between Iraq and / United States is going to go on and and I mean things change. Remember that / it wasn't that long ago in the 1980s that Iraq was America's ally against the evil country of Iran ... But things will change and I- I really it would be hard to predict / how long this situation will go on for and what the final outcome will be. So we'll keep we'll stay tuned. It's an ongoing issue. It's obviously a good choice of an article. It has a lot of / interest for people. Right? / Okay. Nice job. {Applause.}

Presentation 3
    Finally, Extract #3a represents a third presentation by Mike, also a local male student, several weeks later. It confirms and provides elaboration on the pattern that has already emerged from the previous extracts: the teacher's socialization of students' attention and expectations regarding significant, discussion-worthy current news items and issues. The topic in Extract #3a is a serendipitous scientific discovery relating to the early detection of breast cancer by analyzing abnormalities in women's hair.

Extract #3a

01   T   All right. Whenever you think they are paying attention you can {taps twice} go for it. /// All right – the two D's <meaning Duncan and Dean> please give your attention? ///
02   Mi   All right. / Hair test touted as tool for breast cancer diagnosis {reading title, and also reading presentation report}. Sophisticated x-ray studies conducted on a single hair may reveal whether a woman has breast cancer / and could help doctors diag- uh diagnose other cancers. / The leader of this research at the University of New South Wales in Australia / says this new

find is almost unbelievable / unbelievable. It was discovered by
mistake. For years she had studied skin changes in breast cancer
patients. Before she went to Japan / where one of the world's
three large synchrotron's / or x-ray centers / is located she
stopped off at a hospital in England to pick up some skits skin
specimens. When she found that they had been accidentally
thrown out she took hair samples of people / with and without
breast castor breast cancer instead. They x-rayed the hairs and
found that those from cancer patients / had unique abnormalities
compared to those of healthy people. / She says that although this
test appears highly accurate it is being tested on too few women
to know how useful it will be. / I think that this type of cancer
detection is a huge stride in cancer research. It is not only highly
effective but it all- is also very cheap and relatively simple. A few
hairs can be sent by mail for a few dollars to the lab where they
will be tested. / It is much cheaper than current testing with
mammograms and could help a lot of people by detecting cancer
in early stage and possibly save their lives uh life because of this.

03   Ss   {applause for 5.0 seconds}

The presentation then is followed by Mr Jones' assessment, shown in
Extract #3b. As in the presentation by Dean in Extract #2a (but unlike
Duncan's in Extract #1a, who was praised for *not* reading), Mike was mostly
reading his prepared script in Extract #3a (with attendant miscues), but this
is not commented upon by Mr Jones in Extract #3b because the quality of
the news item and presentation seemed to compensate for that aspect. The
register of Mike's summary of the news story is more academic or formal
than Duncan's in Extract #1a and his statement of opinion in the last four
sentences of Turn 2 in Extract #3a is also more sophisticated and forceful.

Extract #3b

04   T   So here we go, so I bet there might be some questions or uh
comments on this uh nice medical finding. Now oftentimes with
a medical finding. {writing in his book}// I'm going to give uh
Mike full credit for choosing this article. I think it's relevant and
I think it may have a controversial aspect / which is what we look
for in current events articles right? If something was all positive
and all that we could uh say is great! Good news! / Then I might
not give him full credit for the article selection because / it may
be important but it's not / something that's going to lead to
discussion. There is believe it or not even about this, often with
medical advances there's two sides. Oh great, a benefit? But there's
a concern. There is a concern with this one. It, it the benefits far

outweigh the concerns but there is a concern. But you can just about what that might be 'cause I want to give a chance first to check / if any before I do my questions and stuff are there any / questions? Comments? It sounds like good news right?

Mr Jones' assessment of the presentation (this 'nice medical finding') is both complimentary and provocative. He again states that finding a 'controversial aspect' (04) in a news report is important. A 'good news' story would not receive full credit but this student has received full credit. There must be some concerns arising from even an ostensibly positive finding. That the topic should generate subsequent questions, discussion, and diverging opinions is made very explicit and Mr Jones asks students for questions or possible 'concerns' in relation to this medical breakthrough. As in other excerpts, he also indicates that he already has some questions and points of his own to raise after students have done so.

Part 2: The discussion phase of current events presentations

As the preceding excerpts and analysis indicate, the purpose of talking about current events in class was to make students more aware about the world around them and to foster their ability to communicate with others about the news, and to think critically, exploring different points of view. Even relatively straightforward and seemingly positive news items, such as finding a diagnostic test for breast cancer, were explored for possible disadvantages or negative points: such as false positives or misdiagnosis and about people opting for radical pre-emptive surgical measures based on genetics or other factors. The serendipitous nature of many scientific discoveries (and the meaning of serendipity) was discussed as well.

The discussion connected with the United States involvement in Iraq was very animated with proponents both for and against US military action, and with questioning by the teacher about whether bombing another country had resolved problems in the past, whether there were parallels between Saddam Hussein and Adolf Hitler, about which countries were backing the United States, and which were not, and why.

In the discussion of the murdered high school student (see Extract #4), for example, issues, language and laws connected with sexual harassment, stalking, premeditation in murder, restraining orders and extradition agreements between countries were raised and exemplified collaboratively (e.g. 23–25). Various local members of the class (both students and the teacher) mentioned that they had some personal knowledge of the case from friends or colleagues attending the school the victim had attended and contributed what they knew (e.g. 26). Their discussion, as in the other two lessons, also provided opportunities for the teacher to instruct them about relevant laws, policies or debates, and to discuss news sources and the recency or validity of their sources or their degree of certainty about their knowledge (25, 37). Students

volunteered questions about whether the united states has extradition agreements with Mexico (36) and why fugitives sometimes flee to Mexico.

Extract #4

023	T	Okay they- the police discovered that he had a plane ticket when he did this / which if that's true that shows
024	S1	Premeditated.
025	T	Premeditation which makes it a more serious under our laws offense than, than unpremeditated murder. And the, the thing that I read was / uh LA- thcy thought he was in LA but that was a day or two ago in the paper so maybe uh you've heard this more recently, Seattle?
026	S2	Some friends from (the victim's school) told me.
027	T	In the States. Okay well the newspaper said he had a plane ticket to LA. The police I believe. And he got on this plane / uh if by the way just a little learning here. If he's caught in America / what happens to him?
028	S3	Death penalty.
029	T	No. <Several students talk> Shh, one at a time. Do they bring him back to Canada?
030	Ss	Yeah.
031	T	Yes they do. And what's that called? John?
032	Jo	Extradition.
033	T	It's called extradition. He would be / extradited / right? / to Canada. Now / does Canada / Canada and the United States have / this arrangement of extradition. Does Canada have that arrangement with every country in the world?
034	Ss	No.
035	T	No. That's something that governments do. Most countries in the world and Canada have that agreement but there are places in the world that you a criminal could go / and if there's no extradition treaty with Canada then /
036	S5	What about (Mexico and the States?)
037	T	They're safe. Both Mexico and the States. I I'm almost certain. Meh – States for a fact. Mexico I'm sure that they do. Uh 'cause Canada wants /
038	S6	Because that's why everyone runs down to the border and hops the fence because they (xxx)
039	T	No they just hope to get lost in Mexico. Right? … The Mexican government really doesn't want to be a haven for criminals flee- ing but traditionally it, it is because it's easier to get lost …

Here, then, we see an extension of the original reporting of a funeral for a
young murder victim to broader social and legal issues both nationally and

internationally, with significant student input and the co-construction of discourse and knowledge along the way.

Discussion

Current events topics were usually selected by students because of their own interests and background knowledge. With skilful assistance from the teacher in the most successful cases, the topic also sparked a much deeper and more extended discussion of different points of view, tensions, laws, the relationship between international events and Canada, and related topics. Students were socialized to be engaged, informed and communicatively competent presenters and citizens, and also attentive, respectful but active audience members and co-discussants. New vocabulary was routinely introduced and illustrated (*serendipitous discoveries, extradition agreements, restraining orders*), historical facts were often introduced (e.g. Canada's alliances with other countries), and intertextual links were established with various other news sources beyond the original articles; and the credibility of those sources was sometimes examined too (Duff, 2004). Class members in this way joined together in building their understandings of the world and their place in it and their personal ideologies and also building their knowledge of academic argument and evidence.

Not surprisingly, perhaps, the least vocal participants in the discussion phase were the newly arrived English language learners, many of whom had been in the country from one to three years but had taken relatively few content courses in English up to that year (Duff, 2002, 2004). Their ability to spontaneously discuss events such as those described here using English was naturally limited in relation to many of their more outspoken local European-Canadian classmates. Furthermore, the quick, animated, and sometimes humorous nature of the exchanges between and among students and Mr Jones, and the often far-ranging topics made it all the more difficult for them to comprehend the discourse, let alone contribute actively to it. Most were silent during entire class periods as a result. Yet, as was the case for the local students, who themselves were still learning to overcome their fears or anxieties about facing the class to make their short presentations and to help lead discussion from the front or answer questions directed at them, this learning experience was part of a much larger and longer trajectory of socialization (Wortham, 2005).

TAKE 2

Introduction

In Chapter 2, 'Teaching Content, Learning Language: Socialising ESL Students into Classroom Practices in Australia', I suggested that particular patterns of interactions occur in classrooms and that these are context dependent. This proposition is also supported by the examination of the transcript data from a Canadian classroom.

In the first three extracts of this data the lesson proceeds in the following manner – the teacher provides the introduction, often setting the parameters of the behaviour that is expected, then a student orally presents on the topic of a current event, the teacher then reflects on both the topic and the attributes of the students presentation, and, finally concludes by inviting questions and comments from the other students. As such the teacher moves from management to content-focused interactions, and in one instance also engages in a genuine communicative exchange. However, although this is the general pattern, there is some fluidity between the types of exchange that occur. Specifically whilst some extracts demonstrate exchanges that consist of just one interactional context (e.g. management exchanges), other examples show the teacher moving swiftly from one context to another (e.g. from management, to content, to communicative and back to management exchanges). In fact it is apparent that there is a greater degree of fluidity in the movement of this teacher between the different interactional contexts than occurred in the Australian example, possibly because of the different goals of these two classes.

In contrast to the first three extracts, the fourth extract proceeds in a slightly different way. Although the initial exchanges in this extract are clearly related to the curriculum, the focus is on the language related to this content. Further, the pattern of interaction the teacher employs to elicit this language is what is commonly referred to as the Initiation–Response–Evaluation (IRE) (Hall & Walsh, 2002) drill/display pattern of teacher interaction. The teacher asks a question or prompts a student response, a student responds accordingly and the teacher then evaluates this response – using it in a spiral fashion as a basis to further the discussion. However, midway through the extract the pattern of exchange changes when a student asks questions of the teacher. At this point the interaction, although still having a curriculum content underpinning, becomes genuinely communicative.

In all the excerpts it can be seen how the interactional contexts within the lesson reflect the various pedagogic goals of the teacher and the roles of the students in the learning process. These contexts include the teacher managing student behaviour and actions; the teacher providing input about or eliciting information from the students related to the curriculum; the teacher developing and extending the students' language (particularly that tied directly to the curriculum); and, there is also genuine communication between the teacher and his students. Therefore, these interactional contexts differ both in terms of intent, but also with regard the way communication flows in the classroom, be it in a one way direction from the teacher to his students, or in two way direction between students and the teacher. It also seems that the different interactional contexts of the lesson determine whether or not the teacher provides feedback to the students, be this about the form or content of the students' contributions.

Management interactions

In Extract #1a it can be seen how the teacher seems to be focusing predominately on managing his students' actions – directing the learners, both individually and as a group, in order to socialise them to behave in ways he deems to be appropriate for the classroom, and for oral presentations in particular. He frames Duncan's presentation initially by encouraging the type of audience behaviour he wishes to see from the class 'when Dean is paying attention' and 'when Susan is a good member of the audience' and also prompts Duncan when to begin 'then we'll start. Yep'. After the presentation has been completed the teacher then outlines to the class those aspects of Duncan's talk that are praiseworthy and thus behaviours that should be emulated: 'That was a nice uh conversational manner you have when you – it's not like you're reading. That's excellent 'cause you're not reading' and 'I mean I'm encouraging that's good/public speaking'. At the end of this extract it also can be seen how the teacher invites the participation of other class members, but does so in such a way that he still controls the interaction – nominating who should talk (i.e. Susan).

Content exchanges

In Extract #1b, which is a continuation of Extract #1a, the teacher shows an apparent shift in intention, moving from a role where he is directing actions and behaviour to one that is more didactic. In doing so he both provides input to his students, and also draws the content from them. In this instance he uses as a stimulus Duncan's presentation, suggesting to the class that the scope of future presentations should be broadened. As a consequence the current topic of discussion also broadens from talk about a single murder to talk about social issues such as stalking, violence and so on.

As part of this exchange the teacher employs such discourse features as repetition and meta-talk, indicating to the students what is important (and what is not) and guiding them in their thinking. For example, it can be seen in the teacher's first turn how he works explicitly to 'broaden' the discussion, using this specific lexical item twice to indicate to the students that this is what they should do. He couples this with meta-talk – inviting the students to think more broadly but also indicating to them the type of direction they should consider. He uses expressions such as 'broader topics' 'tied … to current events', 'broader themes … that are societal concerns'. In his second turn, building upon the suggestion of one of his students, the teacher again uses repetition – this time using the word 'stalking' four times. He also couples this with explicit directions about what the students should consider – 'you can think of those kind of things to flesh out on opinions and tie it into bigger topics'. At the same time he provides exemplification of what these topics might be: 'Stalking. Teen violence'. Finally in this exchange, as he did in Extract #1a, he invites the students to contribute to this discussion, and in doing so, provides them with the opportunity for the students to consolidate their understanding. However, once again he *manages* the interaction, nominating the students who can respond.

In Extract #2 (a, b and c) the teacher follows a similar pattern of exchange as he used in Extract #1 (a and b) moving from *management exchanges* to *content exchanges*. Specifically, in Extract #2a he commences by directing student behaviour, telling Dean 'to not talk too fast', not to 'feel you have to rush through' and to get 'everyone's attention'. The instructions he provides not only serve to assist Dean, but they also work to ensure that the whole class is behaving in an appropriate manner as an audience. In Extract #2b he concludes Dean's presentation by signalling that there may be different opinions. Finally, in Extract #2c, as in Extract #1, the teacher's exchanges become even more didactic when he provides input related to the curriculum 'it wasn't that long ago in the 1980s that Iraq was America's ally' and he also provides feedback about oral presentations: 'It's obviously a good choice of an article. It has a lot of interest for people.'

Communicative exchanges

Within Extract #2a the teacher also engages in a different type of interaction, namely a *communicative exchange*. He does this when he interjects Dean's presentation and seeks clarification by asking the question 'who has?'. This is quite distinct from the display type questions used in other contexts – questions to which the teacher already knows the answer. It is apparent that the teacher has either not heard or misheard the information Dean has given, and thus there is a genuine two-way communication between the teacher and Dean. After Dean responds to this question, the teacher signifies that his question has been clarified 'Okay, right', and the exchange moves back into its original presentational format. This brief interlude illustrates the fluidity of exchanges which occur as the teacher's intentions and roles change within the classroom – in this case from someone who manages and instructs, to a more equal conversational partner. However, unlike in Australian data where the teacher and her students stepped outside the content of curriculum during such interactions the examples of communicative exchanges in this Canadian data were embedded within it.

Once more Extract #3 follows a similar pattern of exchange to that used in the previous two – moving from *management* to *content exchanges*. Again the teacher begins by indicating to the class what they should be doing (Extract #3a). In his initial turn he repeats the word 'attention' to reinforce to the class, and then to two individuals in particular (Duncan and Dean), how they should behave. After Mike gives his presentation, in Extract #3b, the teacher then delivers a monologue with a *content* focus. Firstly he provides the class with a brief summary of Mike's presentation, making the subject very clear by repeating the phrase 'medical finding' twice. Next he indicates to the class why Mike's choice of topic is such a good one. He uses terms such as 'relevant', 'controversial aspect . . . in current events' and 'something that's going to lead to discussion' to illustrate those qualities that he deems positive about the topic selection. He then exemplifies this with further talk clearly showing how this specific topic fulfils these requirements: 'often with medical advances there's two sides . . . a benefit . . . a concern'. He then invites the class to participate in the discussion, asking if there are questions or comments, but not without first concluding in such a way to invite the students to think about and decide their own position in the argument 'It sounds like good news right?'. Thus the teacher provides content input to his students, not only about the topic at hand, but also about the set task, and he does so in such a way to guide and stimulate their thinking.

Language-focused exchanges

The first half of Extract #4 represents a different overall pattern of exchange from that which occurs in the previous extracts. As previously noted, in this extract the teacher engages in what is commonly referred to as the IRF pattern of interaction. This manifests itself in such a way that the teacher, although initially inviting his students to participate in the discussion, firmly controls the communication. Thus his pedagogic intention appears to be to one where he seeks to elicit the *content* from his students, and in particular the vocabulary related to this. Thus the exchange, whilst related to the curriculum, has an explicit *language focus*. Where appropriate he also incorporates linguistic feedback to his students about the form of their language production. For example, when a student responds to the teacher's prompt 'if that's true that shows' with the word 'premeditated', the teacher accepts this response, but changes the form to 'premeditation'. Without interrupting the flow, nor giving his student the opportunity for uptake (i.e. to produce this form for himself) the teacher continues to provide input about the legal consequences of premeditation. In a similar way the teacher works to elicit and then to illustrate the concept of extradition: 'Do they bring him back to Canada?', 'And what's that called? John.' When John responds with the correct word the teacher repeats it and embeds it within an explicit definitional statement 'It's called extradition' thus both acknowledging John's contribution, but also making very clear to the class what the term is. He even reinforces this in his next turn, transforming it from noun to verb, and back again as he repeats the term 'He would be / extradited / right? . . . this arrangement of extradition'. During both these exchanges the teacher maintains his control, at one point even uttering 'Shh one at a time' to *manage* the students' participation.

Later in this extract one student calls out the question 'What about (Mexico and the States?)' and thus the context changes from a pattern of

IRF, where the teacher controls the interaction, to one where there is a true *communicative exchange*. Despite seeming less confident, as indicated by the use of hedges such as 'I'm almost certain' and 'I'm sure that they do', the teacher does answer this student's question. However, he no longer controls the exchange, but instead takes on the role of a responsive conversational partner. Despite this change in his role, and even given his hesitancy, it is clear that the teacher remains the 'content expert' because it is the teacher who provides the answer to the question, and in fact he elaborates on his answer to provide further input to the students.

Therefore Extract # 4 in particular, but all the extracts together, serve to demonstrate the fluidity in the nature of the teacher's exchanges. They also illustrate the diverse interactional contexts of the classroom, the various pedagogic intentions of the teacher, and the complex roles that are played by both the teacher and his students as they interact.

TAKE 3

This is an extract from the same class two months after Extracts #1 to 4 after a series of other presentations. Rather than Mr Jones (T), a new student teacher (ST), two thirds of the way through her teaching degree, is in charge of facilitating class discussions although Mr Jones is still present. The student teacher has been in the class for a couple of weeks already, first observing and then taking charge of the class The student presenter in this case, Jean, is a Taiwanese student who has been in Canada for under two years.

Extract #4

01	ST	'Kay quiet. Let's start.
02	T	Shh. Shh. Jean. Shh.
03	ST	Okay so uh we'll start the current events and / Jean if you want to / come up and / begin please?
04	Je	/ / / / / / Do I have to read the article?
05	ST	Just write your title on the board / / / /
06	T	And to answer your question Jean
07	Je	Hmm?
08	T	To answer your question you've seen / lots of current events presentations.
09	Je	Yeah.
010	T	We don't want you just reading your article right? We want you telling us a summary / of the issue right? / Right? <40 seconds pass; sound of chalk writing on the board and of pages in a book turning. >
011	Je	Um / (entire texts?) um (ice shelves / ice broken up quickly?) and um / it's um because the / um glaciers <pronounced as

glassers> in the (xx) the of the (xx) specialists predict /and um they say that / the ice shelves have lost nearly three hundred square kilometers in the past (xx) years? And um / mm / so they say if the glaciers without the shelves' / protection and this will be / like um melt faster than usual? And um I just choose this from the newspaper 'cause I think um / as the global warming is like get more serious recently 'cause it's lots of cars something like that on the street or and um / and the sea level is rising? And s 'cause we live in the coastline and it it's / keep rising? For years and years? This will affect our lives. Yeah. And so / I think it's kind of (interesting?)

012		<applause>
013	T	I have some quest- you might have some questions.
014	S1	(Course she will?)
015	ST	Questions?
016	S2	Um // how like fast is the sea level is actually rising at.
017	Je	Um this doesn't say 'cause um this like / um / about / it's rise about about / ten centimeter for last (xx) about ten years? / Yeah and if it say um if all the /the i iceberg or the glassers are melting and / the sea level will rise about /eighty /um meters.
018	S3	Eighty meters?
019	Je	Yeah all the / like all the iceberg and the glassers.
020	S3	/// Um.
021	ST	/// So if uh so if the / ocean level does rise say a total of eighty meters what sort of effects would / happen / around the world.
022	Je	Yeah 'cause um /like some sea islands / in the / um near the Indian / Ocean or / like the / some parts of / the country? They are / um like below the / sea level and if the /sea lev. sea level get rise and it's like we'll be (sink under it?) (xxx) // So /this may affect (xxx) /////
023	ST	Do you have any questions?
024	T	No?
025	S4	(xxx)
026	T	Thanks (xxx).
027	Ss	<applause>

Guiding questions for Take 3

(1) How is the teacher assisting the student teacher in understanding her duties as the instructor? How is the teacher also helping Jean understand her duties as a presenter?

(2) What are some of the elements of Jean's speech that indicate she is a second language learner or a newcomer to this academic community?

(3)   How did the student teacher respond to the reporting when Jean
      says that the water level will rise from 10 centimeters to 80 meters
      in turn 21?

Acknowledgements

This research was funded by grants from the Social Sciences and
Humanities Research Council of Canada and the Spencer Foundation/
National Academy of Education to Patricia Duff, who thanks both organi-
zations, the teacher and students in this class, and research assistant Tammy
Slater for their support.

References

Case, R. and Clark, P. (eds) (1997) *The Canadian Anthology of Social Studies*. Burnaby,
   BC: Simon Fraser University.
Duff, P. (1995) An ethnography of communication in immersion classrooms in
   Hungary. *TESOL Quarterly* 29, 505–537.
Duff, P. (2001) Language, literacy, content, and (pop) culture: Challenges
   for ESL students in mainstream courses. *Canadian Modern Language Review* 59,
   103–132.
Duff, P. (2002) The discursive construction of knowledge, identity, and difference:
   An ethnography of communication in the high school mainstream. *Applied
   Linguistics* 23, 289–322.
Duff, P. (2003) New directions and issues in second language socialization research.
   Korean Journal of English Language and Linguistics 3, 309–339.
Duff, P. (2004) Intertextuality and hybrid discourses: The infusion of pop culture in
   educational discourse. *Linguistics and Education* 14, 231–276.
Duff, P. (2007) Problematising academic discourse socialisation. In H. Marriott,
   T. Moore and R. Spence-Brown (eds) *Discourses of Learning and Learning of
   Discourses* (pp. 1–18). Melbourne, Australia. Monash University e-Press/Univer-
   sity of Sydney Press.
Duff, P.A. (2008) Language socialization, participation and identity: Ethnographic
   approaches. In M. Martin-Jones, A-M. de Mejia and N.H. Hornberger (eds) *Ency-
   clopedia of Language and Education. Vol. 3: Discourse and Education* (pp. 107–119).
   Boston: Springer.
Duff, P.A. and Hornberger, N.H. (eds) (2008) *Encyclopedia of Language and Education,
   Vol. 8: Language Socialization*. Boston: Springer.
Hall, J.K. and Walsh, M. (2002) Teacher-student interaction and language learning.
   Annual Review Applied Linguistics 22, 186–203.
Kobayashi, M. (2003) The role of peer support in ESL students' accomplishment of
   oral academic tasks. *Canadian Modern Language Review* 59, 337–368.
Morita, N. (2000) Discourse socialization through oral classroom activities in a TESL
   graduate program. *TESOL Quarterly* 34, 279–310.
Morita, N. and Kobayashi, M. (2008) Academic discourse socialization in a
   second language. In P. Duff and N.H. Hornberger (eds) *Encyclopedia of
   Language and Education. Vol. 8: Language Socialization* (pp. 243–255). Boston:
   Springer.
Ochs, E. and Schieffelin, B. (2008) Language socialization: An historical overview.
   In P. Duff and N.H. Hornberger (eds) *Encyclopedia of Language and Education,
   Vol. 8: Language Socialization* (pp. 3–15). Boston: Springer.

Wortham, S. (2005) Socialization beyond the speech event. *Journal of Linguistic Anthropology* 15, 95–112.

Zappa-Hollman, S. (2007) Becoming socialized into diverse academic communities through oral presentations. *Canadian Modern Language Review* 63, 455–485.

Zuengler, J. and Cole, K. (2005) Language socialization and L2 learning. In E. Hinkel (ed.) *Handbook of Research in Second Language Teaching and Learning* (pp. 301–316). Mahwah, NJ: Lawrence Erlbaum.

Afterword

First Steps

I started transcribing 46 years ago, live transcription, not from audio-tapes or digital recorders. I transcribed exchanges between 12 practice teachers I was supervising as part of my responsibilities at a teachers' college in Nigeria. One catch was that these practice teachers, who were my students, all had from two to 20 years more experience than I had. In addition, they were teaching subjects I knew nothing about such as Nigerian history and geography, and how to calculate costs and expenses in pounds, shillings and pence. So, I transcribed initially to overcome my ignorance. I needed to meet my students, who were practice teaching, every other day to discuss their lessons. I wanted to be able to have discussions that were not a waste of the teachers' time.

There were two streams of Grades 1 to 6. I spent the first half of each period in one stream and the second half of each period in the other stream of the same grade. I wrote down as many comments, questions and answers each teacher made and as many comments, questions and answers their students made. I had conferences with pairs of my students teaching the same grade. During my conferences I reported to both of them what I had transcribed in each stream. The teachers as a result got a clearer idea of what both they and the students were saying and doing. Each teacher also got ideas from what was going on in another class dealing with the identical material. For example, one teacher often introduced an explorer by showing a picture of the person in a book he had borrowed from the library. The teacher in the other stream of the same grade often drew sketches on the blackboard and asked students to come up and add details to show how they imagined the explorer might have looked. Each teacher usually appreciated the details I shared from the transcriptions because they gave each teacher ideas for their subsequent lessons.

In my next position, also at a teacher training college, I was asked to teach a course in classroom observation. We asked potential teachers, who were straight out of college, to enroll in the course so they could visit schools and see what teaching was like. While most of them enjoyed visiting a wide range of schools and grade levels, I found the reports they gave in class on their observations rather general and very judgmental. After each one shared their first reports in class, we all agreed that to learn more about what was going on we had to change the format of the reports. We also agreed that we had to do something about the judgments they were making. We were guests with less experience than the teachers we were observing. In addition, we used the same schools we observed in as practice teaching sites so we decided we had to do something about being judgmental.

The potential teachers in my classes did not limit their judgments to the interactions. They often made judgments about students. Each judgment we make about a student – she's not motivated; he's a hard worker – is a kind of diagnosis. If we are wrong in our diagnosis, we will not be able to provide the right treatment. So, I tried to develop the ability to suspend our judgments of teachers as well as students.

Since I had just returned from Nigeria, transcription was still very much on my mind. So, I suggested that subsequent reports should contain some transcribed exchanges. I suggested that my students visit in pairs so that they could capture more exchanges. In those days, tape recorders were available but they were very heavy and cumbersome so we stuck with live transcription.

Second Steps

As I was teaching the classroom observation course, together with those in the class, I started to look for books and articles about classroom observation. The one I found that initially influenced me the most was Arno Bellack's *The Language of the Classroom* (1966). Since he was teaching at the same teachers' college I was, I had many opportunities to discuss his work with him and his colleagues. Though he had developed a category system, he did not limit himself to category systems in his thinking about classroom observation. He introduced me to many anthropological studies not only of classroom interaction but also of conversational interaction.

I adapted Bellack's categories for ESOL classrooms as a means to concentrate on describing rather than judging (Fanselow, 1977, 1987). However, many of my students made the same types of judgments they previously did as soon as they finished coding a transcript. They used the coding to support their judgments! So, I abandoned my confidence in using coding systems to decrease judgments. However, I did not abandon my confidence in using coding systems as a tool to analyze transcriptions. As we coded, we consistently had to ask ourselves whether a particular communication was in one category or another. And often the answer was that the communication had characteristics that made it difficult to say for sure which category it belonged in.

These discussions of how to code communications led me to my next attempt to find a way to observe so that we could *discover* something rather than to judge what we were observing. But given the very strong tendency most have to judge, I decided to develop a way for observers to use their judgments as a step in their analysis.

When an observer said that a teacher in a transcript was overbearing, I would ask the observer, always working with a partner, to find evidence that the teacher was not overbearing. Of course, not all judgments are negative. But I treated positive judgments in the same way. When an observer claimed that the teacher engaged the students, I would ask the observer and partner to find evidence that showed that the students were not engaged. Of course, this procedure is nothing but a variation of the null hypotheses that is the basis of most research. We try to disprove what we claim. (Fanselow, 1988, 1992; Fanselow & Barnard, 2005).

Another aim of the observation courses I taught was to introduce my students to ways of expanding the range of activities they could use both in their practice teaching and on the job. I wanted teachers to be able to analyze transcripts not only to understand interactions better and see something they had not previously seen. I also wanted teachers to be able to use the transcripts to generate alternative practices, just as I had used my transcripts in Nigeria to suggest alternative practices.

In Nigeria, I saw that when teachers in pairs generated alternative practices together, through seeing each other's teaching, as reflected in my transcriptions, they began to feel more autonomous. Even if supervisors and those who prepare teachers always had many useful suggestions to make to teachers, there are rarely enough supervisors and teacher trainers available to work with all teachers. And the amount of time that teachers have to meet supervisors and teacher trainers is limited. So the more autonomous teachers can be, the more they can learn from each other in the setting they are in, the more likely they are going to continue to expand the range of activities they use.

As you have noticed, I have suggested in a number of places that expanding the range of activities we use in our teaching is valuable. I present a number of reasons in my books to support this claim. But since this claim is not directly related to the theme of this book, I will not re-state the reasons here. I just wanted to point out that I developed two key reasons for analyzing transcripts: see something we had not noticed before – move beyond our initial interpretation and judgment – and expand the range of our teaching practices.

Most Recent Steps

Since the early 1960s, when I started transcribing, there has been a lot of focus on classroom observation and the analysis of interactions. As I look back at the limited view I had of the complexity of interactions when I simply shared what one teacher did in a history lesson with another teacher who had taught the same lesson in a slightly different way I am somewhat bemused.

However, the fact that I have learned how limited my initial work in observation was has been an exhilarating experience. There has been a great deal of thoughtful work since my days in Nigeria. Many of the developments in the field of observation in ESOL are illustrated in a book edited by two of Dick Allwright's former students (Gieve & Miller, 2005) to honor Dick's contributions to the field and his retirement, which contains the chapter Roger and I wrote that this present book is based on. Though it is unlikely we would have written the chapter had Simon Gieve and Inés Miller not invited us to submit a proposal, we had become increasingly frustrated by what we saw as the doctrinaire attitude in some writings about classroom interactions, including some earlier ones of our own! After so many years of transcribing and analyzing transcripts, as well as later audio and video excerpts, we began to wonder how we might combine some of our previous ideas and those of others in an approach that would be more genuinely exploratory.

As we reflected on the idea of moving beyond single interpretations of transcripts, we were reminded of a description of three types of baseball umpires.

Umpire type 1: 'I calls 'em the way I sees 'em.'
Umpire type 2: 'I calls 'em the way they iz.'
Umpire type 3: 'They ain't nothin till I calls 'em.'

The first type of umpire is what the Take 1, Take 2, Take 3 approach is about. We encourage each person to 'call them' as he/she sees them, not pretending to mistake individual interpretations for reality nor thinking that individual interpretations of reality determine what is happening. The second and third types of umpire are those who present one-dimensional interpretations.

Future Steps: Applying the Take 1, Take 2, Take 3 Methodology

As I reflect on the chapters in this book, I think they deal with two of the central problems that pop up in many of the usual conversations about teaching and in many of the analyses of classroom interaction: (1) being doctrinaire and one-dimensional, thus preventing us from seeing something new, and (2) having a limited range of transcribed activities we can use to expand our repertoire of activities.

Regarding the first problem, because two different people independently interpret each set of data, the analyses will less likely be one-dimensional or doctrinaire. We think that when you see the two interpretations of each set of excerpts, you will be liberated to make your own interpretation because you will have seen that two other people made interpretations that are often quite different. Reading two interpretations is also likely to lead you to see something different because they remind you that you do not have to be doctrinaire or one-dimensional.

Of course, we teachers are not the only people who tend to be doctrinaire and one-dimensional. Just as I received the drafts of these chapters, I read in the *New Yorker* (29 January 2007) an excerpt of a book by Jerone Groopman titled *What's the Trouble? How Doctors Think.* The theme of the book is that doctors very often diagnose a patient within the first few seconds of a consultation! The author starts the book by describing a misdiagnosis he made early in his career based on an initial impression rather than a second or third take. A forest ranger in his thirties came into the doctor's office. The ranger was tanned, looked fit and had not an ounce of fat on him. He said that when he climbed up the ranges with his 10-kilo backpack on he often felt a pain in his chest. He said that in the last couple of days he had the pain in his chest even when not climbing with his 10-kilo backpack. The doctor had an electrocardiogram done. He also had a blood test done to check for a couple of items that might indicate a heart problem. But because the ranger looked so fit, the doctor could not believe he had a heart problem. When the results of the electrocardiogram and the couple of blood tests did not reveal any particular problem, the doctor sent the ranger home. That night, the ranger had a heart attack! The doctor writes in his book, and teaches in his classes, that it is very dangerous to base a diagnosis on first impressions because such a diagnosis can lead both to negative conse-quences for patient health and also to potential malpractice suits. He said that he should have ordered additional blood tests and had the ranger spend the night in the hospital under observation. A tanned face and a fit appearance provide a positive first take. But looking beneath the surface, in teaching as in medicine is crucial. Our first take requires looking beneath the surface and even there we could see that there are possible second and third takes.

Regarding the second problem – having a limited range of data – you now have a wide range of data from many countries and many subjects. 'So what?' some might ask. Well, because you have such a rich set of data, we think you will be stimulated to compare and contrast the separate excerpts. In Nigeria, I had transcripts from 12 teachers but all in the same primary school. You have transcripts from nine teachers in nine different countries with a wide range of content areas. And you have Take 1 and Take 2 – two interpretations – on each set of data plus a set of questions for Take 3 – your own interpretation.

We hope that when you reflect on such a wide range of data and interpretations you will feel free to play with activities you use and alter them. Why not try some activities teachers regularly use in Japan or New Zealand or Taiwan or Canada in your own classes? The key aim of Take 3 is to generate alternative moves or scripts from those in the original transcribed excerpt from a lesson.

Patterns in Classroom Discourse and in Conversations about Classroom Discourse

Just as you have seen many similar patterns in classroom discourse, so after reading the chapters in this book, you have seen that there are patterns of discourse in conversations about teaching. We had two aims when we wrote *Take 1, Take 2, Take 3*. One was to encourage everyone to feel free to interpret transcriptions differently – alternative interpretations from those of the first interpreters. Another was to remind us all that one-dimensional or conventional interpretations, as well as unsupported claims, are likely to be false because the meanings in all discourse are complex, full of multiple meanings, ambiguous and likely to be interpreted quite differently by different participants.

We hoped that by introducing the steps we developed in *Take 1, Take 2, Take 3*, everyone would both interpret transcriptions differently and move beyond one-dimensional, conventional interpretations and making claims without support. In the event, I have discovered as I read and re-read the chapters in this book that just as we often are controlled/trapped by rules of classroom discourse, so we are often controlled/trapped by rules of discourse in our conversations about teaching.

I also discovered something that I had failed to notice before: in some one-dimensional interpretations – really judgments since they tend to be black and white, good or bad – I found a tendency to inflate some judgments in a positive way. Thinking that *everyone* would be able to change, as I said we had hoped in the above paragraph was obviously naïve. In each chapter, I found examples of the kinds of interpretations we think reflect the complexity of classroom interaction and some that do not, in different proportions. I found it useful as I read and reread each chapter to identify examples of the usual interpretations and the ones we are advocating. As you read and reread the chapters, you might find it useful to identify each type we advocate as well.

The purpose of the following examples is not to cast aspersions on those who made some of the usual interpretations rather than the alternative interpretations we are advocating. Rather, the purpose is to show that the rules of discourse control us a great deal more than we realize. The more we write down our interpretations, as the educators have in this book, the more we label them, the more we will be able to change our discourse in our discussions of our teaching.

Here are my comments about a few examples of what I consider to be each type: one-dimensional and multi-dimensional, conventional and unconventional, claims supported and not supported by data.

One-dimensional interpretations

Author's interpretation	*Alternative interpretation*
[The teacher] provides a model ... However, ... [the student] ignores this repetition and continues ...	Perhaps the student ignored what the teacher had said. Perhaps the student was engaged in his comment and did not hear what the teacher said. Perhaps the student did not hear any difference between what he had said and what the teacher 'modeled' so maybe the teacher's words were not a model, to name a few other possibilities.
.... the teacher code-mixes the two languages in her utterances in order to get the attention of the learners ...	The teacher might also code-mix because s/he is not sure the students understand either directions or word equivalents in English. Or the teacher might not have had strong command of English to use it more and avoid code mixing. Maybe the teacher had been taught in the same way and felt that code mixing was the expected and normal way to speak in English class.

Multi-dimensional interpretations

Author's interpretation	*Alternative interpretation*
As in the previous segments, she uses the adverbial 'now' as a secondary device because she starts with the 'okay'. 'Okay' is an American US colloquialism implying democracy and consent. Yet, as it has come to be commonly used, and used in this setting, it is a weaker version of consent; it is used in a similar way as 'now' – to call attention to the next move. In this case, evaluation.	The commentator presents three different meanings of 'okay'. Of course there are many more but not that many more in this particular context.

(Continued)

(*Continued*)

Author's interpretation	Alternative interpretation
To a large extent this may be due to a lack of Cognitive Academic Language Proficiency – or even Basic Interactional Conversation Skills (Cummins, 1981) not only on their part but also on their teachers'.	We see four dimensions here: proficiency or skills on the part of the student or teacher.
[These routines] were performed many times throughout the school day ... While the routine is linguistically simple and at first blush may be dismissed as unimportant, the attention granted it by the teacher points to a cultural significance that surpasses its surface simplicity.	The commentator explicitly states that the first interpretation is not adequate and suggests another.

One-dimensional/multi-dimensional interpretations

Conventional interpretations

Author's interpretation	Alternative interpretation
The teacher uses various strategies to reinforce the students' knowledge of English, such as requesting repetition, asking students to name the letters that spell the word while she writes them on the board, and extending their understanding of the meaning by differentiating it from more specific details of the temporal location of their interaction.	While repetition and spelling might reinforce, if students already know the words and can spell them, the repetition and spelling could be a turn off or a way to bore students. There is no indication in the transcript that the students had any difficulty with the words or the spelling.
... the teacher will also change direction, in this case interrupting the reading of the story to engage the class in a discussion about the meaning of the word 'bony'.	In the so-called discussion, one student said 'bones' and one student touched a part of the body with a bone inside. I say 'so called' because if we describe saying one word and pointing to a part of our body a *discussion*, what would we call long comments between two or more people about the same topic?

Unconventional interpretations

How does the teacher use and not use the student's prior knowledge to connect them to the topic of study?	Asking how something might apply and might not apply is what we refer to as testing the null-hypothesis in our original paper. We are more likely to see another dimension of what we are interpreting if we look at both sides. In police work all too often in some places people are determined to be guilty and then evidence is found to support the initial claim. This is one reason the work of defense lawyers is so crucial. And so in exploring teaching, we have to find evidence that does not support our claim as well as evidence that we think does support our claim.
The teacher repeats that the students do not remember (Turns 1, 5 and 9). Is the teacher referring to the content or the language? Can it be both and what evidence can you find for each?	Looking at both sides, or in this case three sides of the same communication.
[The teacher] then feels the need to negotiate the meaning of the key word 'Bony', which occurs four times in succession in the book text. The students' response 'bones' ... suggests that this is understood, but the teacher decides that further negotiation is required and, leaving the book text, elicits a physical response by instructing students to feel their bones. 'bony' ... [is] identified by the teacher as [an item] in the book text which may be problematic for the students to comprehend, and therefore require a form of meaningful negotiation beyond a more comprehension check. This can be seen as a one-sided form of negotiation for meaning, since it is the teacher who determines which words represent items of possible misunderstanding.	By looking from the perspective of the students as well as from the perspective of the teacher, we have two sides to consider rather than one.

Conventional and unconventional interpretations

Claims supported by data

Three aspects of this dynamic exchange merit attention. Firstly, the fast-paced interaction, of which this is a small fragment, is characterized by incomplete and overlapping turns in which suggestions are made and ideas rebound. Children's conversational asides and interruptions, marked by [, are frequently 'taken up' and woven into the flow of talk, revealing how students' interests, rather than the teacher's intentions, can at times divert the pedagogic agenda. Secondly, the tone of the discourse is provisional and speculative, tentativeness reflected in the level of modality, 'could' 'would' and 'probably', and Robert's (Ro) declaration that his idea is 'just a guess'. The teacher's locution 'I bet you' functions as a 'modal adjunct' that entertains the possibility of alternative viewpoints and uncertainty in discourse. Finally, students are speculating and reasoning, problem solving and, crucial to their effectiveness as learners, asking questions.	In addition to the examples cited for each claim shown here, the author refers to many other lines and relates them to her claims.

Claims not supported by data

'You should tip your tongue lower.' Is referred to as a meta-cognitive explanation.	If such a short comment is called an explanation, what would either a longer, more precise comment be called and what would what are normally called explanations – multiple details or reasons – be called?
... the teacher provides a brief evaluation – typically, 'good', 'OK', 'yes' or a similar expression of positive reinforcement ...	When such words are said constantly, after both incorrect and correct responses, the claim that they either evaluate or provide positive reinforcement has to be questioned; when teachers transcribe their teaching, they often are unaware of how frequent they say these words and how indiscriminate their use of the words is.

(Continued)

(Continued)

She commends him on the content of his answer 'Right' and 'very good', but recasts it into a more target-like form – long legs with sharp claws. (Student had said 'She has a long leg, and a skinny leg, and a sharp claws.')	The teacher says the words correctly – whether the teacher heard the student errors or not is unclear so recast is a bit of a claim; also to say that 'Right' and 'very good' are commendations, especially since there response had so many errors seems a bit overstated.
Here … we see … significant student input and the co-construction of discourse and knowledge along the way.	This comment was made after a transcription in which the teacher said 265 words and individual students said around 25 words. If student input that is only 10% of the conversation is 'significant', what would we call 50%?

Claims supported and not supported by data

I mentioned the richness of the data that the nine teachers from nine countries provide. Rich as it is, unless each of us interprets the data in multi-dimensional and unconventional ways and avoids making claims without support, the data will not enrich *us*. We have to interpret from a range of perspectives, including some the exact opposite of those who did both the first and second take. As I said in the preface to the Japanese edition of my book, *Try the Opposite* (Fanselow, 1999: x), '[t]he alternative practices are not presented as better practices. The explanations offered are not presented as different practices, different explanations. One of the tasks for you as a reader in fact will be to generate still other alternative practices and explanations'.

Back to First and Second Steps

I began my exploration of teaching in Nigeria. Limited as my methodology was, many experiences unrelated to transcriptions in Nigeria transformed my life. I did electrical work to earn money for college in Chicago. In the United States, we usually push a wall switch up to turn a ceiling light on and push it down to turn the ceiling light off. When I got to Nigeria and pushed the wall switch up, I turned the ceiling light off rather than on! And when I pushed the wall switch down, I turned the ceiling light on! My first thought was why did the electricians in Nigeria install all the wall switches wrong! Well, in the event, I realized as Hamlet says, in a one-dimensional but thought provoking comment, 'There is nothing either good or bad but thinking that makes it so!' (Act 2, scene 2, 239–251). During my years in Nigeria, as well as Togo and Somalia, I experienced many, many other moments that turned my previous values upside down and inside out – before I heard of Dianna Ross's song with this title.

In our Introduction, we highlighted the powerful influence of cultural practices outside the classroom on practices inside the classroom. The example I just gave about light switches highlights the crucial role that out of class expectations and practices play on practices inside the classroom.

In retrospect, I am a bit chagrined that it took me so long to advocate multiple interpretations of the same data rather than one-dimensional interpretations, unconventional rather than conventional interpretations, and interpretations supported by a great deal of data. I majored in literature in university. My literature professors constantly asked us to develop a range of alternative or unconventional interpretations of scenes in novels or plays and lines in poems. And making claims like 'The play clearly shows how clever Wilde was with words' without any data earned an F in a heartbeat.

In spite of this training, it took me quite a few years to apply these lessons to the analysis of transcripts. Gregory Bateson provides a possible reason:

> [People often miss the obvious] because people are self-corrective systems. They are self-corrective against disturbance, and if the obvious is not of a kind that [we] can easily assimilate without internal disturbance, [our] self-corrective mechanisms work to sidetrack it, to hide it, even to the extent of shutting the eyes if necessary, or shutting off various parts of the process of perception. Disturbing information can be framed like a pearl so that it doesn't make a nuisance of itself ... (Bateson, 1972: 428)

At any rate, when Roger and I wrote *Take 1, Take 2, Take 3*, I finally saw a way to apply the methodology I had developed in my study of literature to transcripts. (Having said 'I finally applied the methodology' does not mean I apply it naturally; I have to work at it just as I am asking you to work at it by labeling interpretations that are multiple versus one-dimensional, conventional versus unconventional and are supported by the data and not inflated rather than not being supported by the data and being inflated.) If we analyze transcripts the same way we analyze lines in plays, we can not only develop a range of interpretations but we can also suspend our judgments. And we can feel free – liberated – to change some of the lines in our subsequent lessons just as we feel free to alter a line in a play or novel or poem to produce a different effect. When our goal is to see something new in what we experience, we eliminate the natural tendency to judge and focus on analysis and multiple interpretations.

Questions about Sampling

At workshops, when we present the types of short transcripts the authors in this book present, many participants raise the question of sampling. 'How can you hope to understand classroom interactions when you deal with such short exchanges?' We cannot prove that short exchanges are representative. But after we have looked at transcripts of entire lessons, we have consistently seen that short excerpts are usually representative of the entire class.

In literature, the same phenomenon obtains. If we read a few pages from *Jane Eyre*, we find the style, theme, characterization, use of images, and so on, is similar to scores of other pages. In medicine, the same phenomenon also obtains. If you want to find out your blood type, cholesterol level, and so on, you do not have to have all of your blood taken out but just a few tubes of blood. As William Blake wrote in *Auguries of Innocence* more than two centuries ago:

To see a World in a Grain of Sand
And a Heaven in a Wild Flower,
Hold Infinity in the palm of your hand
And Eternity in an hour.

John F. Fanselow

References

Bateson, G. (1972) *Steps to an Ecology of Mind*. New York: Ballantine.
Bellack, A., Kliebard, H., Hyman, R. and Smith, L. (1966) *The Language of the Classroom*. New York: Teachers College, Columbia University.
Cummins, J. (1981) *Bilingualism and Minority Language Children*. Ontario, Canada: Ontario Institute for Studies in Education.
Fanselow, J.F. (1977) Beyond *Rashomon*: Conceptualising and observing the teaching act. *TESOL Quarterly 11*, 17–41.
Fanselow, J.F. (1987) *Breaking Rules*. White Plains, NY: Longman.
Fanselow, J.F. (1988) 'Let's see': Contrasting conversations about teaching. *TESOL Quarterly 22* (1), 113–130.
Fanselow, J.F. (1992) *Contrasting Conversations*. White Plains, NY: Longman.
Fanselow, J.F. (1999) *Try the Opposite: Teaching English with Dr. Fanselow* (Naoko Aoki, trans.). Tokyo: Simul Press.
Fanselow, J.F. and Barnard, R. (2005) Take 1, Take 2, Take 3 – A suggested three-stage approach to exploratory practice. In S. Gieve and I. Miller (eds) *Understanding the Language Classroom* (pp. 175–199). Basingstoke: Palgrave MacMillan.
Gieve, S. and Miller, I. (eds) (2005) *Understanding the Language Classroom*. Basingstoke: Palgrave MacMillan.

Index

DATE DUE

Demco, Inc. 38-293